THE LIFE AND MUSIC OF
JAMES WILSON

The Life and Music of James Wilson

Mark Fitzgerald

First published in 2015 by
Cork University Press
Youngline Industrial Estate
Pouladuff Road, Togher
Cork, Ireland

British Library Cataloguing in Publication Data
A CIP catalogue record for this book is available from the British Library.

ISBN 978-1-78205-136-7

Typeset by Tower Books, Ballincollig, County Cork
Printed in Spain by Grafo

www.corkuniversitypress.com

Contents

Acknowledgements   vii

1   Early Life in London   1

2   Arrival in Dublin   17

3   First Compositional Successes   40

4   Consolidation of Career   72

5   Connections with Denmark and Return
    to Opera   104

6   Late Works   140

7   Conclusion   173

Appendix One   184
Appendix Two   190
Bibliography   213
Notes and References   217
Index   237

Acknowledgements

It is perhaps not often that a project's origin is also a terminus. This book originated as a commission from Patrick Zuk and Séamas de Barra for a projected series of monographs on Irish composers to be published by Field Day. Arrangements were made by the editors for me to meet Wilson but our one and only brief meeting coincided with his hospitalisation and death. I had been given a draft copy of some memoirs entitled *From the Top* that Wilson had been working on in the last years of his life. These were put together from memory without checking dates or general chronology and Wilson's statement that there have been 'variations, development sections and doubtless errors of fact' is, if anything, an understatement. I was therefore highly reliant on the assistance of a range of relatives, friends, collaborators and several libraries in putting this work together.

I would first like to thank Nicholas Wilson for his generous support of the project and in particular for his permission to use the letters and other archive material collected, assiduously and with great love, by his mother Clarice Wilson, one of Jim's dearest friends, and the wife of his brother Robert. This collection was particularly important, helping to unravel a lot of biographical issues as well as providing insight into Wilson's own thoughts and ideas. Dr Bernard Meehan, Jane Maxwell and all the staff of the Manuscripts Department of Trinity College Library were extremely helpful and tireless in their assistance, allowing me full access to the Wilson papers. Thanks are also due to Jesper Düring Jørgensen of the Manuscripts Department of the Royal Library, Denmark, for his assistance in locating both parts of the correspondence between Wilson and Elsa Gress and also to Jonathan Grimes and all the staff of the Contemporary Music Centre (CMC) in Dublin, including Eve O'Kelly who was director at the period when this book was written. All the staff at CMC were (and continue to be) incredibly helpful in assisting me with numerous queries. My thanks also to Dr Nicholas Clark of the Britten-Pears Library for his assistance with the Britten-Wilson correspondence. Gerard Lynn, Máire Ní Chonalláin and Tom Desmond of the National Library of Ireland were extremely helpful in isolating and allowing access to parts of the collection of the Music Association of Ireland, helping to throw some light on Wilson's early years in Dublin.

My attempts to build up a picture of Wilson have been greatly assisted by a wide array of people but in particular I would like to thank Jytte Abildstrøm, Lindsay Armstrong, Derek Ball, the late Mary Boydell, John Buckley, Dorothy Dorow, Ian Fox, Jim Harkin, Jane Manning, Viki Moltke, Pádhraic Ó Cuinneagáin, Eve O'Kelly, Martin O'Leary, Colman Pearce and Gillian Smith, all of whom granted extensive interviews. I am particularly grateful to Anne Makower Fitz-Simon who spent considerable time talking to me about Wilson when I first started on this project and has never tired of my e-mail queries since; to Donald and Phyllida McAlpine for their help in illuminating one of the more obscure periods of Wilson's life and for their hospitality; and to the late Brian Grimson for allowing me access to his papers as well as for his refreshing openness in discussing Wilson. It was a particular sadness that Ian Balfour (2nd Baron Balfour of Inchrye) died before this book appeared in print. I remember with great fondness his marvellous hospitality, generosity and friendship, as well as his constant help as this project progressed.

My thanks to Bruce Arnold for his reminiscences and for supplying me with a copy of *A Most Confounded Tory*; to Lesley Bishop for tracking down material in the RTÉ archive; to Aleck Crichton for his information regarding John Campbell and to Neil and Jean Townsend for their support. Raymond Deane, Noreen Doody, Iain Fairweather of the Nairn Book & Arts Festival, Beryl Kington, Niall MacDonagh, Peter Mountain, Alasdair Pettinger from the Scottish Music Centre, Andrew Plant, Brian Thomas of The Marine Society and Sea Cadets and Elizabeth Woodgate of Trinity College London all helped with various queries associated with this project. Professor Gerard Gillen, apart from discussing his memories of Wilson, also provided me with copies of correspondence. Thanks also to Deborah Kelleher for alerting me to the existence of, and allowing me access to, the letters and papers relating to the premiere of *The Hunting of the Snark* donated to the Royal Irish Academy of Music by Randal Henry.

This book was completed some years ago but the ending of the project proved to be another terminus as before my volume reached the editing stage Field Day discontinued their music series. Many people cheerfully regaled me with horror stories regarding the problems assailing those who wished to find a publisher. However, Cork University Press, to whom I sent a proposal, were immediately enthusiastic and encouraging, and Maria O'Donovan and Mike Collins have been extremely helpful throughout the entire process of bringing this book to fruition. The final text also bene-fitted from their rigorous reviewing process and the informed ideas of the three anonymous reviewers.

I am particularly grateful to Áine Sheil and Kerry Houston for reading extracts from the book and to Eoghan Ward who bravely tackled the entire volume in its first draft; their helpful suggestions and comments helped to improve the book and removed many errors. A huge debt of thanks also to Robert Yeo who took on the task of reading the revised draft of the book prepared for Cork University Press and whose comments saved me from various errors and descents into unintelligibility. Particular thanks also to Dónal Rafferty for his prompt and accurate preparation of the musical examples. Finally, I wish to thank my mother who not only read the draft chapters but also provided the solution to one of the more perplexing issues raised by the research for this book.

NOTE:

After Wilson's death his papers and manuscripts were transferred to Trinity College Manuscripts Library. All references to material in the collection are identified in the text with the catalogue designation TCD MS 11240. All references to *From the Top* are, unless otherwise specified, to the final draft. To avoid confusion page numbers are my own as this draft does not contain consecutively numbered pages. Instead it was drawn from several separate documents revised at various times resulting in bewildering page number duplications and discontinuities. The letters to Clarice Wilson, Gerard Gillen and Ian Balfour are all held in private collections unless otherwise identified in the endnotes.

1 Early Life in London

James Walter Wilson was born on 27 September 1922 at number 356 Essex Road, Islington, London. His father Edgar Wilson was a pharmacist whose family was originally from Yorkshire. After his marriage Edgar Wilson had settled in the house on Essex Road, the ground floor of which was used as a chemist's shop. Wilson later described 1920s Essex Road as 'cheerfully scruffy' and the house with its sitting room, bathroom, two bedrooms, attic and cellar as 'not . . . an elegant dwelling'.[1] Wilson's mother Margaret Alice Wilson (née Eldridge) was from the Buckinghamshire village of Ellesborough and had been working during the First World War as a shop walker in Crouch End, north London. Wilson himself was the youngest of three boys. His earliest memories were of a quasi-Victorian London of trams, gas-lit houses (though his parents' house had electricity), lamplighters and barrel organs played by street musicians. In contrast to this was the quiet village life of his grandmother and assorted aunts in Ellesborough, where trade was still sometimes conducted by a barter system and the family had owned the nearby forge in Terrick for four hundred years.

In his memoirs, Wilson recalled being fascinated by music from an early age, mentioning how he was attracted to the pianos and harmoniums that were a staple feature of middle-class homes of the time, the pianos having the added advantage for a young boy that they could be played from beneath the keys even when the lid was locked. In a broadcast to mark his sixtieth birthday he remembered 'leaning over the garden gate listening to the church bells fascinated by the way in which so many other notes seemed to swarm around each principal note', something he also recalled in his later memoirs.[2] Neither of his parents had any great interest in music, though his mother played the piano a little and enjoyed singing light songs and playing salon pieces such as Gustav Lange's *Blumenlied*.[3] Wilson's father died when he was four and his mother was left to look after the three children, the eldest Alex and Rob aged ten and nine respectively, and a business with two assistants. Her family advised her to forget her plans to send the children on to secondary education but she ignored this advice and all three children attended Highbury County School, a short walk from their home.[4] This grammar school had been founded in 1922 on a site that had previously housed a missionary society, a truant school and an industrial school. Its original catchment was mainly working class due to competition from more established grammar schools in the area, and in later years it contained a wide mix of ethnic groups.[5] Wilson was sent to Miss Clara Tappe's school until he was old enough to go to secondary school. He recalled studying grammar and etiquette, singing songs to the accompaniment of Miss Tappe's violin and taking part in plays each summer ranging from *Puss in Boots* to a presumably reduced version of *As you like it* in which he played Orlando.[6]

A friend of his mother, Miss Percival, would often play pieces, primarily hymns, to him and allowed him to play her piano, but it was not until he was about nine years old that he began formal piano lessons with a Miss Mary Maskall. Apart from occasional ventures into Beethoven, the musical diet at these lessons consisted of the lighter pieces of composers such as Coleridge Taylor and Chaminade, which helped to give Wilson a lifelong aversion to what he called 'coffee-table' music.[7] Like many young children learning to play an instrument, Wilson made some forays into writing his own pieces, one of which survives. The title page of this reads: 'Dedicated to my dear friend and teacher Mary H.E. Maskall; A Tone Poem by Jimmy Maestro.' It is a short thirty-three-bar piece in A minor with a number of chromatic notes and sevenths.[8] It is probably this piece that Wilson was thinking of when he spoke of a piano work written at this time, which originally ended with a seventh. Maskall then added a cadence in A minor saying 'not bloody likely'.[9]

At about the time this was written he entered Highbury County School. The basic rudiments of music were taught in the school, but in such a poor manner as to fail to arouse Wilson's interest. The exception was a school trip to a concert that included a performance of Bizet's incidental music to Daudet's *L'Arlésienne*, which impressed him.[10] Lessons in French and English proved more stimulating, the French lessons marking the beginning of a lifelong passion for all things French. Poetry was at first a chore to be endured and rather joylessly learnt by heart, though interestingly he frequently returned to the poetry encountered in school when composing songs in later life. His attitude was changed utterly when he came across W.B. Yeats' *The Lake Isle of Innisfree*, while his taste was extended further by his sixth-form tutor, who introduced him to T.S. Eliot's *The Waste Land*. The same tutor also cultivated the students' interest in contemporary art, showing them photographs of works by Henry Moore among others.[11] There was also a very active dramatic society in the school and each year a play by contemporary authors such as Karel Čapek, John Galsworthy, John Drinkwater and R.C. Sherriff was put on in addition to works by Shakespeare and other classics.[12]

The greater part of Wilson's artistic education was extracurricular. He became acquainted with another boy called Reg Tait who was relatively proficient on both piano and violin and together they played through four-hand arrangements of the Beethoven symphonies and violin sonatas by Mozart and Schubert, an exercise that Wilson felt taught him something of how to structure music. As time went on they plundered the local library and played through scores by more modern composers such as Debussy, Ravel and Stravinsky as well as music that is no longer part of the standard repertoire including operas by Meyerbeer.[13] He later recalled these as 'my happiest days in music: discovering some new and splendid work, and knowing that I was only glimpsing the entrance to a vast treasury.'[14] Wilson was also an avid reader of literature from Dickens (a complete edition of whose works his mother owned) to more recent authors such as D.H. Lawrence and Aldous Huxley. The latter were given to him by a Mr Walker who worked for a time as a dispenser in the family shop. Wilson described him and his sixth-form tutor as the only men he knew at this time 'who thought that an interest in the arts was reasonable in a teenage boy'.[15]

When Wilson came to the age of being confirmed he informed the vicar that he did not believe anything he had been taught about religious belief. His mother's response was to bring him to a variety of different meetings run by Quakers, Christian Scientists and revivalists to see if there was anything else that appealed to him. He recalled at one stage having what his brothers described as a brief attack of religious mania after a revivalist meeting and wryly commented that he wished to be saved but was not sure from what.[16] However, none of these forms of belief had any lasting impact and Wilson remained an atheist for the rest of his life.[17]

The greatest influence on the young Wilson was his mother with whom he developed a particularly close bond. While his brothers, who were five and six years older than him, tended to play together, Wilson's mother brought him to galleries and museums at weekends, instilling an enduring love of art and architecture. She also brought him to the theatre where they saw works by Shaw, Ibsen and Chekhov, and occasionally to the cinema. She was also responsible for introducing him in the early 1930s to opera:

> There was a Saturday afternoon when I came home disgruntled. The sixpenny seats at the Carlton Cinema – an eccentric building in Essex-Road-Egyptian style – were full. My mother

was at the kitchen stove when I came in. When I had com-
plained about the injustice of the world towards me, she turned
and said 'Why don't you go to Sadler's Wells?' Sadler's Wells was
accessible; just the other side of the Angel. 'But that's opera, or
something awful, isn't it?' I asked. She looked at me. 'Why don't
you try it?' I went. Joan Cross was singing Mimi in *La Bohème*. I
was hooked.[18]

Other operas quickly followed; standard repertoire such as *Carmen* and *Il
Trovatore*, recent English operas such as Ethel Smyth's *The Wreckers* (premiered in Leipzig in 1906 and revived at Sadler's Wells in 1939) and
Vaughan Williams' *Hugh the Drover* (premiered in 1922, performed in the
1936–37 season) as well as more unusual fare such as Rimsky-Korsakov's
The Snow Maiden (performed in 1933). The greatest revelation, however,
was Mozart's *Don Giovanni,* and Mozart's operas were to remain one of the
key models behind his own dramatic works for the rest of his life.

Sadler's Wells was also home to a ballet company that had evolved from
a group of artists associated with the *Ballets Russes* which had dissolved after
the death of Sergei Diaghilev. This regrouped under a variety of names: the
Sunday Ballet Club, the Camargo Society, the Vic-Wells and finally the
Sadler's Wells Ballet.[19] Unlike some of the groups splintered from the *Ballets
Russes*, this group, directed by Dame Ninette de Valois, with Constant
Lambert, another Diaghilev protégé, as music director, offered a distinctive
mix of standard pieces and works associated with the Diaghilev company.
More importantly, it also continued to posit ballet as the innovative art
form of the future with a range of new commissions. Audiences at the Wells
witnessed, in 1934, the first production of *The Nutcracker* outside Russia,
while in 1938 Lambert conducted Tchaikovsky's *The Sleeping Princess*,
which had previously only been performed in England by Diaghilev's company. The new ballets produced played an important role in introducing
Wilson to, and shaping his views on, contemporary music and among the
productions he attended were Gavin Gordon's *The Rake's Progress* and
Stravinsky's *Le baiser de la fée*, performed in the 1935 season; Arthur Bliss'
Checkmate premiered in 1937 and Lambert's *Horoscope* premiered in
1938.[20] Indeed, while Wilson was not unaware of the symphonic repertoire,
it is probably fair to say that his musical tastes and experience were moulded
to a greater extent by his exposure to dramatic works rather than engagement with the Austro-German symphonic repertoire.

In 1937, Wilson travelled abroad for the first time when his mother
paid for him to join a cruise along the coast of Norway organised by the

School Journeys Association. This first trip abroad aroused Wilson's interest in Scandinavia, something that was to increase as he developed stronger ties with artists in the region later in his career. When he completed his secondary education at Highbury County School, Wilson applied for a position in the civil service and after sitting the entrance exam began work in the Admiralty in May 1939. University education was out of the question, something that Wilson later regretted. In the final version of his memoirs, Wilson refers rather obliquely to this, stating 'Highbury County School did not set its standards very high. Pupils were guided into nice safe jobs with pensions: the Civil Service, the Banks, and failing these, the Metropolitan Water Board.'[21] In the draft outline for the memoirs, however, in a list of post-war events, is the phrase 'my longing to go to university' while on another occasion he referred to 'the university education that I'd helplessly coveted during my years in the Navy'.[22] Wilson's insecurity about his formal education is also reflected in the memoirs, where he describes how he was deprived of the chance to study Latin, the basis of a classical education, in school, saying 'I am still a bit ashamed of not having studied it.'[23] This may have been exacerbated by the background of his later partner John Campbell and many of their social circle.

While Wilson found his job at the Admiralty dull, it paid for a number of treats, such as books on art and tickets to see de Basil's Russian Ballet when it visited London.[24] After this experience he felt that Sadler's Wells was never quite as glamorous as it had previously seemed.[25] A curious by-product of these early experiences of ballet was to emerge near the end of Wilson's career. *Les Sylphides* was a classic of the early years of the Diaghilev ballet but the score has had a particularly convoluted history which has resulted in various people re-orchestrating the work for different companies over the last century.[26] In 1998 Wilson created his own version of the score, inscribing it with the words 'In homage to Frédéric Chopin and Maurice Ravel.' The work, apparently written with no performance in mind and to date unperformed, would seem to be as much an affectionate homage to the dance companies that gave him his early musical education and the glamorous world of the Russian ballet that lay behind them as it is to the virtuosic orchestration of one of his favourite composers.

The outbreak of war in September 1939 did not immediately affect Wilson, but Churchill's ruling that naval signals should be dealt with by civilians rather than through service channels resulted in Wilson being transferred to the cipher and coding department. In a commentary on government arts policy he described this period:

> During the Blitz on London, I spent most nights working under-
> ground in Whitehall. On a number of occasions, the building in
> which I worked was hit by a bomb. After something like four-
> teen hours' work, I would go home, not always in the best
> possible state. And when I got home, before I had a wash or a
> cup of tea, I sat at the piano for ten minutes playing Mozart.
> That is what made it possible to carry on.[27]

When Wilson's mother decided to move from blitzed London to the greater
safety of her family's home in Wendover, a short distance from Ellesborough,
he moved with her, commuting by train to Whitehall. He was later to refer
to this as 'the most testing time of our lives' and the toll it exacted is demonstrated by his description of this period, 'when I was quite desperate and near
suicidal, trying to cope with a job that was far too demanding for anyone of
my age, short of sleep and inadequately fed.'[28] On a more positive note, he
was still able occasionally to play Mozart with his friend Tait, as they were in
the same department of the civil service, and they also took a walking
holiday together in Sussex. It was through his work in the Admiralty that
Wilson met Clarice Jeffery, who was the same age as him and with whom he
was to keep up an important correspondence until her death in 2005. He
later introduced her to his brother Robert, whom she married in 1947.[29]

With the closure of many venues and the removal of orchestras from the
city, the National Gallery, across Trafalgar Square from his workplace,
became the centre of Wilson's other artistic experiences at this time. Each
month one masterpiece was selected from the gallery's collection, which was
in storage in Wales, and exhibited, providing the public with an extraordinary opportunity to examine and get to know single paintings in isolation.
Wilson felt that it was only in these circumstances that he learnt to look at
paintings. The gallery was also host to a series of lunchtime concerts organised by Myra Hess, which ran throughout the war. It was at these that
Wilson heard what was to remain one of his favourite compositions,
Mozart's Oboe Quartet K370, a work he described as containing 'the quin-
tessence of all music'.[30]

In late 1942, at the age of twenty, Wilson was called up for active
service in the Royal Navy, the Fleet Air Arm having turned him down on
account of his colour blindness. He commenced training on 31 December
1942 in Skegness. This was followed by six months' study of radio theory at
Northampton Polytechnic and practical radar training on the Isle of Man.
His training and later work at radar also gave him a rudimentary introduction to electronics which he was later to capitalise on in his radio work. At

first Wilson served on a mailboat from Scapa Flow to Reykjavik, whose tedium and routine he was only to appreciate when this was exchanged for work with the Arctic convoys. These had been authorised by Churchill despite the dangers posed, to convey materials necessary for the Soviet war effort to Murmansk in the fear that Stalin would otherwise make a separate peace pact with Hitler.[31] During summer, the sun never set, leaving convoys open to attack from the air, while dense fogs which made navigation tremendously difficult for those on the ships did not necessarily provide cover for the masts from air surveillance. The winter, with its perpetual twilight, provided greater cover but exposed the crews to high winds, violent storms and freezing temperatures. Much time had to be spent by crews removing the ice which built up on the ships to prevent them capsizing. The chances of survival if a boat capsized or sank were very small due to the low temperatures; death from hypothermia would occur after, at most, three minutes in the water. Wilson's post as radio mechanic presented its own dangers, as he discovered on the first convoy; when attempting to steady himself while fixing an electronic fault with the radar set, he accidentally electrocuted himself by touching the transmitter. The accident left a small hole in the top joint of one finger that took a long time to heal.[32]

Wilson took part in four convoys through the Arctic. On the second of these, Wilson's ship, the destroyer HMS *Impulsive*, was involved in the sinking of the German battleship *Scharnhorst* on 26 December 1943, one of the key military engagements of the naval war in the north.[33] In February 1944, Wilson took part in his third convoy in which another of the destroyers in the convoy, HMS *Mahratta*, was torpedoed by U990 and sank.[34] Breaking orders, *Impulsive* stopped to rescue men from the sea, despite attack from further U-boats. Only seventeen men from a crew of around two hundred were taken from the water alive and one of these subsequently died from hypothermia. Wilson recalled that when the convoy returned to Scapa, it was immediately sent back to Russia with further provisions.[35]

Unlikely as it may at first seem, it was during this period of active service on HMS *Impulsive* that Wilson began to engage seriously with the possibility of music as a profession. He had brought pocket scores of Sibelius' fifth symphony, Brahms' third symphony and the *Fantasia on a Theme by Thomas Tallis* by Vaughan Williams with him, and a copy of Forsyth's *Orchestration*.[36] To these was later added a score of Pergolesi's *Stabat Mater*.[37] One of the officers who knew of Wilson's interests lent him his wind-up gramophone and collection of records, which included

Brahms' fourth symphony and Elizabeth Schumann singing *Bist du bei mir*. During a short period, when HMS *Impulsive* was based at Portsmouth, he was able to go ashore and play through music by Schubert with a violinist who had joined the crew. Apart from this, the experience of hearing music was limited to occasional pieces heard on the communal radio on board and concerts attended when on leave. Wilson had also brought a few French and English books on board. While most of his fellow sailors were not interested in music and literature in the same way as Wilson, he forged a strong and lasting friendship with Thorkild Harboe, a young man originally from Denmark, who had spent the previous years with his parents in Rio de Janeiro. Their acquaintance was initially founded on their shared love of books and music, as well as their shared sexuality. They remained in contact after the war and Harboe was to play a crucial role in developing Wilson's career in Denmark thirty years later.

More importantly, active service was also Wilson's pathway to his first formal training in composition. In 1938, the College of the Sea had been founded as an extension of the earlier Seafarers Education Service, and sailors had the opportunity to do correspondence courses in various subjects, the standard and pace being dictated by the ability and time available to each candidate.[38] One of the main tutors in the music-theory section at the time was Gordon Jacob; however, it is not clear who Wilson's own tutor was.[39] Wilson began his course in late 1944 and, despite the difficult conditions, seems to have composed quite an amount of music while at sea. In October 1944, he drafted a piano sonata and quickly followed this with a violin sonata, which he got a chance to play to a violinist in December.[40] In his memoirs he recalled a setting he made of Edith Sitwell's *Street Songs* for soprano, flute and piano. Most ambitiously, in December 1944 he began a setting of *The Waste Land*, despite what he referred to as his 'very small' knowledge of orchestration:

> I'm opening with a picture of the waste land, drum rolls, pianis
> simo, on C and D flat, with shakes on harp and harpsichord, a
> fourth apart, which should sound very bleak. By page three,
> when I have reached the line 'Summer surprised us, coming over
> the Starnbergersee,' I have made use of the above instruments
> plus bass clarinet, 'cello, double bass, three flutes, horn, bassoon
> and muted trombone.[41]

With the establishment of Allied supremacy in the Arctic, HMS *Impulsive* was dispatched for other duties. The remainder of the war saw Wilson involved in escorting US ships, supporting the Normandy landings, and taking part in the liberation of Guernsey. After a short illness, Wilson spent time at various shore postings, including Doonfoot in Ayr in Burns' country, before ending up in Derry on HMS *Pitcairn*, his first experience of Ireland. In one of his last interviews he recalled, 'I suppose I fell in love with Ireland. I used to go across the border whenever I could because you could get nice steaks and things, which you couldn't anywhere else; it was a very beautiful country.'[42] While in Derry, he was diagnosed with tuberculosis and sent to the Isle of Wight for treatment. He was finally invalided out of the navy with a disability pension of three pounds a week for the next three years and a post-war gratuity.[43] Wilson's war experiences left their mark in the anti-war stance taken in such compositions as *A Passionate Man* and *Virata*, and colleagues noted his strong views on such matters.[44] However, in interview he once enigmatically described the war as something he 'would not have missed for anything', adding that it gave him a wealth of experiences, both musical and non-musical that he would never have otherwise had.[45] He also discussed the way in which it developed his character, bringing out a ruthless side he had not known existed and developing a toughness which was to be essential in his struggle to survive as a composer in later life.[46]

Wilson spent his demobilisation leave in France, visiting among other places Arles, where Van Gogh had produced many of his most famous paintings, and when he received his gratuity, half of it was spent on a copy of *À la recherche du temps perdu*. The other half of the gratuity was spent on composition lessons at Trinity College of Music, London, where he also enrolled for harpsichord lessons with Christopher Wood and piano lessons with Irving Hinchcliffe.[47] His composition teacher was Alec Rowley, another London-born composer, perhaps best known today for his educational music. Like Wilson, Rowley was a confirmed Francophile. His interests were wide-ranging, however, and he encouraged his students to explore lesser known works and composers as well as encouraging their interest in the other arts. His own tastes included the music of his English contemporaries and friends such as Bridge and Warlock and French composers ranging from Fauré and Debussy to Milhaud and Poulenc. While lamenting the lack of 'romantic beauty' in modern music he admired the music of Bartók but failed to empathise with the music of the Second Viennese School.[48] Wilson was back working in the military branch of the Admiralty at this time and he attended weekly lessons with Rowley in the evenings, frequently accompanying him for supper in a local Italian restaurant afterwards. While Wilson always found Rowley's advice well founded, Rowley never explained exactly why something in a composition was wrong. Of this time Wilson recalled:

> I set a number of sonnets by Pierre de Ronsard, which was foolish of me, since Alec Rowley didn't speak French. Also, I did not know nearly enough about the language to understand subtleties of rhythm and pronunciation. But one day when I had written a setting of Leigh Hunt's poem *Jenny kissed me*, I was told 'That's your first proper song.'[49]

Wilson's *Six Chansons de Ronsard pour des voix divers* have a certain curiosity value as they are the only compositions still extant from this period of his career. The surviving score is dedicated to Isla Morante and is dated 26 November 1950.[50] They bear out Wilson's comments about their lack of understanding regarding rhythmic subtlety and how to set the French words; the vocal line tends to be regular, syllabic and lacking in memorable melodic shaping. The piano part is quite awkward to play in a number of places, which is surprising considering Wilson's own ability at the instrument, but more noticeable is the awkwardness of the harmonic writing. Extra voices fill in the gaps between the treble and bass in a sometimes quite arbitrary manner. Despite these problems, what can be discerned in the work is a penchant for modal inflections and parallel chords, and while all songs end firmly in the key in which they began, the central passages of the songs tend to modulate sometimes to quite unexpected regions in a manner that suggests lack of traditional harmonic training. The influence of French music shares an equal platform with that from the English neo-Renaissance modal songwriters.

Looking back at this period of study with Rowley in the 1980s Wilson commented:

> I really didn't spend nearly long enough in hindsight being taught. What I was writing with him was piano music and songs. I'd just started writing for a small orchestra but I only had something like 18 months with him after which I was on my own. But I learned a lot I think, about song writing especially, from him and I have always since then been very interested in writing songs.[51]

In reality, it was to be many years before Wilson tackled songwriting again and, in some ways, it is surprising that Wilson seems to have abandoned this mode of expression after settling in Ireland, but perhaps at this stage he did not place as high a value on songwriting, preoccupied as he was with the idea of writing for the stage. When Wilson moved to Dublin he lost contact with Rowley, intending to renew contact when he had made a breakthrough. This did not happen before Rowley's death in 1958, something that Wilson always regretted.

Wilson's letters and later writings give us some sense of his musical position at this period. Writing in 1982 in a half-ironical way about his own development he noted:

> I suppose that every composer begins by imitating someone. In my youth in London, we were all writing Vaughan Williams: now the kids are would-be Stockhausens and Ligetis. After a bit of time at this, most of us find a second composer at the other end of the contemporary spectrum (in my case it was Prokofiev) and write strange amalgams that we imagine to be works of flaming genius and originality. Provided that we do not let ourselves be entirely discouraged by the reception that is rightly afforded to our products, we may in course of time find something of our own to say. If we don't, maybe we will reach the stage when we can produce first-class imitations of our favoured model, but we would be better employed doing some honest work, such as knitting or accountancy or home brewing.[52]

The admiration he cites for the music of Vaughan Williams is not surprising, as for most musicians of that generation Vaughan Williams dominated the London contemporary music scene in the 1920s and 1930s, Elgar having more or less ceased to compose after the death of his wife in 1920. The *Fantasia on a Theme by Thomas Tallis* had been one of the three scores he had with him while on active service and there are other references to Vaughan Williams in his letters from the period. As he worked on his own setting of *The Waste Land*, Wilson commented 'I am still hoping that it is not too late for Vaughan Williams to write the incidental music for *Murder in the Cathedral*.'[53] Most of Wilson's earliest music no longer exists but traces of Vaughan Williams can still be found, as late as 1969, in his first large-scale opera *Twelfth Night* and he continued to cite Vaughan Williams in later interviews, noting in 2002, 'To me Vaughan Williams is one of the great song-writers. I think he's rather underestimated in general for that.'[54]

The Prokofiev influence is clearer from some of his surviving works, such as the first symphony from 1960, and Colman Pearce recalled seeing an early orchestral piece in which there was an inadvertent quotation from Prokofiev.[55] Other influences in the early years included Stravinsky, whose ballets in particular were familiar to Wilson, and Bartók, whose music he seems to have begun discovering during the war years. During one of his periods of leave, he attended a performance of Bartók's Sonata for Two Pianos and Percussion, though it was abandoned before the conclusion due to a musically timed explosion of a flying bomb, which left the performers convulsed with laughter.[56] His wartime letters contain glowing praise for the recently premiered second violin concerto.[57] The music of Debussy and Ravel was always of tremendous importance to him and he also admired what he had heard of the music of Frank Bridge and Arthur Honegger, in particular the latter's *Le roi David*, which remained a favourite work.[58] He was also greatly interested in the music of Dvořák and particularly Smetana, ranking *The Bartered Bride* as one of the most satisfying of all operas at this time, but also admiring the orchestral works.[59] What is striking about the composers cited by Wilson in interview, and letters is that there is less stated interest in the nineteenth-century Austro-Germanic school than in music of composers from other traditions. Indeed, in a pre-concert interview, he described himself as being, when young, 'more familiar with Stravinsky than Beethoven'.[60]

The sense of a lack of interest in this music is increased by comments in later interviews, such as one from 2005 where, upon being asked to discuss what had influenced his music, he replied, 'Mozart, and then there's probably a gap until you get to Debussy and Ravel, Stravinsky, Prokofiev.'[61] It is important, however, when examining Wilson's work not to overlook his interest in a number of figures from the Austro-Germanic school even though his temperament inclined him more towards French music. Mozart and Schubert were two of his favourite composers and he also had a high regard for the music of Schumann. More unlikely on a surface level was his interest in Brahms. For Wilson, the most interesting aspect of Brahms was the economy of the writing, something it shares with the fifth symphony of Sibelius which, with Brahms' third symphony and the Vaughan Williams score, made up his music library during the war years. Another early letter from the 1940s comments on how his listening had been dominated by 'lots of Brahms'.[62] He acknowledged in a number of interviews that Brahms' ability to derive large structures from quite small motivic cells remained an important model for him, stating 'that's what I like doing. Getting the maximum effect from the minimum of means',[63] while, when lambasting minimalism, saying it was 'really fairly disastrous, I mean it's like painting by numbers – any fool can write that kind of thing', he declared that real minimalism was to be found in the disciplined music of Brahms.[64]

The post-war music scene in London offered Wilson plenty of new experiences at both ends of the music spectrum. His interest in early music was served by Walter Goehr's performance of Monteverdi's 1610 vespers in Hans Redlich's edition with the Morley College Choir and Orchestra, and he also attended performances of Bach's B-minor Mass and *Die Kunst der Fuge* among other works. The Henry Wood Promenade Concerts gave him his first real introduction to the standard orchestral repertoire. Apart from his love of Vaughan Williams and Bartók, he was also interested in the music of Stravinsky and attended a performance of *Les Noces*, and he also sought out concerts of music by Frank Martin, Honnegger, Hindemith and Berg. He attended the first English production of *Fancy Free* by Bernstein in 1946 and saw Richard Strauss conduct the Philharmonia Orchestra in his *Sinfonia Domestica, Don Juan*, the waltzes from *Der Rosenkavalier* and the Burlesque for Piano and Orchestra on 19 October 1947. Other notable concerts attended included the premiere of Vaughan Williams' sixth symphony on 21 April 1948 and a double bill of Schoenberg's *Pierrot Lunaire* with the unlikely coupling of Walton's *Façade*; while he found the Schoenberg intriguing he was much more taken by the Walton.[65]

This was also the period when Benjamin Britten moved from being a promising young composer to the dominant figure among British composers. Wilson was already familiar with the *Variations on a Theme of Frank Bridge* (1937) and *Les Illuminations* (1940) from performances by Boyd Neel and his string orchestra.[66] He attended one of the early performances of *Peter Grimes* in June 1945 at Sadler's Wells and bought a copy of poems by Crabbe in St Paul's churchyard in the hope of finding some reference to Grimes.[67] He also attended early performances of *The Rape of Lucretia* (1946), *Albert Herring* (1947) and Britten's arrangement of John Gay's *The Beggar's Opera* (1948), as well as a performance of *The Young Person's Guide to the Orchestra* and the Sea Interludes from *Peter Grimes* at the Proms in 1948.[68]

Wilson's music has frequently been compared to that of Britten, partly because of the prominent position opera takes in the output of both composers. The comparison probably originated in the fact that the first work with which Wilson came to prominence was a children's opera and most of the publicity drew parallels with the works for children by Britten, though Wilson himself tended to compare it instead with the work of Ravel. Britten certainly was the major figure in post-war London, particularly for a composer interested in theatre. However, after the vivid impressions made by the premiere of *Peter Grimes*, Wilson found his later operas less interesting. *The*

Rape of Lucretia he found disappointingly undramatic – he jokingly commented that Britten should have been sued for false advertising, as the audience does not get to see the rape – but the general idea behind *The Beggar's Opera* was to remain in the back of his mind when he wrote his own *A Passionate Man*.[69] In retrospect he felt that Britten was a great song composer, though not necessarily a great opera composer and a list of 'favourite things' for a radio programme, of which only the first half survives, includes *Les Illuminations*.[70] Britten's approach to text setting, clarity of word delivery, and avoidance of extremes of range that might inhibit text audibility, served as an exemplar for Wilson, as did his tailoring of music for the qualities of specific performers, but beyond this any perceived resemblance is purely superficial.

It was at some stage in the mid-1940s that Wilson first met John Campbell, who was to remain his partner until Campbell's death in 1975. Born James Harper Poynter Campbell in 1901, apart from being older than Wilson, John Campbell came from a different social background and had been educated at Eton and King's College, Cambridge. He competed in the pole vault event at the 1924 Olympic Games, and took on the role of works and production manager of the wine importers Moussec Ltd.[71] In 1929 he sailed with a friend, Philip Merton, across the Atlantic to the West Indies and the US in a yacht called the *Daydream*. Merton died shortly before the war and Campbell volunteered, helping with the evacuation of Crete.[72] He later became commander of the Aegean Raiding Forces ('Comaro One') and it was in conversations between Campbell and Paddy Leigh Fermor that the successful plan to kidnap General von Kreipe, the German commander of Crete, originated.[73] He was also responsible for landing Greek agents and evacuating refugees, as well as organising raids which succeeded in keeping large numbers of German troops engaged with a minimum use of allied manpower. With these operations, Campbell won the awards of DSO and DSC.[74] A vivid picture of Campbell was drawn by Xan Fielding in his account of this period:

> John spoke through clenched teeth in monosyllables – except during rare outbursts of temper, when he showed an equally masterly command of invective. Tall and powerful, with a tenacity and singleness of purpose bordering on fanaticism, he was saved from what might otherwise have been an appearance of sinister ruthlessness by conventional good looks that were far above the average and by an elegance that asserted itself even in the impersonal accoutrements of war-time service dress.[75]

Summing him up, Wilson recalled 'he was everything that I was not', and also said that he had 'one of the best brains that I have ever encountered.'[76] After the war, Campbell returned to Dublin and settled in Monkstown, having sold his property in Sligo. He made frequent visits to London, where he met Wilson. Campbell introduced Wilson to his circle of friends in London and it was through him that Wilson met Boyd Neel at a dinner party. Neel and Wilson soon became friends, going dancing in the East End and discussing shared musical interests, ranging from the works of Gilbert and Sullivan to those of Berlioz.[77] Neel remained in contact with Wilson for the rest of his life and helped to arrange performances of several of his compositions over the years.

In the late 1940s, Wilson decided to take the civil service executive examination, but having passed the written part he failed the interview section. This setback seems to have made Wilson reassess his position carefully. He had been quite determined throughout the war that he was going to be a composer. He knew that the military branch of the Admiralty would soon be disbanded and a less interesting job would be the most likely outcome.[78] He was also beginning to feel that he needed to obtain some distance from the cultural saturation of London:

> What I really needed I think was to get down into myself and discover what I could do, and the danger for a young composer in London was over-stimulation; there were too many concerts, there were too many exhibitions, too many new operas and plays and things to distract you from sitting down and working on your own. And that is what I had to do. I had to sit down and stop listening to what other people were doing and looking sideways and get on with what I was going to write.[79]

The ascendancy of Britten must also have been a factor and Wilson may have felt it would be easier to establish himself in Dublin where there was no such dominating force. Another factor which may have played a part in Wilson's decision-making was that the prosecution of homosexuals in London peaked at this period in the late 1940s, reaching what was to be the highest level of the century, and high-profile prosecutions continued into the 1950s.[80] Although Irish society was considerably more repressive in many other ways, Wilson recalled that homosexuals 'were left more or less alone'.[81] While there were prosecutions in Ireland, the Irish authorities did not mount a campaign against homosexuals equivalent to that which existed in London. There were also no high-profile prosecutions of public figures in Ireland whereas in England those prosecuted included John Gielgud, who was a friend of Campbell's.[82] It would seem that Campbell did not retain his close ties with London after this period and seldom visited the country. The development of his relationship with Campbell presumably sealed Wilson's resolve. Whether it was initially intended as a permanent move or not is unclear, but after one or two holidays spent in Ireland with Campbell, he resigned from the Admiralty, thus forfeiting his pension, and left Britain to settle in the newly declared republic in 1949, determined to become a composer.[83]

2 Arrival in Dublin

Wilson's first years in Dublin were anything but auspicious. John Campbell was at the time in the throes of writing an account of his wartime operations, *Fragments of Stone*, and Wilson began the task of editing and typing the memoir. He also made a number of ink drawings to illustrate the volume. The memoir was submitted to Chatto & Windus in 1950 on the recommendation of Compton Mackenzie, but was rejected, due to the repetitive nature of the operations described and Campbell's rather dry writing style.[1] Before Wilson had completed his editorial task he decided to take a job in the firm of Charles Pilkington, an interior decorators in Kildare Street.[2] In every interview and in his memoirs, Wilson stressed how much he hated this job and that this time was the most miserable of his life. After about eighteen months he left the job and Ireland to sail around the Mediterranean with Campbell.

The Mediterranean had been the original destination for Campbell's earlier sailing trip with Philip Merton, but they had been persuaded to sail across the Atlantic instead. This was an opportunity for Campbell to realise the earlier plans as well as an opportunity to return to the Greek Islands, which he had played a major role in liberating. In July 1950, Wilson and Campbell set off in Campbell's yacht, *Vistona*, a thirty-ton gaff cutter. Campbell took care of the navigation and Wilson looked after the cooking. Everything else that had to be done was divided between the two of them, and with friends that joined them for parts of the journey, and with the various hands they employed. The first stretch of the journey took them from Dún Laoghaire to the north-west of Spain at Corcubión and then gradually down the coast, stopping at Lisbon and Cádiz, before reaching Gibraltar. In Gibraltar Wilson spent much time listening to a flamenco troupe and even took castanet lessons. Wilson recorded his impressions of the dancers:

> In two places I have seen perfect dancing. Once it was near Murmansk where some Russian soldiers entertained the Royal Navy, and once in a pub in Gibraltar where eight girls, Spanish gypsies from La Linea, every evening in gorgeous dresses perform the *jota* and the classical *paso doble*, stared at by soldiers and

sailors over pints of beer. At the end of the evening they danced the *Sevillanas* together, and eight pairs of castanets sprang into life, the high heels stamped, beating out the dance with mechanical precision as they moved through the formal figures.[3]

On 4 September they left Gibraltar and headed towards Majorca before moving on to Sardinia. On 20 September they left Cagliari for Ischia, where Campbell's sister lived. After spending a few weeks exploring southern Italy they began the journey to Greece, where they stayed for the winter. The following April, they continued their exploration of the Greek Islands, before returning via Italy to the Côte d'Azur. It would seem they went back to Ireland in December and returned to the Côte d'Azur in June 1952. They stayed in the area until September when John Campbell sold *Vistona* at Cannes and returned to Dublin, feeling that he had accomplished what he had wanted to do.[4]

There had been no time for composition on board the yacht. A wind-up gramophone on board was restricted to recordings of Mozart's *Die Zauberflöte* Overture and Piano Concerto in C minor K491 and a selection of ballet music; Stravinsky's *Firebird*, Tchaikovsky's *Sleeping Princess* and *Sylvia* by Delibes.[5] The trip did enable Wilson to spend considerable time studying and listening to the folk music of Spain, Greece and Turkey, while in Sardinia he recorded:

> We left . . . but not before we heard recordings of some Sardinian folk songs, thanks to the musical director of the radio station. The Society of St Cecilia, Italy's main musical organisation, is making a collection of this music in order to save much of it from extinction. I have never heard any folk music that impressed me more.[6]

The effect on his approach to composition was of huge importance:

> Before that I think I thought in terms of two in a bar, three in a bar and then I started thinking in terms of 7 and 11 and 13 in a bar and followed by bars of four/four and mixing them all up and so on and it gave me an entirely new idea about writing music.[7]

His interest in non-standard metres and rhythms remained a feature throughout his output, though it later became less constantly applied than in his earliest music, which prompted a commentator to characterise him as 'a composer with an interest in unusual time-signatures'.[8] It was, however, always more of a surface feature of the music and Wilson was not interested in the type of rhythmic or metric complexity found in the music of Stravinsky or more recent composers, but rather in the vitality he felt irregular rhythms gave to the music.[9] He was also inspired by some of the folk instruments, particularly a double-reed Moroccan instrument, the raita, and tried to imitate its sound in some of his compositions. With the exposure this trip gave Wilson to sights, cultures, history and above all music, it is not surprising that he referred to this period as his 'equivalent to going to university'.[10]

Returning to a Dublin Wilson recalled as rather drab and settling back into ordinary life there can not have been easy; Wilson later recalled Ireland at this time as a 'rather difficult climate to live and work in'.[11] The sense of the dominance of the Catholic church was particularly strong in these years in the wake of the failed Mother and Child Scheme of Dr Noël Browne.[12] Censorship of literature had reached ludicrous levels, particularly since the amendments to the Censorship Act of 1946, allowing greater powers to the censorship board and customs officials, and most contemporary literature of quality was banned. Severe censorship also applied to cinema and theatre.[13] However, it is clear that like other people outside the dominant social grouping, Wilson and Campbell managed to establish a comfortable environment in which they could operate. Despite the censorship, it seems from Wilson's letters that he had no particular difficulty in obtaining books that were not commercially available in Dublin. Socially, Wilson and Campbell became part of Dublin's homosexual society, but they also culti-vated strong links with Anglo-Irish and wealthy society. Indeed Wilson's letters are teeming with titles and ambassadors; as Mary Boydell wryly noted, 'they liked grand people'.[14] Their lifestyle together was remembered by Brian Grimson as being redolent of '1930s England, Noel Coward and that atmosphere', with cocktails, dressing for dinner and each course served by a servant summoned by an electric bell installed beside Campbell's place at the table.

Wilson quickly made efforts to integrate himself into the musical life of the city, which was slowly entering a significant phase of regeneration. The Music Association of Ireland (MAI), which was to be the driving force behind most of the musical activity in the country throughout the next few decades, had been founded in 1948 and in the same year the national broadcaster Radio Éireann had established its symphony orchestra. The other orchestra in Dublin, the amateur Dublin Orchestral Players, had a wider repertoire though the standard of performance was often not partic-ularly high due to the mixed standard of the personnel. Although it would seem Wilson spent the vast majority of 1951 away from Ireland, he joined the MAI that year realising that this was essential for furthering his career. The artist Norah McGuinness advised him that 'if you want to know about music here, you've got to meet Brian Boydell' and by the end of 1952, at the latest, Wilson was in contact with him.[15] His friendship with Brian Boydell quickly bore fruit, with the first performance of some of his music in a concert given by the Dublin Orchestral Players conducted by Boydell in the Abbey Lecture Hall on Thursday, 18 June 1953. The leader of the orchestra was Carol Acton, wife of Charles Acton, who was soon to be appointed music critic of *The Irish Times*, and the programme also included works by J.C. Bach and Järnefelt, Bruch's first violin concerto and Beethoven's first symphony.

The music performed was two extracts from a three-act ballet *Esther*, based on the biblical Book of Esther, to a scenario devised by the artist Eric Horsbrugh Porter.[16] Wilson wrote a short note for the programme:

> The two dances to be played tonight are taken from the first of the three acts. Ahasuerus, King of Medes and Persians, has put away his first wife and seeks another. In the great hall of his palace, maidens dance a Sarabande, and are unveiled as they dance. The king is indifferent until the young Jewess Esther is brought in by her father Mordecai, and made against her will to dance. After the hesitant beginning of the music she too is unveiled and the King's awakened desire is roused to frenzy. The Sarabande is scored for strings only, and is a straightforward piece in conventional form. Esther's dance has a persistent rhythmical bass, against which clash the other rhythms introduced by the dance.[17]

The reviews of the dances variously described as being by 'a young Dublin composer' and 'the Irish composer Jim Wilson' were in general favourable. Robert Johnstone, writing in the *Irish Press*, reported that they were 'well laid out for orchestra':

> He has managed to produce pages that are uncomplicated without triteness, the interior design of the movements is transparently clear, while the material and the uses to which it is put are attractive and forcefully expounded.

Joseph O'Neill in the *Irish Independent* noted their 'effective Eastern atmosphere' and 'orchestral inventiveness and musical imagination', though perhaps troubled by its metrical novelty, felt that more firmness could have been given to 'the accent beat' to give a better outline to the music. An anonymous review noted: 'They are very attractively, but simply, scored, and indicate that the composer's style has not fully matured yet.' Denis Donoghue reported, 'At first hearing, this music has a reticence and taste which are delightful. On its own, the "Sarabande" has no special significance, but "Esther's Dance" has a gay glitter. This dance has at least two passages of real excitement.'

This early success must have been extremely encouraging for Wilson, but he soon found that it would not be an easy matter to capitalise on this. In 1954 composers in the MAI formed a group which Wilson recalled as 'a sort of Composers' Group, which met occasionally over tea and buns to listen to recordings and to be polite about one another's work'.[18] They also organised concerts and in their first year four concerts took place in Trinity College, Dublin, including music by Seóirse Bodley, Brian Boydell, Frederick May, John Reidy (Seán Ó Riada) and Archie Potter. Wilson's work was not featured and he wryly commented in his memoirs that 'nobody wanted any of my works, and they were quite right, because I didn't know enough about the job of composition.'[19] While none of this music survives to enable one to make definitive judgements, it would appear from the surviving evidence that the main reason for this, and his subsequent failure to make any significant breakthrough in the 1950s, is that, unlike the composers mentioned above who had produced a range of songs and chamber music, Wilson seems to have concentrated his energies on writing large-scale pieces for big forces. Apart from his three-act *Esther*, he embarked at some point in the 1950s on an opera based on Selma Lagerlöf's *Gösta Berling's Saga*, a long colourful tale which mixes folklore and the supernatural with scenes of Swedish peasant life, its hero being a former clergyman who becomes entangled with a powerful landowner and her collection of vagrant cavaliers. This project seems to have been shelved at some point.[20] However, in 1955 he completed a two-act ballet *Le Roi de l'Ille*, of approximately forty-five minutes' duration with a scenario by John Campbell's sister, Isla Morante, for a large orchestra including triple wind, alto saxophone, piano and mandolin. The impracticality of this in a city with no ballet company and a small orchestra in difficult economic times is obvious.[21] It is, however, possible that Wilson had not got an Irish performance in mind as is suggested by his next ballet project.

Mo and Eric Horsbrugh Porter's daughter Phyllida had married ballet dancer Donald McAlpine. McAlpine had danced with Sadler's Wells Ballet for four years and at this point both he and his wife were dancing for London Festival Ballet. They devised a scenario for Wilson based loosely around a Russian play Phyllida had heard on the radio. Wilson suggested the name *Cynara* as the poem by Ernest Dowson with its recurrent refrain 'But I was desolate and sick of an old passion . . . I have been faithful to thee, Cynara! In my fashion' was the nearest thing he could think of that related to the idea explored in the ballet of faithfulness after death.[22] Porter designed costumes for the ballet and McAlpine then tried unsuccessfully to interest Julian Braunschweg and Anton Dolin in the project.[23] He also gave a copy of the score to the music director of the company Geoffrey Corbett, but Corbett mislaid it while touring Italy and the ballet was never performed.[24]

His next success was to occur outside the Republic. At this time Wilson changed his approach and began to compose with specific people in mind, in the hope of securing performances. He completed his Divertimento for Strings in 1957, which he dedicated to his friend Boyd Neel, who was by this time resident in Canada and dean of the Royal Conservatory of Music and head of the music faculty of Toronto University.[25] Neel played it through with his students, but more encouragingly, the work was broadcast by BBC Northern Ireland on 23 July 1957 in a performance by the BBC Midland Orchestra, conducted by Leo Wurmser.[26] Donald McAlpine heard the broadcast and recognised the work's balletic potential but it was to be many years before he got the opportunity to stage the work.[27] This is one of the few works from this period that has survived, the other ballets having presumably been destroyed by the composer at some point. The four movements demonstrate how Wilson was amalgamating ideas he had gathered on his Mediterranean journey with a style redolent of the lighter English composers from the pre-war period. The first movement is based on a type of folk dance he witnessed on the island of Ischia, while the second movement is a tarantella whose melody is based on the Lydian mode. Throughout the work the tonality is enriched by harmonies in parallel fourths and fifths or in some cases in parallel minor thirds resulting in combinations such as a chord of E and G followed by either G-sharp and B or C and E flat. These bitonal colourings never destabilise the tonality to any great degree and the work is an attractive if relatively lightweight piece.

This was followed by a suite for brass band, while a performance by the Greek pianist Gina Bachauer at the Wexford Festival inspired him to write a piano concerto again with large orchestra. When Bachauer returned to Ireland in June 1959 to perform Brahms' second concerto with Barbirolli, Wilson met her to talk through aspects of the piece. She attempted to get the

BBC to perform it, but it was rejected by their reading panel. A further work for orchestra, *Poema Sarda,* was worked on until the end of 1959, but again Wilson failed to get anyone interested in performing it.

In the absence of opportunities to establish himself through performances, Wilson got increasingly involved in the work of the Music Association of Ireland. In 1957 the MAI decided to bring the Belfast Chamber Opera Group and its conductor Dr Havelock Nelson to Dublin with their staging of Benjamin Britten's *Let's Make an Opera.* For this project they were able to enlist the support of Lady Dorothy Mayer. Dorothy Mayer (née Moulton; 1886–1974) had begun her career as a singer, specialising in contemporary repertoire. She was one of the first singers to perform Stravinsky and Schoenberg in England and also introduced contemporary English works in mainland Europe.[28] After her marriage to Sir Robert Mayer (1879–1985), they founded a famous series of children's concerts in London, modelled on concerts she had witnessed in New York conducted by Walter Damrosch. She was a firm supporter of the MAI throughout the 1950s and 1960s and was particularly concerned about the lack of opportunities for young people and children to hear music. In the publicity material the MAI announced:

> In an endeavour to create an interest in good modern music among young people, The Music Association of Ireland are presenting Benjamin Britten's *Let's Make An Opera* at the Royal Irish Academy of Music during the Christmas holiday period . . . We hope to make children realise that music is written to be enjoyed, and that the music of classical composers can give as much pleasure as any other kind.[29]

Wilson was appointed stage manager for the production, but also took care of press conferences and a myriad of other duties associated with the performance. There were six evening performances and two matinees between 29 December 1958 and 3 January 1959. The production was extremely successful, with later performances completely sold out. It also gave Wilson his first experience in staging and management.

The year 1959 was the bicentenary of Handel's death and the MAI marked the occasion with an ambitious range of concerts around the country. Wilson chaired the committee formed for the occasion and was in charge of an exhibition housed in the Civic Museum. The exhibition contained manuscripts from Mercer's Hospital and Marsh's Library, a double bassoon from the National Museum believed to have been used in Handel performances in London, word books for Handel operas and oratorios, reproductions and facsimiles of Handel manuscripts, portraits, engravings and other Handelian relics. Once again Wilson appeared at various press conferences and was described merely as 'a member of the committee' rather than as a composer.

In 1960, his *Poema Sarda* completed, Wilson decided to embark on a symphony. The timing seemed propitious. Fundraising had begun for a new concert hall and the Hungarian conductor Tibor Paul, whom Wilson described in a letter as 'the best thing that ever happened to the Radio Éireann orchestra', was appointed as principal conductor in 1961, ushering a period of higher standards of performance.[30] Encouraged by these events and the news that Boyd Neel had performed his divertimento and was hoping to secure a broadcast of it on Canadian radio, Wilson also began work on a sinfonietta at this time. The sinfonietta would seem to have been written with the Dublin Orchestral Players in mind. He told Clarice Wilson:

> The work lasts 20–25 minutes, and is scored for small orchestra without trumpets (whom we have to pay, and who play badly anyway, because we can't afford to pay them to come until the last rehearsal). It is in three movements, I think, or perhaps in one with a slow middle: anyway, the same two themes keep cropping up all the way through. It's difficult to say whether it is tonal, atonal, or polytonal, but there are no key-signatures.[31]

Despite his precautions the piece was not performed.

The symphony, meanwhile, was sent to RTÉ in 1962 and a letter was addressed to Tibor Paul. After some initial interest from RTÉ and vague promises of a performance in September of 1963 or the following January, Tibor Paul turned the work down after one rehearsal, declaring it unplayable.[32] Attempts to extract further details as to why his piece had been refused from Gerard Victory, Paul's deputy director of music, only elicited some enigmatic comments about problems with the horn parts, which Wilson himself could find no fault with.[33] This rejection was an immense blow to Wilson and, in an interview given less than a month before his death, he described it as the lowlight of his career.[34] Undoubtedly the news of Paul's dismissal of the work would have been damaging to Wilson's reputation in Dublin. Compounding Wilson's problems in making a decisive breakthrough in Dublin's musical life was the fact that at this time he was regarded as something of an amateur or dilettante, and this rejection would have strengthened the view. He had arrived from Britain without a portfolio of work to demonstrate ability and it is clear that some aspects of his technique were shaky. This in itself should not have been problematic as a number of Irish composers had a similarly insecure technique due to a lack of thorough training.[35] However, the combination of his lack of training and his outsider status made it more difficult for him to be taken seriously. As Mary Boydell recollected:

> He was seen as an amateur because he was obviously being financially backed by John Campbell and there was that sort of aura, of somebody who did not need to work. It would mitigate against you. And then of course he was not of Irish origin.[36]

Brian Grimson recalled a similar impression and suggests that it may have been exacerbated by Campbell's ascendency background and their homosexuality.[37] Wilson worked extremely hard at overcoming his deficiencies in technique, and from the surviving diaries of the period he clearly took the opportunity whenever meeting musicians to gather details about such things as instrumental capabilities. This became a lifelong habit ensuring that he eventually had an encyclopaedic knowledge of such technical matters.

While the symphony was being considered by RTÉ, Wilson composed a violin concerto for the violinist Michel Chauveton, who had performed the Berg concerto in Dublin. This was sent off to him in September, 1962, but again no performance resulted. In 1967, the concerto was one of seven works chosen by a foreign jury appointed by the Cultural Relations Committee of Ireland to be professionally copied for performance and further dissemination.[38] Despite this, the work was never performed. Several other works were composed and left unperformed; a sonata for Gina Bachauer, a string quartet and a piece for string orchestra called *Ceremonies*, which he sent to Boyd Neel. Each of these pieces was also given to Olive Smith of the MAI, who often sent works on to foreign performers planning to visit Ireland in the usually vain hope of persuading them to perform something Irish. He was also in negotiation with Donagh Mac Donagh about a collaboration, though this project seems to have fallen through at an early stage.[39]

In 1962, the MAI decided to follow up the success of *Let's Make an Opera* by inviting Havelock Nelson to bring his Studio Opera Group production of Britten's *Noye's Fludde* to Trinity College, Dublin for two performances on 29 September, though ironically this failed to draw the large crowds of the previous venture due to heavy rain. Wilson was part of the organisational committee with David Laing and Victor Leeson. This gave Wilson more experience of staging and he also designed and painted a series of gold masks, which decorated the windows of the Examination Hall in Trinity.

It was a further performance of *The Little Sweep* from *Let's Make an Opera* conducted by Brian Grimson, the assistant conductor of the Dublin Orchestral Players, which Wilson attended in March 1963 in Wesley College, Dublin that was to be the turning point in Wilson's career. Grimson had contacted Brian Boydell to obtain permission to borrow the Dublin Orchestral Players' timpani and Boydell suggested that Grimson should contact Havelock Nelson for advice. Nelson in turn put Grimson in contact with Wilson, who suggested approaching Lady Dorothy Mayer for support. She agreed to support the performance and attended it in Wilson's company.[40] In his memoirs he recalled that 'at the end, Dorothy turned to me and said "Wouldn't it be splendid if you wrote something like this". I answered, "You commission me, and I will". "Done", she said.'[41] If Wilson's recollection is correct, what in all likelihood was a throwaway remark on the part of Dorothy Mayer was seized by Wilson as a make-or-break opportunity.[42] With no prospect of any of his other music being performed and no discernible interest on the part of Irish musicians to take up his music or commission pieces, he knew this opportunity was crucial if he wanted to continue as a composer. He later recalled 'When I sat down to write it I said, "I'm going to put everything I know into this, and if it fails maybe I'll take up knitting or something instead of writing music."'[43] At the end of March Wilson wrote to Mayer suggesting *The Hunting of the Snark* by Lewis Carroll as a suitable text upon which to base the work and by 4 April he was able to send her a draft libretto along with a series of suggestions for the production:

> As to the libretto: it is only a first draft, and you will see that it is too long in some places, too short in others. Also that I have called for stage effects of some complexity: they represent what I would like if it were possible, and may be omitted without serious loss. But certain of them, for instance, the gradual materialisation of the island jungle before the eyes of the audience, could be exciting and beautiful. I think Milner is the man to make something of this.
>
> My idea is that there should be a big baritone part, that of the Bellman; a fair-sized part for a tenor, the Baker; and the principal treble, the Beaver. This part would be taken by this year's 'Sammy' and needs enlarging from what I have got written down. Between them, these three would make the plot comprehensible. The rest

of the singers would be given unison or two-part simple singing and rhythmic chanting, apart from odd remarks in character. The whole thing would last between one and one and a half hours.

There is a good dancer available, I'm told, to choreograph and dance the part of the Bonnet Maker. The Frumious Bird and Snark merely mime.[44]

It was originally envisaged that the production would be mounted by Wesley College, while the part of the Bonnet Maker was devised by Wilson with Phyllida McAlpine in mind. However, the earlier production of the Britten had actually taken place due to the hard work of Grimson and a housemaster, Guy Milner, in a general atmosphere of hostility against the project within the school. On the day of the dress rehearsal, Grimson was summoned by the headmaster and told that, for no particular reason, the rehearsal could not take place. Grimson decided to ignore this command, as the orchestra was made up of professional musicians who had already been booked. As a result of this he was informed that his services were no longer required at the school.[45] Wilson was aware of this turn of events and, after years of writing pieces which did not reach performance, was wary of starting another large piece without some sort of guarantee. He therefore approached Mayer directly to see if she would formally commission the work:

> If I do sit down and write the thing, it will mean working solidly at it from my return here at the end of June until next Christmas, or thereabouts. It's not worth doing at all unless I make a good solid job of it.
>
> This I can't do simply as an act of faith in Wesley College amateur operatics. Would you be at all interested in commissioning it? I can see possibilities of future presentations: in England, for groups of young people who have done *The Little Sweep*, by Havelock Nelson in Ulster, Radio Eireann, possibly Wexford. If it is good.
>
> What do you think? If you think not, please don't hesitate to say so. I shall not take umbrage, as you know.[46]

Wilson had already asked the opinion of Milner and Grimson – who apart from his work with the Dublin Orchestral Players was by this time employed by Sandford Park School regarding his choice of text. However, Mayer, fearing the text may have dated, first showed the libretto to some children to gain their approval, before writing to Wilson on 9 April offering a commission of £50. With this guarantee Wilson began work on the opera in earnest, reporting a short while later to Clarice that he had completed the first three numbers and had started on the fourth, 'What's the good of Mercator's North Poles and Equators.' In order to complete the work on time he divided his days strictly, with the morning reserved for composing and shopping, the afternoons for gardening and writing letters and the evenings for making a new carpet for the house with Campbell.[47] He was working on the first scene of the second act by August and by the end of the year had completed the work and sent the score to a copyist. At this point he began thinking ahead to the production:

> I am considering all the things I don't understand, in the way of production and so on. This alarms me a bit, because I shall not have time to find out enough before we put the thing on: nevertheless I want to do it myself, because I have quite clear ideas on the effects I need.[48]

Dorothy Mayer remained a major source of support throughout the project. When Wesley College decided not to produce the work in early 1963, she encouraged Wilson to continue on the basis that it could be presented in the Dagg Hall of the Royal Irish Academy of Music as a Christmas entertainment for young people.[49] She met with Wilson in the autumn and he played the entire piece to her and showed her his various designs for the sets. On returning to London at the beginning of November, she sent Wilson a cheque for an amount larger than the original commissioning fee to show her approval of the work. The copied score was sent to Mayer on time for Christmas. The other key figure in ensuring the opera reached the stage was the secretary of the Music Association of Ireland, Olive Smith. As with Mayer, Wilson played the score to Smith and showed her his stage designs before asking her if the MAI could support the production of the event. In a gesture of reciprocation for this support, Wilson agreed in April 1964 to take on the editorship of the MAI bulletin, a position he retained until 1969. A huge amount of pre-performance publicity was created with an official launch of the project by Mayer held at the Gresham Hotel at the beginning of December, where it was announced as the first such work ever to be written, composed and produced in Dublin. In addition the MAI had played an important part in raising money for the production.

Victor Leeson, who had worked with Wilson as part of the organisational committee for Nelson's performances of the Britten operas, agreed to take on the part of the Baker. For the important role of the Bellman, Wilson's attention was directed in early May 1963 to an American baritone, Herbert

Moulton, then appearing in a touring production of a musical, *Glory Be*. Charles Acton had heard him singing and was actively encouraging him to give a solo recital in Dublin. When contacted by Wilson, Moulton expressed an interest in the work, but also suggested that Wilson might like to write some songs specifically for him.[50] Wilson sent Moulton a copy of the libretto and the Bellman's aria in December 1963 for consideration and by October of 1964 Moulton had agreed to take on the role of the Bellman, turning down the rather more lucrative option of singing in the pantomime that year. When it became clear that Phyllida McAlpine would not be available to take the role of the Bonnet Maker, it was given to Nadia Stiven, a ballet teacher in Dublin whose husband Simon Quick was Eric and Mo Porter's lawyer.[51]

The children were drawn from Grimson's pupils at Sandford Park School and the assignment of solo roles was finalised by October 1964. Intensive rehearsals with the boys began under Grimson, with Wilson acting as répétiteur. Grimson recalls feeling that he had more experience at rehearsing and producing performances even though he was twenty years younger than Wilson, and a letter survives from the rehearsal period where Grimson points out the necessity of getting the children to learn the music thoroughly before advancing to stage rehearsals with props.[52] Originally it was intended that the orchestra would be drawn from the Dublin Orchestral Players. On seeing the score, however, it was realised that some professional players would be needed to assist and so a number of players were drafted in from the symphony orchestra for the performances, while Bay Jellett, sister of the artist Mainie Jellett, played for the rehearsals.[53] The costumes were made by a team of people led by Mary Boydell. The sets and props were designed and made by Campbell and Wilson with the assistance of members of Sandford Park School. Rehearsals were held throughout the end of December and beginning of January, while the production ran from 5 to 9 January 1965, with extra matinee performances on the Thursday and Saturday. Mary Boydell remembered the way in which the importance of this performance for Wilson was reflected in the formality with which he treated the premiere:

> I remember Jim and the Commander so well at the opening night. At that time there was a little box in the Dagg Hall up on the left and the two of them appeared in evening dress which no one else was wearing. They looked so wonderful with carnations in their button holes and they were going through this lovely fantasy. It was most engaging.[54]

The first performance was extremely successful and was very well received by the Dublin critics, with the result that later performances were fully booked out, and Wilson felt that only the need for the boys to return to school prevented them from hosting another week of sell-out performances.

Carroll's tale is a lengthy mock-epic poem in eight sections – or as the title page describes it, 'An Agony in Eight Fits' – in which ten oddly assorted characters all beginning with the letter B sail to a distant land in search of a Snark.[55] One of these, the Baker, has been warned that he will suddenly vanish if he comes across the variety of Snark known as a Boojum. Inevitably, after the crew have encountered the Jubjub bird and a fearsome Bandersnatch, the Baker is the one to track down a Snark and it turns out to be a Boojum. The structure of the opera follows the original text quite closely, with both acts divided into four 'fits'. The first and second fits of the poem rearranged provide the text for the first two fits of act one. The main purpose of this rearrangement is to enable Wilson to set the first part of the work on board ship, with a subsequent sighting of land and disembarking of the crew. This adds some dramatic action to the opening, while the transformation of the stage set from ship to island jungle was one of the initial ideas Wilson had when envisaging the work. The third and fourth fits are abridged and the act ends with cries of 'Callooh Callay' lifted from Carroll's poem *Jabberwocky*. For dramatic concision the fifth and eight fits of the poem are again cut somewhat and form the opening and close of act two, but the sixth and seventh fits are more radically altered. 'The Barrister's Dream', which forms the fifth fit of the poem, was felt by Wilson to be unsuitable for stage treatment, especially as it is quite incidental to the plot and might be confusing for those unfamiliar with the text. He replaced it with a ballet for the Bonnet Maker, who encounters the Frumious Bird that she manages to charm by rapidly improvising a bonnet and presenting it to the bird. Wilson also decided on a rather more gruesome end for the encounter between the Bandersnatch and the Banker in the following fit; the Banker is chased offstage and the Bandersnatch returns some moments later eating the Banker's hat, having presumably already consumed the Banker. Both of these scenes are presented as mimes.

Because of the nature of the pre-performance publicity, which linked the opera to the previous successful performances of *The Little Sweep*, the scoring of the work and the circumstances of the commission, many commentators assumed a direct link between the music of Wilson and Britten's work. However, the striking divergences in approach of the two composers, not to mention the huge difference in style, are more obvious than any perceived similarities. *The Little Sweep* – with its wealthy English children, nursery maid and housekeeper in a big house, and the sometimes-arch dialogue – can seem rather dated today. Wilson's choice of Lewis Carroll's nonsense poem *The Hunting of the Snark*, on the other hand, ensures that the work retains its freshness and has not fallen victim to changes in social conditions or fashion. For Wilson, part of the attraction of the text was the dark undertow beneath the nonsense surface:

> Snark is not a 'pretty' piece: it has none of the tweeness of Disneyland. It is fanciful, I hope it is funny, and it has some of the disquieting quality that one meets in other Victorian fantasy. In the doings of Lewis Carroll's Red Queen, for instance, or the Long-Legged Scissor Man, or the Pied Piper of Hamelin.[56]

When discussing the musical language of the piece, Wilson tended to cite the influence of Ravel, in particular, in collaboration with Colette, his *L'enfant et les sortilèges*, while, writing to his family about the music, he also noted:

> Certain parts, such as the march, are meant to sound spiky, and a good deal is meant to sound oriental. I had Indonesian shadow-plays in mind, some of the time. If you don't like spikes and orients, you won't like a good deal of the music, though I thought that the barcarolle, the nocturne and so on gave adequate lyricism. But much of the music is illustrative of the text, and you do need to have read the text before you criticise.[57]

As Wilson's comment that he determined to put everything he knew into the work might suggest, it is a heterogeneous gathering of material that is encountered throughout the two acts of the work. Ravel's opera gave him the precedent of a fantastical tale that, within its short duration, encompasses a wide range of styles, from the artless simplicity of passages such as the Child's 'Toi, le coeur de la rose' to the dance parodies of the ragtime of the Teacup and waltz of the Dragonfly, or the mysterious nocturnal soundscape Ravel creates to depict the garden populated by insects, frogs, toads and owls. The type of stylistic parody that abounds in Ravel's opera is used by Wilson in a number of places, such as the opening of the Bellman's speech about Snarks, which is riddled with quotations to match the text: 'Friends, Romans, countrymen lend me your ears – We are all of us fond of quotations', or, in a less literal sense, in the lachrymose waltz marked to be played in the Viennese style for the Baker's narrative in the second fit where he tells his life story in 'antediluvian tones'.

In general terms the style is most frequently determined by the voices used in each particular section. The simplest music is that reserved for the boys when unsupported by the professional singers. The scene between the Beaver and the Butcher in the fifth fit, in which they struggle with the mathematical complexity of adding two to one, demonstrates Wilson's approach to the challenges of writing for children. For the opening section, where they hear the mysterious cry of the Jubjub, the text is declaimed rhythmically. This moves into a lyrical melody for the Beaver, which was envisaged as the most important of the children's roles to be given to the best singer available.

Example 2.1: *The Hunting of the Snark*, Act II Scene i, 82–89

The middle section of the scene switches back to rhythmically declaimed text before there is a return to the Beaver's melody, now with a second part added for the Butcher, with an option to double the voices if necessary on the piano. The final section for offstage trebles can be bolstered by adults as it was at the premiere and the more awkward leaps are carefully worked into the violin line.

When the adult parts of the Bellman and the Baker are combined with the choir, their parts tend to be more complex either melodically or metrically. The chorus marking the landing on the island 'Just the place for a Snark' utilises a syrtos rhythm in 7/8 that Wilson collected in Greece, and alternates between the children and adults with a high degree of repetition to counterbalance the novel metre.

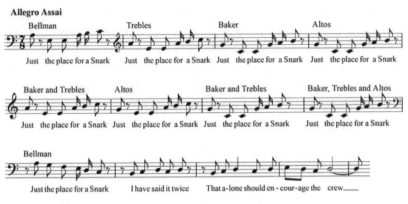

Example 2.2: *The Hunting of the Snark*, Act I Scene i, 303–314

In key places Wilson combines these approaches for particular effects. The chorus in the final fit 'Hurray for what's his name' is based on repetitions of a melody first sung by the Beaver and then by all the children, with judicious doublings in the orchestral parts. As the piece progresses the Bellman first supports the voices and then breaks into a countermelody. Finally the trebles add a descant which is again doubled by the violins, the melody having been repeated so often by this stage that it does not cause any undue complications for those holding the main line.

The most adventurous writing is to be found in the purely instrumental sections, the largest of which are found in the second act. Tonal ambiguity is a feature of these from the opening pages of the work onwards, where we are presented with a three-note idea that Wilson uses at a number of key points in the work, the distinctive bitonal sonorities helping to link disparate sections of the work together.

Example 2.3: *The Hunting of the Snark*, Act I Scene i, 1–9

This can be seen in the nocturne for strings that opens the second act where a variant of the music in bar 5 of Example 2.3 is created by swapping the accidentals in each pair of notes, and this idea punctuates each section of the chromatic melody heard first on unaccompanied cello, and then in varied form on viola and two violins until the nocturne concludes with all the string parts joining together in a quasi-canonic presentation of the melody.

Example 2.4: *The Hunting of the Snark*, Act II Scene i, 9–28

The ballet for the Bonnet Maker and the Frumious Bird is set to a virtuosic toccata of intense rhythmic propulsion for the two pianos, while the scene with the Banker is scored for percussion only. The absence of any singing for much of the second act gives a slight sense of imbalance between the two acts, with the first seeming to be more musically rewarding, and it is possibly for this reason that a cut was made in the Bonnet Maker's scene in later per-formances.[58] Despite this, the work stands as an appealing piece for children, with some impressive dramatic sequences. Most notable in this regard is Wilson's handling of the act one finale, a five-minute stretch of material that he builds steadily from unaccompanied rhythmic chanting at the opening until all the forces are used for the cries of 'Callooh, Callay'. The music then gradually dies away as the cast, who leave the stage and march through the audience, exit via the auditorium door while still singing.

From very early on in the process of composition Mayer and Wilson were busy thinking up different ways of using the production to further Wilson's career not just in Ireland but also abroad through further dissem-ination of the work. It was hoped, following the success of Britten's works and the emergence of a large market for works which could be performed by schoolchildren, that one of the major publishing companies would be willing to sign Wilson on to their books. In the letter agreeing to commis-sion the opera from Wilson, Mayer suggested the possibility of showing the libretto to Oxford University Press and John Calder. It is not clear if she went ahead with this plan, but by the end of the year she was suggesting showing the score to a representative from Boosey & Hawkes.[59]

In January 1964, Wilson tried to involve Hilton Edwards in the forth-coming production, who, apart from his role in the Gate Theatre, was also head of drama in the relatively new state television broadcaster.[60] However, Edwards was about to leave for London where a Gate production of *The Roses are Real* by Patrick Paterson was to open and they did not meet to discuss the opera until June.[61] While Edwards was happy to give general advice and both he and his partner Micheál MacLiammóir became friends and regular visitors to Wilson and Campbell's dinners, nothing ever came of plans to collaborate on *Snark* or other mooted projects.[62] In November, Mayer tried unsuccessfully to interest Humphrey Burton from the BBC in the project, giving him the score and suggesting he send a television team over. A final attempt to interest RTÉ television in late January 1965 led to Wilson arranging a meeting with RTÉ producer Anne Makower. Makower was also a soprano and while this particular meeting came to nothing it did mark the beginning of a friendship which was to result in a number of col-laborations over the rest of Wilson's life.

In late 1964, Mayer tried to interest J&W Chester Ltd but there was no initial response. In January 1965, Wilson sent them a selection of the posi-tive reviews from the press in the hope that it might prompt them into action. On the surface it seemed as if the publication of a work for children at this time would have to be a success, but one of these positive reviews had managed in the midst of its praise to put its finger on the main problem:

> Comparisons with 'The Little Sweep' are inevitable, in spite of the differences in content. On the whole I prefer 'Snark' to 'Sweep.' Not only on account of the imaginative staging: more because I found the music more fun. Mr Wilson's tunes (which he rightly plugs suitably) are infectious and catchy. The music of the percussion and the two pianos is lively and apt: the small group of strings adds line and support, though their music sounds unduly difficult.[63]

While the vocal parts were manageable with rehearsal, the instrumental parts necessitated the employment of professional musicians for any performance, and this severely limited the market for the work, particularly in Irish schools.[64] This was the reason given for refusal by Chester later in January, and it recurs in a number of other refusals from schools to which Wilson sent the score. In 1967, he wrote to a representative of Boosey & Hawkes, who had received a copy of the manuscript, suggesting a number of cuts to the score to be confirmed before he prepared a revised vocal score.[65] Wilson finally tried to interest some companies in recording the work before leaving the piece aside to concentrate on other things. It did, however, get a revival performance in March 1974 when it was performed in Mount Temple School, with the music again conducted by Brian Grimson and the staging directed by Anne Makower. The opening night was attended by the president of Ireland, Erskine Childers.

Despite Wilson's inability to secure any commitment from publishers, broadcasters or English schools, one important encouragement was to emerge from his efforts. Through a series of intermediaries, Wilson managed to get the score of *Snark* brought to the attention of Benjamin Britten, who wrote a short letter to one of these, Andrew Winser, mixing advice and praise. Wilson treasured this letter from a composer he greatly admired, confirming him in his decision to compose. After initial apologies for the delay in responding, Britten wrote:

> It is certainly a lively piece written with a considerable sense of humour – both musically and dramatically; in fact, it is quite a neat stage adaptation of the poem. It is not easy, but with a lively musical direction should not be impossible for prep. school boys, provided that experienced and capable men (for baritone and tenor parts) are available. The instrumental parts are not easy either, and would, I should have thought, have needed to be all

professionals (although Mr Wilson said they had three amateurs in the Dublin orchestra – they must have been gifted!). I should not be afraid of cutting – not only because it is very long and there is a great deal for the boys to learn, but also because I feel there are too many episodes not necessary for the drama (particularly balletic) and a few of the numbers are too long for their content. The music is very direct, and should be interesting for the boys to learn. 1 [*sic*] weakness I find is a lack of melodic warmth (and I do not mean sweetness, but richness) – but I do not think that will worry you too much.

It needs an excellent resourceful producer, and vivid but not necessarily complicated scenery. One practical suggestion: in my experience the chorus should *not* be hidden – which is often boring for the performers and worrying (and obscure) for the audience. If they do not take part in the action – let them be in a stage box at the side or something (crazily dressed).

I have not time to write separately to Mr Wilson. I should be grateful if you would tell him the gist of this letter, and thank him for his nice letter to me. I think he certainly is gifted, and is on the right lines![66]

Wilson replied to Britten in July:

May I thank you most sincerely for taking the trouble to write. At present I'm feeling happy at the pleasant things you say, but your strictures regarding melodic style and difficulty of performance will probably remain longer in my mind, and be of value for the future.[67]

The Hunting of the Snark was not Wilson's last work for children and his other major children's opera does not show many signs of Wilson paying heed to Britten's strictures. In 1973, Wilson was asked to write something for the Finchley Children's Group and quickly put together a libretto based on John Ruskin's story *The King of the Golden River*.[68] The story is about a boy called Gluck who lives with his two evil drunken brothers Hans and Schwarz. When the brothers refuse to offer hospitality to the South West Wind, he persuades all the winds to refrain from visiting the valley the brothers live in. The resultant drought turns their land into a desert, so the brothers turn to work as goldsmiths to try and raise some money. In this way they encounter the King of the Golden River, who claims that the person who throws three drops of holy water into the river will succeed in turning the river into gold. Hans and Schwarz both attempt the challenge, but because of their refusal to help an old man, a dog and a child en route they are instead turned into black stones. It is only when Gluck undertakes the journey that the river is diverted through the valley, which comes to life again, allowing Gluck to live in prosperity.

It would seem the commission fell through and Wilson did nothing more about this project until more than ten years later when, under the impression that funding was available to commission it, he composed the first half of the work. When he found out there was no money available, he decided to finish the work anyway, completing it in 1987. It was originally scored for an orchestra of fifteen players consisting of single wind and brass, harp, percussion and strings. The work also requires two tenors to play the South West Wind and Hans and two basses to play Schwartz and the King of the Golden River. Gluck can be played by a soprano and there is a choral part for the other children. Much of the music is based on a wedge-shaped motif of increasing intervals, chosen because Wilson felt it looked like a picture of a meandering river.[69]

Example 2.5: *The King of the Golden River*, basic motif

Lasting roughly an hour, if the demanding role of Gluck is given to a soprano, the work does not provide a huge amount of opportunities for solo work by children, and the orchestral parts are once again too demanding and would require adult musicians. The choral parts are generally fairly straightforward and are carefully doubled by instruments, but in some places, such as the long chorus that opens the second act, the music places very high demands on a children's chorus. In general the language is more complex and less tonal than *The Hunting of the Snark* and it is probably fair to suggest that the concept of the work seems to place a greater emphasis on appealing to a young audience rather than to be performed by children in the way *Snark* was. In 1992, in the hope of getting a performance of the work in the tiny Riddersalen Theatre in Denmark, he rescored the work for five players: clarinet doubling bass clarinet, violin, cello, piano and synthesiser.[70] The effects called for in the libretto, such as the roof of the house being lifted off by the wind, the glacier the three brothers cross, the river and the conclusion where 'the river bursts through the rocks' and 'the chorus are transformed to trees, plants, birds' would be ideal for the sort of techniques the Riddersalen has perfected in its children's theatre and puppet performances. However, the costs were presumably prohibitive, as the work requires a large children's choir that can be split into three groups, along with the principal characters and the instrumental parts which need professional performers. The work has never been performed.

A more accessible piece is his *Canticle for Christmas* from 1967. The text was based on a selection of texts on a Christmas theme mainly taken from an anthology of religious verse he had received from Herbert Moulton. On the score Wilson notes:

> This has been written on similar lines to Britten's setting of Psalm 150, with an orchestra that can be varied to suit the available forces. Minimum requirements are piano, four hands; a treble instrument (preferably woodwind, but violin or trumpet will do) and a drum. Other parts are optional, and it follows that anything found too difficult by the players of these supplementary parts can be omitted. The organ can be replaced by accordion or harmonium.

Jottings in his notebooks regarding the piece show that he was considering flute, recorder, oboe or clarinet as the best options for the principal treble instrument.[71] However, it is clear from surviving recordings that even the 'minimum requirements' could be altered to suit the instrumentalists available, and in his memoirs he noted that the orchestra could 'consist of almost anything, provided that there was a top line and a bottom line'.[72] One recording, which does not list the performers and survives in particularly murky sound, seems to omit the piano and uses recorders, harp and possibly organ or harmonium along with a range of percussion.[73] The vocal parts designated as soprano and alto can be sung by children and generally move in rhythmic unison with simple harmonies. The work would make an attractive and fresh addition to the repertoire at the Christmas season and because of the flexibility of its scoring is accessible for non-specialist schools in a way that Wilson's operas for children are not.

3 First Compositional Successes

The main result of the *Snark* performances was that at the age of forty-two Wilson had finally reached a stage where a number of Irish musicians no longer saw him as an amateur dabbler but instead as a considerable talent. This impression of an important new force was increased by the appearance of another work of Wilson's in the Gaiety Theatre at the end of February 1965 when the Harlequin Ballet visited Dublin for a week's residency. Harlequin Ballet had been founded in 1959 by John Gregory (1914–1996), as a natural outgrowth of his earlier School of Russian Ballet, opened by Alicia Markova and Anton Dolin ten years earlier.[1] Donald McAlpine had joined the company as dancer and choreographer and as part of their 1965 programme Harlequin presented his *Divertimento* for one male and two female dancers dealing with the theme of rejected love, utilising Wilson's String Divertimento opus 1, in a revised format rescored for flute, violin, cello and piano, as the score. For the ballet Wilson added an eighteen-bar introduction which, shortened by four bars, doubled as the finale. The performances were a success and the company brought the work on tour around Britain with a new finale, giving over fifty performances. The music was praised by critics for its attractiveness, and when performed in Bournemouth was singled out as the only work on the programme to achieve any emotional impact.[2]

As a result of the success of this venture Gregory and Wilson began to discuss the possibility of a three-act ballet based on J.M. Barrie's *Peter Pan*, featuring a major ballet star in the lead. There were a number of difficulties in obtaining copyright permission, but an agreement was eventually made with Great Ormond Street Hospital and Wilson began work on a *pas de deux*. At this point disagreements arose between Wilson and Gregory, who was unhappy with the style of the music Wilson provided and after a lot of discussions the project was abandoned.[3] Harlequin was disbanded in 1968.

This setback was outweighed by the change in attitude wrought in Dublin by the performances of the opera and ballet; instead of having to ask people to play his music, performers started to ask Wilson for music. Rather poignantly he noted to his family when discussing the ballet premiere:

40

I feared the worst for my poor score on Tuesday, when the orchestra got together for the first time. But by Thursday the flautist and the 'cellist were liking the music to the extent of saying please would I write them each something for recitals. I've already written a sonatina for the pianist and a pet clarinettist he recitals with. You don't know what it feels like after all these years to have people clamouring for your music.[4]

The long struggle to reach a stage where he could get music performed, not to mention commissioned, may be the reason why, even at this stage in his career, the reaction of an audience was not of huge concern to Wilson and did not cause pre-concert anxieties; he attended premieres with what he described as a 'calm die-is-cast feeling'.[5] In an interview with Eve O'Kelly, he discussed this aspect of the importance of performance of his work in more detail:

I think I get more out of writing the piece than hearing it performed. The most important thing is that the performers should like it. If other people like it, that's a fringe benefit, really, but if the performers like it that means it's properly written. When I've heard a work of mine for the first time I've often thought the performers made the music sound much better than it really is, but I've never been very surprised at what comes out. It does matter whether or not something achieves a performance, though. You don't feel it exists until it's been performed; it's not real, it's just blobs on paper.[6]

Crucially as regards the development of his reputation with an audience, the late 1960s saw Wilson shifting his attention to smaller scale works which could be more easily performed. The most important of these commissions, in terms of the contribution it made to the development of Wilson's musical language, came from Hans Waldemar Rosen, the director of the RTÉ Singers, who after hearing *Snark* decided to commission a choral work. With the exception of *Snark*, with its particular demands for simplicity, Wilson had avoided composing vocal music up to this time:

For many years I hadn't written any vocal music, largely because I couldn't reconcile the demands of the voice, which is a tonal instrument, lets face it, with the kind of music I was writing which was not tonal and then I really owe it entirely to Hans Rosen; he put me on to writing choral music.[7]

The result of the commission was a setting of the anonymous sixteenth-century text *Tom O'Bedlam* for choir, percussion, harp and piano. For Wilson it was a major breakthrough and he described the premiere as the first performance of his music he had enjoyed. It resulted in a sudden surge in vocal composition, in which Rosen strongly supported Wilson:

> The choir are taking the piece [*Tom O'Bedlam*] to Germany this year, and have accepted a half-hour-long Burns cycle for broadcasting. They're also considering another big setting of *Tam O'Shanter*. Another choir have taken a new setting: *Ode on a Favourite Cat, Drowned in a Tub of Goldfishes* (women's voices and piano) and asked me for a religious work, with soloists, for themselves and string orchestra. So I've written that too . . . Future plans are: a song cycle to Eric Porter's poems (commission!!) and another to a selection from the Penguin Book of Chinese Verse . . . Sorry to sound so full of myself, but it does feel nice to be working like stink and having things taken. *The Snark* did me a lot of good, public relations wise.[8]

Wilson always claimed that the experience of composing these choral works was crucial in unlocking his ability to write for voice; without the experience of writing these works he would not have been able to tackle the song cycles and operatic works that dominate his output.

The most interesting of the works is the half-hour Robert Burns cycle entitled *Burns Night* also composed in 1965. Wilson noted:

> Burns is a marvellous poet to set to music. I discovered how clever his rhythms are, and how much he cares about words. But the singer must understand the proper dialect. If the words are sung in a refined middle-class way, they don't rhyme and the jokes fall flat.[9]

The cycle started out as a setting for unaccompanied choir of the poem 'Peg Nicholson' ('Elegy on Willie Nicol's Mare'). Presumably the sardonic anti-clericalism in this description of the carcass of the mare floating along the River Nith appealed to Wilson:

> Peg Nicholson was a good bay mare,
> An' the priest he rode her sair;
> And much oppress'd and bruis'd she was,
> As priest-rid cattle are.

To heighten this aspect Wilson sets the work as if he was writing religious responses, with a tenor intoning the opening lines of each stanza answered by the main choir. Wilson offered the piece to Hans Waldemar Rosen who felt the short work could not be performed on its own, possibly not just for musical reasons; its anti-clericalism and parodistic vein would have been more noticeable if it was performed in isolation. Wilson therefore composed a further five Burns songs to go with 'Peg Nicholson' and described it as a portrait of Burns. The score is dedicated 'to JHPC', his partner John Campbell. The use of initials is reminiscent of Britten's *Les Illuminations*, where individual songs are dedicated using initials.[10] This idea may be supported by the opening song in which Wilson combines two Burns texts, 'O whistle, an' I'll come to ye, my lad' and 'Jamie come try me' – Campbell's original name was also James. Throughout the song the two texts alternate, the first in 2/4 and the second in 6/8, until the close of the work when the two are combined.

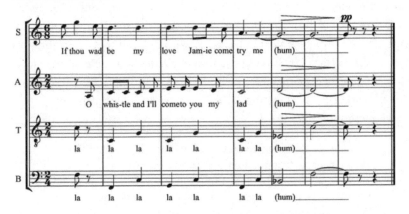

Example 3.1: *Burns Night*, 'O whistle, an' I'll come to ye', bars 137–143

This personal connection to the work may also be the reason why Wilson continued to single out this work from his earlier period for mention in later interviews.

The premiere of the Burns cycle *Burns Night* originally scheduled for 25 November 1966 had to be postponed at short notice when Tibor Paul decided he wanted the hall for a rehearsal, and it was rescheduled for 24 January 1967.[11] Despite this inauspicious beginning it was well received critically and was taken up by other choirs. The Guinness Choir won third prize at the Llangollen Eisteddfod singing 'Peg Nicholson' from the cycle, and part of the cycle was performed by the RTÉ Singers at the 1968 Cork Choral Festival. The work had an additional significance in that the premiere was, in the words of *The Irish Times* critic, 'the first adequate performance of music by James Wilson that I have heard'.[12] Later Wilson made a radiophonic version of the work entitled *Rab*.

This experience of writing choral music also led Wilson to compose a number of song cycles. The necessity of finding a text that could be added to through a musical setting meant that Wilson usually set works by lesser known poets, though there are a number of important exceptions to this in his output:

> By and large, I avoid setting great poetry, apart from Yeats, because it doesn't need any help from you – it has got its music. People like Burns, Alexander Pope or Browning – people who aren't quite at the top . . . you can cast a new light on the poems or possibly add something.[13]

Once the poem was chosen the manner of the setting had to be determined and for Wilson this had to be dictated by something within the text: 'Every poem ever written has a keyword . . . and this determines the style of the music.'[14] In his later memoirs he reiterated some of these ideas while also raising the necessity of finding a text that would work harmoniously with a musical setting rather than being in competition with or even submerging the music:

> Writing for the voice presents a composer with a special set of problems. The first question that he must answer is: 'Does this poem really need any help from you?' If you think that the answer is Yes, then the next thing is to get inside the mind of the writer. Each and every poetic voice needs its own specific treatment: the composer is on unfamiliar ground. The only way in which I can write a song is to forget anything that I have done in the past, and work as though this is the first song that I have ever written . . . I always write with a specific performer in mind, and often I ask the singer to suggest a text that I might set. This means that he or she is already involved in the work, and I do not have to 'sell' my own idea of a text.[15]

The other advantage to writing works tailored specifically for particular singers was that it increased the chances of the work reaching a performance. For Bernadette Greevy he composed *Three Birds* based on poems by Shelley, Tennyson and Clare, premiered in Trinity College in 1967, and also his *Fourth Canticle* (1967). For Herbert Moulton and his wife, the Swedish mezzo-soprano Gun Kronzell, he composed *Trefoil* (1966–67), which they performed on tour in Germany and Ireland.

Two song-cycle commissions in 1966 demonstrate his tendency to allow singers to choose texts, but also presented to him a greater challenge than his other cycles from the period due to the choices made by the singers in question. The first was written for Gráinne Yeats, daughter-in-law of William Butler Yeats, a singer who also performed on the Irish harp. Wilson admired her singing and when he approached her to see if she would be interested in performing a new work by him, she instantly suggested the set of poems by Yeats, *A Woman Young and Old* . Wilson noted:

> These poems . . . are many-faceted, and merciless in their explo-
> ration of the mind of a lover. Had Gráinne not asked me to do
> so, I would not have presumed to set them to music . . . I would
> find myself, on finishing a setting, saying 'Damn. It doesn't mean
> that at all.' Or perhaps it did mean that, but it meant half a
> dozen other things as well. One poem, *Chosen*, I set five times
> before I thought I had it right.[16]

With Gráinne Yeats' particular abilities in mind, Wilson set the cycle for soprano and Irish harp. What Wilson did not at first realise was that this decision was to necessitate a fundamental rethink about his compositional process:

> I set one poem and showed it to Gráinne. She said, 'It's alright,
> but there's an awful lot of blading involved.' The Irish harp,
> for anyone who does not know, is built diatonically, usually in
> the key of E flat. Unlike those of the concert harp, each string
> is tuned independently, by means of a metal blade at the top,
> which can raise the pitch by a semitone. And when playing my
> setting of the song, poor Gráinne looked as though she was
> knitting while she was singing. The song was rewritten, and
> any changes in blading were made in between songs. The
> result was that I found myself writing harmonies that I might
> never have thought of, until working with the harp made it
> necessary.[17]

One song from the cycle, 'Her vision in the woods,' was not performed by Yeats as she felt it was too big for the harp.[18] Partly, as a result of this, Wilson decided in 1970 to orchestrate the cycle, and he also provided an arrangement of the work for voice and piano at the same time. The orchestral version was premiered by Yeats in 1971 and was performed a second time, in Dublin in 1978, by Jane Manning.

Wilson decided to take another cycle focusing on the life of a woman – Schumann's 1840 song cycle *Frauenliebe und Leben* to texts by Adelbert von Chamisso – as the model for his piece. Chamisso's rather sentimental texts describe a young girl falling in love, her discovery that her love is reciprocated, her marriage, the birth of a child, the happiness of motherhood and finally her despair at the death of her husband. At the close of this final song the woman retreats to her inner self and memories of her happiness with her late husband, and Schumann marks this in the music with a change from the bleak quasi-recitative of the first half of the song to a return of the melodic material of the first song from the cycle on the piano, a wordless memory. To link his setting to the Schumann, Wilson cut the poems that are not addressed directly by the woman to the reader (no. 1 'Father and Child' and no. 11 'From the *Antigonae*') or that involve dialogue between characters (no. 7 'Parting' and no. 10 'Meeting'). This left him with a chronological journey from a young woman applying her make-up at the opening to the older woman looking back across her life. He then framed the work with a wordless cantilena which precedes the first text and returns to close the work. After this the similarities between the two works really cease. Yeats' texts are the antitheses of Chamisso's in their frank sexuality and pitiless honesty. The complexity of language and image in many of the poems also removes them from the world of the Schumann settings where the music adds to the text rather than struggling with it. The unaltered return to the opening vocalise at the end of the Wilson cycle is also quite a different musical effect from the piano's postlude meditating on earlier musical ideas in the Schumann. In a sense Wilson's work could be seen to suggest the progression of youth to age is a constant and unchanging one, with a generation of the old replaced by another young one. Wilson himself commented that it is meant to indicate that 'the old woman of "A Last Confession" is unchanged from the girl gazing into her mirror of the first song', an unusual statement considering the psychological journey that has taken place between the first and last song.[19] However, this may reflect a view that the various events that impinge on a person over their life merely uncover the inner essence of the character rather than actually changing it.

The language of the song cycle is mainly written in an enriched tonality, which eschews any destabilising chromaticism. This is typified by the opening cantilena which rocks gently between a variety of chords suggestive of E flat and an inversion of a B-major chord. Despite the avoidance of an unambiguous E-flat chord, the sense of rootedness in this pitch area is clear both here and at the end of the piece.

Example 3.2: *A Woman Young and Old*, bars 1–4

The constraints of using the Irish harp, with the necessary resultant sim-plicity of language and approach in some places, work to Wilson's advantage, particularly in the opening songs of the cycle. The artlessness of the opening song mirrors the directness of the young girl as she applies her makeup. In a rather different way the music of 'Her Vision in the Wood', dominated by a rhythmic figuration of a bar's duration that appears almost throughout the entire song, acts as a balance against the brutality and com-plexity of the text. It also helps to maintain tension throughout what is one of the longer songs of the cycle. Conversely the folk-like feel to the opening of the final song as the woman asks 'What likely lad most pleasured me of all that with me lay?' captures something of the humour of the text but misses the starkness of the later lines:

> Flinging from his arms I laughed
> To think his passion such
> He fancied that I gave a soul

Did but our bodies touch,
And laughed upon his breast to think
Beast gave beast as much.

Example 3.3: *A Woman Young and Old*, 'A last confession', bars 1–12

Stranger at first is the disjunction between the andante semplice of the fourth song and the words:

How could passion run so deep
Had I never thought
That the crime of being born
Blackens all our lot?

Wilson seems to have honed in on the title 'Consolation' when setting this particular text and the concluding lines 'But where the crime's committed/ The crime can be forgot.' The restraint of Wilson's final setting of 'Chosen' may not convey all aspects of the text set and the subdued sensuality means that it requires a perceptive interpreter to bring the darker elements to the fore. This simplicity of setting and emphasis on diatonic formations also helps to point up the drama and terror of 'Her vision in the Wood', making it the pivotal song of the cycle. In its orchestral garb, the influence of Ravel and other French composers on the cycle becomes clearer, whether in the delicate colouring at the opening of 'Chosen' or the expansive outburst from singer and orchestra in 'Her Triumph' to mark the lines 'And now we stare astonished at the sea,/ And a miraculous strange bird shrieks at us.'

Charles Acton, who later reviewed the orchestral version of the songs enthusiastically, was rather more negative and quixotic in his review of the original harp premiere. After noting that this was the third song cycle of Wilson's to be premiered that month (the others being *Carrion Comfort* and *Trefoil*), he added:

> It would seem that Mr Wilson is particularly stimulated by words and that he has a wide-ranging mind in his choice of words. He is adventurous and imaginative and is musically stirred by them. Yet at the same time he is in danger of allowing himself to become an illustrator rather than a composer. He tends to let his word-painting become an *unendliche Melodie*, but more a declamation or recitative than melody.
>
> In these Yeats songs I think that he missed the rhythm of the words, while trying too hard to catch their meaning. On the other hand, with the exception of too many tremolandos (which are almost becoming a mannerism with him), the harp part was very welcome to the listener, especially in his ability at getting away from the cloying sweetness which is too readily associated with the instrument.
>
> The really lovely melismatic vocalise with which he opens and closes, (beautifully sung by Mrs Yeats), shows that Mr Wilson can write melody when not distracted by the words. I would ask him to do the impossible and keep these vocalises with virtually all the harp part, and see if he can re-set the words so that they have both melody and the rhythmic feel of verse. To paraphrase the poet, it cost him the devil of a lot to put these words into verse so let no man set them to music that is prose.[20]

The lack of a traditional melodic approach to songwriting bemoaned by Acton is something which was to be a feature of many of Wilson's later song settings, but it is hard to align with the tonal and predominantly melodic writing in this cycle, particularly in the simple melodic setting of 'Consolation'. Ironically, the one song which quite clearly eschews melodic writing is 'Her vision in the wood', which was not included in the original harp performance.

The second cycle from 1966 was the commission from baritone Herbert Moulton for the 1968 Belfast Festival, and again the singer chose a particularly difficult text for Wilson to grapple with:

> I asked him if he wanted a song-cycle from me, to which he answered 'What about the Terrible Sonnets of Gerard Manley Hopkins?' 'Don't be an idiot' I said. 'They're quite impossible to put to music.' They certainly are intractable material; so

condensed, so contorted. Think about 'Angels fall, they are towers, from Heaven.' Where's your vocal line there? If he had written 'Angels fall from Heaven; they are towers,' you would be on the pig's back. But in Hopkins' poem you have that wild swoop in the middle of the line. But Herb said 'Well, have a go.' *Carrion Comfort*, from which that intractable line came, was the result.[21]

For the cycle Wilson set seven of the late sonnets of Hopkins: 'The shepherd's brow, fronting forked lightening', 'Not, I'll not, carrion comfort, Despair, not feast on thee', 'No worst, there is none', 'I wake and feel the fell of dark, not day', 'Patience, hard thing! the hard thing but to pray', 'My own heart let me more have pity on' and 'Thou art indeed just, Lord, if I contend with thee'. Perhaps surprisingly for an atheist, Wilson found the experience of setting these texts highly involving emotionally and later recalled that many times he was reduced to tears by the material.[22] The general tone of disappointment, futility and despair that runs throughout the chosen works evidently resonated with Wilson, who had struggled privately with his creative urges during the first fifteen years of his residence in Ireland, with no prospect of being taken seriously as a composer, and in a programme note he related the cycle to his later opera dealing with a misunderstood artist, *Letters to Theo*. He decided to counterbalance the emotion of the texts with a highly formal approach to the musical setting, utilising devices such as canon and passacaglia, noting, 'Anyone who has learned to play Bach knows that the most intense emotion often results from strict form.'[23] Shortly before the premiere Wilson declared 'If any of my works are important, this one is',[24] while towards the end of his life he wrote '*Carrion Comfort* is an early work, but it expresses something important to me.'[25]

The cycle forms a progression from the satirical bitterness of the opening sonnet to the equivocal final song in which the poet, in an echo of Jeremiah, acknowledges the just qualities of God, before moving through creative despair to a plea for assistance at the close. The texts, therefore, apart from the intransigence of much of the language, also pose a problem in the darkness of the tone throughout; at no point is there any contrasting lightness to provide relief from their gloom, something that is intensified by the settings, which, with the exception of the third song and the furioso opening section of the first song, eschew fast speeds.

Of the challenging piano part Wilson recalled:

> [Havelock Nelson] was a notable pianist, and could play almost anything on sight. This can, mind you, have its disadvantages.

> On one occasion . . . when I knew that Havelock was to be the
> accompanist in a new song-cycle of mine, I deliberately made the
> piano part wildly difficult, so that he would have to look it over
> on the night before the premiere.[26]

Rather than giving the piano a virtuosic part that would foreground itself at
the expense of the vocal line, much of the piano part consists of ostinato
figures. Indeed considerable amounts of the cycle sound rather like accompanied recitative. This is particularly acute in the final song, which is the
most loosely structured song of the cycle. The first song is perhaps the most
disparate in tone. It begins dramatically with a tumultuous piano solo, after
which the first four lines of the text are set to a fast, repeating five-quaver
figure in the piano. There is then a very decisive break and the texture
switches to static chords and a recitative-style vocal part for the following
four lines, resulting in a dissipation of the energy created at the opening.
The remainder of the song marries ideas from these two contrasting parts
and concludes with a repeat of the opening bar from the piano part. Several
of the other songs are organised around repeating ostinato figures in the
piano. The third 'No worst, there is none' is the strictest, as the majority of
the piano part consists of transpositions of the opening figure made from a
combination of repeated third semiquavers, while a rising and falling fourth
motive is repeated throughout most of the song on the pitches B flat and E
flat. Much of the fifth 'Patience, hard thing!' centres on the use of a rising
second figure, while the outer sections of the second 'Not, I'll not, carrion
comfort, despair' use distinctive chords which are repeated in a short-long
pattern. Two of the songs use the strict forms Wilson observed in Bach. The
fourth song, 'I wake and feel the fell of dark, not day', sets the octave of the
sonnet to a fairly strictly observed and densely chromatic three-part canon
in the piano part, with a vocal line based on similar rhythms and intervals.

Example 3.4: *Carrion Comfort*, 'I wake and feel the fell of dark, not day', bars 1–16

'My own heart let me more have pity on' is a carefully shaped passacaglia with the short four-bar-bass idea repeating nineteen times untransposed.

The contrast between these two cycles from 1966 could hardly be greater. In place of the more rhapsodic style of the Yeats settings and the strongly tonal feel of those works is a more formal approach welded to a highly dissonant language which tends to avoid tonal inflections. Emphasis is placed throughout on semitonal dissonance either through the use of clusters of adjacent pitches, such as those that run through the fifth song, through adjacent tonal triads, or such as the chords of E (E, G sharp and B) and E flat (E flat, G natural and B flat) that provide the pitch material at the opening of the third song or contrapuntal lines such as the canon of the fourth, where the lines enter successively on the pitches E, F sharp and A flat. Indeed it may not be entirely coincidental that the opening idea of the darkly nocturnal fourth song (E, G, E flat) is the same as the basic cell of the passacaglia 'Nacht' from Schoenberg's *Pierrot Lunaire*, one of the Schoenberg pieces that Wilson had long been familiar with. At its best, such as in the controlled passacaglia of the fourth song or the obsessive terror of

the third, the work convinces as one of Wilson's most profound achieve-
ment, but places high demands not just on the listener but also both
technically and interpretatively on the performers, who need to ensure that
the work does not begin to sound self-indulgent in its languorous gloom.

Despite or perhaps even because of the extreme challenges the setting of
these texts placed on Wilson, he returned several times to both poets in his
later songs. Three further Yeats songs written for Gráinne Yeats date from
1970, setting the 'Lullaby' from *Words for Music Perhaps*, 'Sweet Dancer'
and 'The Cat and the Moon'. This latter was reset in 1972 to form a new
group along with 'A Coat' and 'Long-legged Fly' for unaccompanied
soprano. The unaccompanied version has a far more ornate melismatic line
than the first setting, as Wilson attempted to encapsulate in the vocal part
the meanings of the individual words. Hopkins, meanwhile, provided texts
for the *Fourth Canticle* (1967), a setting with orchestral accompaniment for
Bernadette Greevy of sections from *The Wreck of the Deutschland*, a work
that has yet to receive a performance. In 1979 he grouped three Hopkins
poems to form a mini-cycle for Jane Manning and the clarinettist Alan
Hacker, and in 1991 he made a setting of 'The Leaden Echo and the
Golden Echo' for soprano and piano.

In 1966, Wilson also began work on what is probably his best-known
and most performed chamber compositions, a result of the visit by the
Danish accordionist Mogens Ellegaard to Ireland in December of that year.
He requested a meeting with any Irish composers who were available in the
General Post Office, then the base for RTÉ radio, to demonstrate his
custom-built accordion, play some of the works which had been composed
for him and show the capabilities of the instrument.

> A group of us assembled in RTÉ's not particularly luxurious
> premises above the Post Office, to meet Mogens and his accor-
> dion. This was a massive machine ranging seven and a half
> octaves – more notes than a concert grand piano – which he had
> designed himself. He played several short pieces for us, and
> explained something of the possibilities of the instrument. The
> accordion has been looked down on by most classical musicians,
> although Tchaikovsky wrote for two accordions in one of his
> orchestral suites. Mogens had been obliged to fill out recitals
> with arrangements of works written for other instruments. 'If
> any of you want to write something for me, and if it's playable,
> I'll play it' he said. I had been about to start work on a string
> quartet, but decided to expand it to a quintet with accordion.[27]

Never one to miss a performance opportunity like this, particularly with the possibility of performances outside Ireland, Wilson thought carefully about the possibilities and limitations of the accordion. As a pianist he found it difficult to adjust to these, but found the sound effects that could be achieved attractive. Writing about it in *Counterpoint* he described it as:

> an instrument capable of every dynamic subtlety; of tremendous rhythmic incisiveness, and of a pitch range of seven octaves . . . There are things that the modern accordion can do superbly and others that it cannot attempt. It cannot for instance bring out one strand in a complex piece of writing as a piano does all the time; in fact it has a regrettable tendency to sound bottom-heavy, the bass note predominating . . . And despite the considerable variety of tone colours that it can produce, (through coupling in various harmonics by the use of the stops), it cannot ravish you with beautiful tone, like a violin or an oboe. Scale passages are usually easy to perform, but pianistic arpeggios may be extremely difficult, owing to the disposition of the buttons. Give it too many notes at once and it sounds like a harmonium or that gloomy machine the Ondes Martenot . . . The accordion, like the piano, is mainly a rhythmic or percussive instrument. Added to that it can sustain a note as effectively as can a violin, and is capable of several highly effective types of tremolo. The bellows tremolo in particular, which sounds much like the bowed tremolo of a stringed instrument, is very useful, though it demands a good deal of physical strength from the player. The glissando, in single notes or in chord clusters is spectacular.[28]

In a letter to Ian Balfour on the same topic, he noted that to avoid the bottom-heavy effect, the left-hand part should be kept 'very thin':

> Single notes preferably and you can leave it completely out for long stretches. Its best feature is its marvellous dynamic variety. sfp, crescendo and diminuendo are very telling, also the bellows shake, which sounds rather like a string-bowed tremolo. Agility is virtually limitless. It's good for note-clusters, also single-note or cluster glissandi, though this kind of thing is becoming rather a cliché.[29]

While Wilson claimed that the work originated in ideas he had for a string quartet, perhaps inevitably no traces of these origins remain in the completed work. Rather than being a chamber-like meeting of equals, the piece is rather like an accordion concerto with string-quartet accompaniment. It consists of three movements that are performed without a break, giving the sense of a multi-sectional single-movement work. This effect is heightened by the final section of the last movement, which begins with a restatement of the opening bars of the quintet, followed by a cadenza for the accordion and slow conclusion in which the accordion's melody is underpinned by sul-tasto chords and a descending figure on the first violin played pizzicato with the nail.

The accordion's first entry introduces a four-note motif that is the basis of the entire piece.

Example 3.5: Accordion Quintet, bars 1–7

This is altered in various ways, with, for example, a rhythmically augmented version of it providing something akin to a second subject at bar 40, while the intervals also underpin much of the passagework given to the accordion throughout the first movement. The use of mutes for the strings for the central section of the movement helps to maintain the accordion's dominance, though the relatively simple writing for the strings may be a by-product of Wilson's lack of experience with solo-string writing at this date. A short static passage marked *Calmato* at bar 162 leads imperceptibly into the second movement. In this short forty-six-bar section, Wilson attempts a greater integration of the instruments at the opening, with the accordion playing a single melodic line, as if it were the first violin, accompanied by the viola and later the cello. The first part of the movement consists of slow contrapuntal writing that is divided up by sudden long notes that act like full stops in the line. The second half of the movement is a 12/8 section from which a slow melody gradually emerges on the first violin. As Wilson recommended to others, most of the accordion part in these first two movements is a single line and occasionally the accordion is used to provide a bassline for the ensemble. The final movement gathers itself together slowly, starting with just a 2 plus 3 rhythmic figure played pizzicato by the lower strings, over which the accordion has its longest stretch of chordal writing. Again the material in this movement is clearly related to the intervals of the original motto figure.

Example 3.6: Accordion Quintet, bars 338–43

Despite this, the overall structural trajectory of the piece is somewhat insecure and the sudden return of the opening is not prepared in a way that would make it sound inevitable. The work, however, is light and attractive if relatively insubstantial.

The quintet provided Wilson with his first taste of success abroad:

> I wrote my quintet and sent it off to Mogens. I forgot about it after that: I am always more interested in the work that I have on the stocks than in something that I have completed. A year later, a tape of a performance by Mogens and the Copenhagen String Quartet arrived in the post. It was a fine performance, and I was rather surprised to find that I liked the work. I sent a copy of the tape to Boyd Neel, who was now Dean of the Faculty of music in Toronto University.[30]

On the advice of a friend in Boosey & Hawkes, Wilson also sent the score to the composer Alexander Tcherepnin, who was involved in the accordion renaissance in the US. Highly impressed by the work, Tcherepnin sent it to an accordionist in Toronto, Joe Marcerollo, who had already received the piece from Boyd Neel. Marcerollo arranged for Wilson to visit for a performance of the work in Toronto University at Easter 1969 by Marcerollo, with the Orford Quartet. *Counterpoint* reported:

> Although Mr Wilson says little of the American premiere of his Accordion Quintet, it was received very well, and John Kraglund, the senior Canadian critic, reviewed it with obvious delight, describing it as 'the kind of work that may earn for the accordion a respectable place among musical instruments.'[31]

Wilson composed a number of other works for accordion, many of them specifically written for Ellegaard, such as the Double Concerto of 1969, *Music for a Temple*, for the eccentric line-up of accordion, electric guitar and percussion, and *Epithalamion* for two accordions. Marcerollo meanwhile arranged for publication of the quintet by Waterloo Music Company Ontario.[32] This led to a commission for two books of studies for use in the Royal Toronto Conservatoire from the publisher in 1970. Ellegaard arranged for the European publication of the studies by a Munich firm, Musikverlag Josef Preissler.[33]

The year 1967 began with the long-delayed premiere of Wilson's first symphony by the RTÉ Symphony Orchestra conducted by Colman Pearce, which was broadcast the following month. While Wilson had completed a number of orchestral works prior to his first symphony, this was the first of his pieces for full orchestra that he got to hear performed by a professional orchestra. The only performance prior to this was of the dances from his ballet *Esther* given by the amateur Dublin Orchestral Players, a performance which he was grateful for but remembered as being terrible in execution.[34] The performance of the symphony was therefore not merely a chance to hear the piece but also his first opportunity to evaluate his approach to orchestration and to test his handling of larger forms. The piece is scored for a standard-sized orchestra with double wind, four horns, two trumpets and one trombone. A particularly prominent role is given to the piano, which frequently presents primary melodic material in octaves, and there are also parts for harp, celeste and percussion.

The four-movement symphony is very much the work of a composer beginning to find his own voice and is indebted to earlier English symphonies such as Walton's, and, in particular, the symphonic works of Sergei Prokofiev; in some places, such as the passage around bar 48 of the first movement, where the piano is underpinned by pulsating wind and horns, the resemblance is particularly striking.[35] In the same movement, a passage of four-part dissonant chords in the lowest register of the piano, pitted against a high violin ostinato, is reminiscent of parts of Prokofiev's Second Symphony, while the largamente restatement of the theme at the close recalls passages of both the Second and Third symphonies, though the result in the Wilson is not as effective due to the static nature of the material. A 5/4 andante follows which is a little too languidly paced for the processional movement to be entirely effective. The third movement is a scherzo marked brillante, and again the string glissandi evoke Prokofiev's Third, though in the Wilson there is less of a sense of direction in the music and the glissandi seem rather randomly applied. This is the least successful of the four movements as it is lacking in melodic invention and the result of the constant ostinato passages is complete stasis. In the final movement, the dominant influence seems to be the orchestral passacaglias of Britten (such as the act two interlude from *Peter Grimes* or the final movement of the Violin Concerto). The movement builds to an impressive and loud climax before dying away to a short and enigmatic conclusion.

The work received a radio broadcast in 1967 after which Wilson wrote to his family reporting on the reception of the work:

> I intend to spend the remainder of this letter boasting about my symphony, so you may stop reading if you wish. But there is only one first performance of one's first symphony in one's life, and one must make the most of it, must one not? I have had delighted telephone calls from England: rapturous letters from the Head of the Arts Council, Northern Ireland, and the Professor of Music, University College Cork.[36]

However, in Wilson's case, there was in a sense to be more than one first performance of his first symphony as, after the initial excitement had died away, listening to the tape of the performance Wilson realised that the work suffered from structural problems and, with Colman Pearce's assistance, he made a number of revisions to the work.[37] Revision of a work after its performance was a practice Wilson generally avoided and his lack of enthusiasm for the undertaking is evident in the letters to his family:

> Previously my curiosity has not got the better of me to the extent of writing, as I've been revising my symphony for a concert performance. A major task, believe you me, and an unattractive one: it's not like composing, and leaves little feeling of satisfaction. But it's finished now.[38]

This reluctance to revise or revisit old scores was something that Wilson rarely managed to overcome in his career and in a late interview he noted:

> I enjoy what I'm writing at the time, whatever it is. While I'm doing it, it's the most enjoyable thing I could be doing. I don't revise much; I find it very difficult. I think I've only done it in a major way twice. For me, in general, once I've finished a work I lose interest in it. It's gone and the next piece is nearly always totally different; I'm dealing with a different set of problems and I'm no longer interested in the problems of the last work. Once a thing has been written you're a different person, another reason why I don't like tinkering with old scores.[39]

The revisions made to the symphony after its premiere fall into two categories. Some are technical, concerning issues of balance and playability while others are structural. In general the orchestration in the revised version is heavier. String parts are brought down an octave in a considerable number of places, making them more manageable in performance.[40] There is a small cut in the first movement and a linking passage was added between it and the second movement. The second movement was extended to improve the structural balance. The last sixteen bars of the third movement were cut, excising a slightly disjointed presentation of ideas. It also removes a gradual diminuendo to solo clarinet, thereby helping to avoid the sense of all movements ending the same way. The largest cut was made to the fourth movement and considerable changes were also made here to the trumpet line through rewriting of the existing line and the addition of the trumpet to climactic passages. Wilson had to wait until June, 1971 for a concert performance of the revised work to materialise. By this time it had no doubt been overshadowed by greater triumphs – the first performance of *Twelfth Night*, the performances around the world of his accordion quintet – and so perhaps it is not surprising that the performance gets only a brief mention in his correspondence some time after the performance: 'My symphony in its revised version, had a hearing and a broadcast recently. It got a good performance, and was well received. I'm glad I reworked it.'[41] Wilson remained particularly grateful to Pearce for rescuing his symphony and the two developed a warm friendship, with Pearce directing the premieres of many of Wilson's compositions.

While Wilson concentrated most of this time on small-scale compositions, which in general promised a quick turnaround of performance, he still hankered after his original ideal of composition of large-scale works for the stage, and in 1967 began planning a piece based on another of those

Victorian fantasies with a dark undertow, Browning's *The Pied Piper of Hamelin*. Writing to the Nederlands Dans Theater, Wilson described his plans for the work:

> Apart from the tape and the words of the choral works, I enclose the scenario of the work on which I am engaged at present, a setting of Browning's poem *The Pied Piper of Hamelin*. I am setting it largely to jazz rhythms, for choir and eight-piece orchestra. My idea is that it should be presented rather like Stravinsky's *Les Noces*: the singers on stage, and the dancers in the middle, dancing before screens on which the sets are projected from behind. I anticipate a concert performance here, but there are no adequate dancers, and I am interested in having the work staged elsewhere. The music is not at all the pretty, fairytale sort of thing that has been wrongly associated with Browning's harsh and satirical poem in the past: I have tried to get back to what Browning wanted and to ignore the sentimentality.[42]

In the notebook Wilson kept at this time he began to work out his ideas for the piece and the possibilities of performance in Ireland. The first page notes 'A masque rather than ballet or opera'. Following this is a list of possible performers and a further list appears three pages later. From these lists it is clear that he had the RTÉ Singers in mind for the vocal parts from the start. For instrumentalists there is merely a suggestion that they should be 'used to jazz', though he also lists the various sizes of recorders and their ranges, suggesting perhaps a rather different approach. He was clearly toying with the idea of a televised production as Hilton Edwards' name appears along with several references to television. Other names include Ninette de Valois and Joan Denise Moriarty, with their respective ballet companies, Sadler's Wells and Cork Ballet Company. When Wilson moves away from the issues of venues and performers, uncertainty is replaced by a very definite visual sense of what the production should look like, along with brief and sharp characterisations of the principal figures in the drama:

> Chorus wear monkish habits, dark brown. The women coifs of white linen. Burghers of Hamelin again in brown, the women with elaborate coifs after van der Weyden portraits. The Mayor short and fat with elaborate brown and purple slashed costume and gold chain. Hat like a big purple pudding. Your most hated small town politician. Piper in crimson and gold tawny spiral stripes. A disquieting person; tall, thin and gypsy looking. Magnificent cloak.[43]

For his set Wilson envisaged 'an oppressive Gothic fantasy: spires, flying buttresses, castellations, crockets, pinnacles, outlined in white on a deep brown ground as though of old weathered wood.' Three soloists are drawn from the choir to represent the main protagonists. The singers were to process in at the opening in front of a curtain on which could be seen an old yellowing map of Hamelin. After the curtain went up, they were to be placed in Gothic stalls at either side of the stage. After completing a detailed scenario, Wilson began work on the music. For this the model was not Stravinsky but rather Kurt Weill's *Aufstieg und Fall der Stadt Mahagonny*. The choir is accompanied by a small ensemble of flute (representing the Piper), horn (representing the Mayor), harp, string quintet and percussion.

Much of the material is derived from the semiquaver figure given to the first violin in the opening bars, an introduction Wilson felt conjured up a baroque atmosphere. Mildly jazzy and blues-inspired rhythms, with prominent seventh chords, are used to depict the rats, the people of the town and the council and to underline satirical moments. The effect depends to a great extent on the delivery of the material and Wilson goes to some pains to delineate in the score the manner in which the Mayor withdraws from his agreement with the Piper, the key turning point of the drama:

> The next nineteen bars give the character of the Mayor on which the story hinges. For this reason, the way in which his lines should be delivered is indicated in detail in square brackets.
>
> [Ruvido] So friend we are not the folks to shrink
> From the duty [sly] of giving you something for drink,
> [unctuous] And a matter of money [sly] to put in your poke;
> But, as for the guilders, what we spoke
> Of them, as you very well know, was in joke. [shrill titter]
> Beside, [sanctimonious] our losses have made us thrifty.
> A thousand guilders! [chuckle] Come, [grovelling] take fifty!

The Piper's arrival is marked by more-tonally-ambiguous material and in particular with a striking fanfare-type figure of ascending and descending parallel major triads over a B-flat pedal. It could be argued, however, that the gentle *tempo di valse* to which the Piper leads the children away lacks the menace that Wilson declared attracted him to the topic. Indeed the sense of threat is not particularly strong throughout the work and there is also a certain diffuseness about the work that mitigates the sense of drama. Wilson recognised this after the first performance and proposed to solve the problem with a number of cuts to the work should any further performance take place.[44]

In the event the work was not staged and received its premiere in a radio broadcast by the RTÉ Singers and members of the Symphony Orchestra under Hans Waldemar Rosen, whose stiff unjazz-like style and polished pronunciation did nothing to help the work.[45] To the broadcast performance were added a number of recorded sounds such as bells, the tapping of a wooden crutch, crowd noises and electronically produced effects to simulate a staged performance of the work. RTÉ chose the piece as its entry for the Italia Prize Competition in 1968 and the recording was later used by Ian Fox and Jim Harkin when they mounted a glove-puppet version of the work for two performances in White's Hotel at the Wexford Festival in 1969. These performances were, however, overshadowed by the premiere of Wilson's first full length opera as a fringe event at the same year's festival.

Wilson had already considered some other possible works for operatic treatment and seems to have had the idea of an operatic setting of *Twelfth Night* in mind for some time. In 1966 or 1967 he apparently discussed this with Herbert Moulton while they worked on his song cycle *Carrion Comfort*. Moulton was also rather taken by this idea and by mid-summer of 1967 he had sent Wilson an unsolicited complete libretto for the opera.[46] Moulton tried to interest some companies in Germany, where he was then based, while Wilson contacted a number of groups, including the BBC, with the rather unlikely hope of obtaining a commission. Throughout his career, Wilson found it impossible to interest any of the British companies in his work. Dublin's now-defunct opera company, Dublin Grand Opera Society (later Opera Ireland), never showed an interest in performing new Irish repertoire, the sole exception being Gerard Victory's *The Music hath Mischief*, performed in 1968.[47] The Wexford Festival has shown a similar disinterest in commissioning repertoire, causing Wilson to refer to its repertoire in one letter as a 'series of housemaids' novels set to mid-nineteenth century music'.[48] It was only with the formation of companies such as Irish National Opera, and later the Opera Theatre Company (which replaced INO) that the possibility of new Irish operas being produced emerged, albeit with reduced forces.

When Wilson was collecting the reviews of *The Hunting of the Snark* in 1965, his eye may have been caught by the review in the *Sunday Press*, which ended with the words:

> Mr Wilson might also do well should he join the newly formed Irish National Opera which will give their first public performance on January 24, in the Dean Crowe Memorial Hall, Athlone.[49]

The name and address of Irish National Opera's director Tony Ó Dálaigh appears in Wilson's appointment diary on the day following the final performance. Irish National Opera focused around a group of Irish singers frustrated by the lack of opportunities to obtain leading operatic roles in the companies based in Ireland. In its first years, the company presented operas by Mozart, Rossini and Puccini in a wide range of venues around the country, including schools and training colleges, as well as a concert performance of *Fidelio* in collaboration with Tibor Paul and the RTÉ Symphony Orchestra.[50]

At some point early in 1968, Wilson invited Ó Dálaigh to dinner and suggested the possibility of his company taking on *Twelfth Night*. After this initial contact, Wilson drew up some more detailed plans for the opera to send to Ó Dálaigh for consideration. Two lists survive in his sketch notebooks giving the characters of the opera and the voice types Wilson had in mind. Each of the characters is linked to figures in other operas, most of them by Mozart. Orsino was associated with Don Ottavio and later Belmonte, though in the event he became a lyric baritone; Maria was modelled on Despina, Viola on Constanze, Sir Andrew on Don Basilio and Olivia was at first seen as akin to Donna Elvira, before being changed to the Countess in *Le Nozze di Figaro*. Sir Toby was linked to Verdi's Falstaff throughout, while Feste was originally conceived as a lyric mezzo in the mould of Siebel in Gounod's *Faust*.[51] To these lists were appended the names of a number of singers, some of them Irish National Opera regulars such as Patrick Ring, Anne Makower and Peter McBrien; some of them friends such as Bernadette Greevy and Herbert Moulton, and his wife Gun Knouzell. Ó Dálaigh suggested that the designation of Feste as a mezzo-soprano role might prove confusing for the audience, as Viola spends most of the opera disguised as a man, and Wilson adopted his suggestion of using a tenor for the role.[52]

In March 1968, Wilson again met with Ó Dálaigh, Gerry Duffy, a regular singer for Irish National Opera, and Paddy Ryan, the company's stage director and designer, and played them sections of the music from the opening three scenes that he had roughly completed.[53] Once he received a commitment from Irish National Opera that it would attempt to produce the piece, Wilson began work in earnest, completing the vocal score by the beginning of December. In a change from his normal practice, he refrained from orchestrating the work until he knew if Irish National Opera had secured funding for the performance and what size orchestra it could afford.[54] In the event, the opera was scored for a fifteen-piece orchestra, and Wilson undertook this task in early 1969, orchestrating roughly two scenes per week.[55]

At first, the Gate Theatre in Dublin was considered as a venue for the premiere. In late 1968, a friend of Wilson's, the artist Derek Hill, having heard about the opera, offered to discuss the work with Brian Dickie, the artistic director of the Wexford Festival. Dickie came to Ireland from Glyndebourne, where he worked, in March 1969 to discuss the possibility of mounting the opera, with the result that *Twelfth Night* was given a single matinee performance at the Festival on 1 November as a fringe event by Irish National Opera. The orchestra was drawn from the RTÉ Symphony Orchestra, organised by Patrick McElwee, the principal horn player, and the performance was conducted by Hans Waldemar Rosen, Wilson's chief champion at the time. Singers included his friend Anne Makower as well as a number of members of the RTÉ Singers. The circumstances for the premiere were quite fraught. The cast only had a chance to see the stage and set on the morning of the performance. Unlike the main festival operas, which each had twelve orchestral rehearsals, *Twelfth Night* had only four and, as the copyist had failed to prepare the orchestral parts adequately, much of the time was wasted trying to sort textual problems. Despite this, the performance seems to have taken place with only one major mishap towards the end of the second act when orchestra and singers fell out of step with each other, and the work was received extremely well by the audience and by the Irish critics.[56]

Twelfth Night for Wilson was a comedy of deceptions, disguises and sexual ambiguity that posited the work in a direct line with such operatic precedents as Mozart's *Le Nozze di Figaro*, Beethoven's *Fidelio* and Richard Strauss' *Der Rosenkavalier*, *Ariadne auf Naxos* or *Arabella*. Viola, cast ashore on Illyria, disguises herself as a man, Cesario, and captures not just the heart of Olivia, whom she woos on behalf of Orsino, but also of the Duke who, while apparently more in love with the idea of being in love with Olivia, within a mere three days can tell Viola/Cesario that he has 'unclasp'd to thee the book even of my secret soul'. Her brother Sebastian, meanwhile, arrives with Antonio and while their two scenes are telescoped and cut in the opera, with most of the direct expressions of affection removed, Wilson saw this scene as 'something quite near a homosexual love scene'.[57]

Interestingly, Wilson had no sympathy for the character of Orsino, dismissing him in all his descriptions as a moping, drooling drip. The character of Malvolio, on the other hand, increasingly fascinated him as composition of the opera progressed. This created a slight problem as he was unsure how to treat Malvolio's imprisonment; it was clear that his punishment was far in excess of his crime and the scene can sit uneasily with a modern audience. Writing about it years later he commented:

> Until this point in the story, we have been lead to believe that the Lighter People – Sir Toby, Sir Andrew and Maria – are nice cosy no nonsense folk, laughing at pomposity. Feste is another matter: perhaps he is simply melancholy, perhaps he is something darker. But then, just as the play is coming to an end, here is jolly Sir Toby, and here is that gay humming bird of a Maria, both of whom are now busy about the torture of Olivia's steward. So what do you, the composer, do? You can't leave the scene out. My own solution was to treat the scene as a completely heartless Danse Macabre: Toby and Maria become two-dimensional caricatures, as Falstaff does in *The Merry Wives of Windsor*. The idea of theatrical alienation goes a long way back beyond the Twentieth Century.[58]

This scene, the penultimate one in the opera, was for Wilson one of two 'black scenes' framing the work; at the other end is the second scene in which Viola arrives in Illyria believing her brother dead. This symmetry is more immediately apparent in Wilson's use of Feste's closing song, 'When that I was and a little tiny boy/ With hey ho, the wind and the rain', at the beginning of the opera as well as at the close, signalling the return to normality after the sexual and social confusion of the previous acts. The central scene of his middle act is Shakespeare's act II scene v, in which the plot against Malvolio is hatched, and Wilson described this, rather than any of Viola's scenes, as the heart of the opera.

As part of his preparation for composing the work, Wilson read Leslie Hotson's *The First Night of Twelfth Night* and took from this Hotson's interpretation of the MOAI riddle sent to Malvolio. Hotson interpreted this as a reference to the four elements: Mare–Sea, Orbis–Earth, Aer–Air and Ignis–Fire, adding 'the word *element* comes more frequently into *Twelfth Night* than into any other play of Shakespeare's'.[59] Wilson incorporated this into his conception of the work, marking each appearance in the libretto and identifying them musically with an 'elements' motif, G, C, E, F sharp. For some reason, Wilson did not incorporate Hotson's correction of the text of 'Come away, come away death' (in which Shakespeare's 'Fye away' had been changed by Nicholas Rowe to 'Fly away'), despite marking it in the draft libretto. His decision not to incorporate Hotson's interpretation of Feste's farewell song as an obscene drunkard's progress is easier to understand as it would not fit well with the role it has to play in the opera as the 'dying fall' that characterises Orsino's court.[60] The character Fabian was omitted – with his lines reassigned to Feste and Maria – as was Curio.

Apart from the various references to the elements, Wilson utilised a basic leitmotif technique for the opera, giving most of the characters a particular cell or idea and also associating a separate motive with the ring given to Viola by Olivia. The exception to this is the character of Sir Andrew Aguecheek, who merely echoes the thoughts and motifs of the other characters. The opening of the opera demonstrates Wilson's use of the technique. To capture the sense of deception and illusion, which was for Wilson the basis of the opera, the opera begins with a rising arpeggio that seems to outline A minor but almost imperceptibly segues into an A-flat-major chord. It is followed by the sound of Feste singing offstage, the music representing Orsino's court and his song 'When that I was and a little tiny boy'.

Example 3.7: *Twelfth Night*, Act I Scene i, bars 1–18

Wilson perceived a dichotomy between the characters of Malvolio as 'denier' and Viola as 'affirmer' and so Malvolio was associated with a descending seventh and Viola with an ascending one.[61] This seventh is embedded in the A/A-flat chord of the opening, but is more clearly articulated within the music accompanying these characters. When Viola disguises herself as Cesario, the motif is inverted.

While the individual characters are each clearly delineated with leitmotifs, the opera is more of an ensemble work than a work of notable arias. This sense is increased by Wilson's elevation of the minor characters in importance to compete with the 'main' characters, Olivia, Cesario, Orsino and Sebastian. Despite the encouragements of his librettist, who saw opportunities for set pieces of vocal display in the work, Wilson tended to avoid this type of setting. Indeed Moulton placed Olivia's scene, where she muses on the departed Cesario's words and finally realises she has fallen in love with him/her (Shakespeare's Act I Scene v) at the close of the first act, and noted in his libretto: 'To my way of thinking, this could be a brilliant très très sec Stretto à la Anne Truelove's Weber-esque aria at the end of Act One in *The Rake's Progress*.'[62] This was all scored out by Wilson, who set the passage as a slow and thoughtful aria which brings the act to a quiet end. Similarly 'Come away death', which is given by Moulton to Viola to sing, quickly develops into an impressive ensemble for Viola, Orsino, Feste and Valentine. The central scene, which Wilson set such store by, is again dominated by ensemble work and features none of the main characters of the opera. After Feste's setting of 'Oh mistress mine, where are you wandering?' the drunken carousing of Sir Toby Belch and his companions provides scope for an ensemble referred to by Wilson as 'an orgy of counterpoint'.[63] Malvolio's bad-tempered intervention leads to a further ensemble for Maria, Sir Toby, Sir Andrew and Feste, based on interpolated text by Moulton. The lyricism of this ensemble and the earlier material is in deliberate contrast with the harsher dissonant music given to Malvolio, who disturbs this nocturnal scene. (see example 3.8)

Critical reaction to the work was almost entirely favourable. Most noted Wilson's use of the orchestra to carry the main melodic ideas rather than necessarily giving them to the voice, as in a nineteenth-century Italian opera, while highest praise was reserved for the numerous ensembles.[64] Indeed so positive was the response and the interest generated by press reports of this single performance that Irish National Opera was able to secure extra funding from the Arts Council to give two performances of the work on Saturday 20 and Sunday 21 June 1970 in the Abbey Theatre, Dublin, the first opera to be performed in the new Michael Scott-designed theatre. The building was being used that week by RTÉ to film a variety show, but this finished early, enabling the cast to rehearse in it on the Friday. Further expense was saved by the fact that RTÉ radio had decided to broadcast a recording of extended excerpts from the opera. The fortuitous timing of this meant that the cost of the orchestral rehearsals for the Dublin performance was covered by the broadcaster.[65] The performances in the Abbey were more secure than the premiere, but were hampered by the highly unsuitable acoustic of the theatre and one critic noted that the set utilised 'the gauze panels from *The Cherry Orchard* and the boulders from *The Well of the Saints*'.[66]

Example 3.8: *Twelfth Night*, Act II Scene v, bars 619–622

The 1970 performances in Dublin confirmed the opinions of all critics, that, even if the opera was a little long, it was an important new work deserving a fully professional production. Ten years later Charles Acton, discussing the Wexford Festival, noted:

> The brilliant success of [Carlisle Floyd's] *Of Mice and Men* . . . and . . . the audiences' response to modern opera would make me hope that in, say, 1982, Wexford would present James Wilson's *Twelfth Night*. We first heard this in 1969. It had two other performances in, (of all acoustically difficult places), the Abbey Theatre. The Wexford premiere was an inadequately rehearsed show done on the cheap by INO on the fringe. And yet, after more than a decade, three or four numbers haunt my memory – of how many one-off operas can you say that? If Mr Slack were to give Wilson's *Twelfth Night* the same treatment he has given to *La Vestale* or *Of Mice and Men*, the audience and my distinguished foreign colleagues might be surprised.[67]

The experience of writing and seeing *Twelfth Night* performed was invaluable to Wilson, who felt that it was an extraordinary learning experience. With hindsight, he could see that the dramatic pacing was too slow. This was partly because Moulton and he, like Britten and Pears in their Shakespeare opera *A Midsummer Night's Dream* of 1960, had been too respectful of the original text and had not cut enough of it, and partly because there were too many unnecessary orchestral postludes and orchestral passages for which there was no complimentary stage action. Indeed Wilson cut a number of these for the performances in the Abbey. Summing up the opera he noted:

> My own feeling about my Twelfth Night, in retrospect, is that it gets off the ground at the Drunk Scene and after that it is reasonably good. But the only way to find out how to write an opera is to write one, and I think that my next three-acter, if I ever write it, will be viable.[68]

For many years Wilson tried unsuccessfully to get *Twelfth Night* performed at a variety of opera houses outside Ireland, including Sadler's Wells, Scottish Opera and Glyndebourne, as well as houses in Vienna, Graz and the Stratford Shakespearian Festival Foundation in Ontario. Several of these indicated that if they were to produce a new work they would prefer to programme something by a local composer rather than an unknown composer based in a different country. He also approached the BBC in 1972, when it was turned down by Julian Budden, and again in 1980, when Chris de Souza said he would recommend it for an outside broadcast if Wilson managed to secure a performance anywhere but not for a studio recording. Had Wilson managed to persuade another company to perform the work he would undoubtedly have tidied it up further and tightened the structure. As it stands, *Twelfth Night* contains some of the most lyrical music Wilson ever composed and marks an important stage in his output as a summation of the first part of his compositional development. With its emphasis on ensembles and use of a small orchestra, it would be ideally suited to a small company or even possibly a presentation by advanced students.

4 Consolidation of Career

The late 1960s had seen a huge amount of music composed by Wilson as he raced to fulfil all the commissions he had managed to obtain, and this pace of composition was something that became habitual with him. For Wilson the act of composition was something that he was simply compelled to do, and it drove him relentlessly, which made him greatly resent anyone who viewed his talent as a hobby or a gift.[1] He later qualified his decision to abandon composition if *The Hunting of the Snark* failed by saying 'I don't know if I really would have stopped writing. Perhaps I wouldn't have been able to. You don't really have much choice.'[2]

Wilson claimed that he preferred to work out the details of a composition in his head rather than sketching on paper, though the existence of some sketches for his final opera suggests that, sometimes at least, he did sketch material before writing up the full score. He tended to maintain that if a musical idea was good enough there was no need to write it down as it would be easily remembered, though again this did not preclude him from notating what look like aide-memoires in his diaries and in other places. Writing came at a late stage in the conception of a work and, because of the amount of preparatory work already undertaken, it was a rapid process:

> I do write fast but I never start writing until I know what I'm going to write. So I never have this problem of scribbling things down and throwing them away because they're wrong. I wait until I know what it should be and get the overall shape of it in my mind, and the kind of harmony.[3]

Generally he composed at the piano, though there were a number of exceptions to this, such as his second symphony.[4] His preference was to write straight into full score rather than starting with a reduced or piano score, something which is indicative of the importance colour had in his music, not just as something added at a later stage but as fundamental to the conception of a piece. As soon as he had finished one composition he moved immediately on to the next one, with John Buckley noting:

> He wrote very quickly from what I could gather . . . I mean you'd
> speak to him one week about what he was working on and if you
> asked about it the next week he'd say 'Oh, that's finished' and he
> would be on to yet another piece that he had planned for
> someone.[5]

Partly as a result of this method of composition, when collaborating with
other artists he tended not to enter into too much detailed discussion about
the work, preferring to work out the problems of a piece to his own satisfaction. Anne Makower, who wrote the libretto for his last unfinished opera
and worked with him on several other projects, recalled:

> I knew it [the libretto] was too long and asked him if I should
> cut it or if he would like to cut it and he said, 'No, I'd like to cut
> it.' So I gave him the uncut version and he made cuts, and
> mostly I think they were good cuts; I can only judge on the first
> act, which is all he got to do. But I would have liked really to be
> able to talk about it and I think it might have been beneficial to
> him if I had been able to talk about it and put criticisms and
> points across but that simply wasn't the way he worked. It wasn't
> arrogance; it just wasn't the way his mind worked.[6]

By contrast, when the work was complete he would consult with the designated performers and was willing to make any changes that were suggested
to him, sometimes giving performers used to dealing with more exacting
composers a sense that he was either unsure about what he had written or
lacking in self-confidence. Others, and in particular singers, were apprecia-
tive of his willingness to adjust material to suit their particular abilities.
Wilson's correspondence with the organist Gerard Gillen, for whom he composed his 1969 *Divertimento on a Theme of Handel*, gives an insight into the
collaborative approach he always took when composing with a particular
performer in mind:

> As there are likely to be revisions after you have looked through
> it, I have not bound the pages . . . I have not put in any indica-
> tions of register, apart from the essential 4', 8' or 16', because
> you will be altogether more competent to suggest tone-colours
> than I am in regard to the organ . . . Please don't hesitate to tell
> me of any particular awkwardnesses that you think can be
> improved. I always work in collaboration with the performer,
> because I think that this produces the most worthwhile music.[7]

Wilson himself felt that this approach was simply pragmatic, noting 'When
the piece is written I go over it with [the performers] plenty of times and keep

changing it until we get it right. Singers can't put over a song unless they're confident. If they're not, the voice goes.'[8] It was only after this revision work with the performer that he felt the composition was complete. Discussing song composition in 1970, he elaborated on his approach, highlighting the benefits for the composer of adjusting the songs during rehearsals:

> Always in writing a song-cycle I start with the singer. Sometimes I am asked for a work, sometimes I suggest it. Then it is a matter of studying the singer's personality, the individual characteristics and excellence of the voice, before I decide on the poems I will use . . . When I have roughed out my songs, I go through them with the singer. Not until then is my work done. There will be something in my sketch that does not suit the voice; an awkward interval, a wrong accentuation, insufficient time for a breath to be taken. Or, perhaps, in hearing the words sung, I become annoyingly conscious that they contain some meaning beyond what I had understood, and I have to revise my setting.[9]

Wilson's move from being an unknown composer of unwanted compositions to a figure who could not only get large-scale works performed in Ireland, but could also muster some performances abroad was extremely rapid, but he was to find in the early 1970s that attempting to develop his career further was very difficult. Ireland's musical infrastructure was still, despite advances in previous decades, woefully inadequate in many respects. Some of these impacted directly on Wilson because of his particular interest in writing for the stage. Immediately after the premiere of *Twelfth Night*, he began to consider another Shakespeare opera with Moulton and Irish National Opera. The chosen text this time was *Julius Caesar* and once again, after some initial discussions, Moulton produced a complete libretto for consideration, suggesting that he and his wife could take part in the performance. An application was made to the Gulbenkian Foundation for a grant, but the foundation needed a firm commitment of a production date. Wilson was unable to provide this as Irish National Opera, which relied on box-office takings for survival and whose funding from the Arts Council was unpredictable, was unable to give an absolute guarantee of performance. After further attempts to find funding, the project was abandoned and the opera remained unwritten. It was a sharp reminder of the obstacles any such undertaking in Ireland was bound to encounter, and, coupled with his inability to interest any other company in performing *Twelfth Night*, led to him abandoning the genre of opera. It was only in the 1980s that he returned to full-scale dramatic works for the stage.

In the absence of any significant amount of musicological commentary in Ireland until recent years, newspaper critics with various degrees of musical training were the main commentators on new Irish music. The standard of reviews tended to vary wildly and could frequently be capricious and lacking in discernment. While Wilson's output was variable in quality there was no guarantee that this would be reflected in the reviews his work received. Though in later years Wilson declared that he did not bother to read any reviews, he kept scrapbooks of reviews throughout the 1960s and into the 1970s; after this, his approach seems to have been more selective. Negative reviews tended to affect him deeply. In a letter he noted:

> Isn't it absurd that we care about these gibbering critics and their grumbles? Bastards. Sons of bitches, one and all. Let them ride their earwigs to hell. But when they admonish us, in the columns of newspapers, we can't help being hurt. We are children again, offering daisy chains to someone we adore, and being laughed at.[10]

Twelfth Night had garnered fifteen reviews, almost all of which were positive, yet the one that Wilson could remember and quote from over thirty years later was William Mann's review in *The Times* which compounded its negativity by misnaming the composer:

> Mr Walker's music contains some effective chamber-orchestral music, several ensembles that go well (but are dramatically contrived in context), and a dumbfounding insensibility about the place of singing characters in opera. Except in the Shakespeare songs ('come away death' &c) which are tunefully but dully set, the composer puts these famous often inspiring lines into featureless semi-recitative or parlando. When greater musical intensity is needed he makes the singers vocalise on *Ah!*[11]

Wilson wrote to the paper to complain about the critic's inability to get his name right, and while his letter was not printed, Mann apologised for the confusion to Wilson and the composer he had mistaken him for – James Walker – at the end of his next review. In 1974, however, *The Irish Times* printed a letter Wilson had been goaded into writing by a dismissive review of the revival of his *The Hunting of the Snark* by Charles Acton, who had given the premiere in 1965 a good review:

> I learn from Mr Acton's review . . . that the music I wrote for it is too high, except where it is too low; that it is in any case too long;

that the words are inaudible; that it is in any case a slight thing, presumably hardly worth the trouble of revision. When in 1965 Mr Acton reviewed the first production of the piece, he compared it with an opera by Britten – to Britten's disadvantage. I must therefore assume that his opinion of Britten is yet lower than his opinion of me. That being so, I am happy to share my pillory with a great man. Incidentally you may be interested to know that Britten thinks highly of my opera. I have a letter from him, in which he says so.[12]

His relationship with Acton was to remain an uneasy one, though he did dedicate his 1970 choral work *Xanadu* to him, perhaps out of a sense of pragmatism. In 1976, he dismissed Acton whose review of Wilson's String Quartet no. 1 was in that day's paper, describing him as 'a fat slob of intellectual pretension' who had patronised his piece. '"A good addition to our quartet library" he says. "Testicles" say I.'[13] Other artists recalled similar dismissive statements being made by Wilson about Acton and his successors.

Wilson continued his policy of writing pieces specifically for particular performers in the hope of gaining performances and was able to take advantage of a local tradition of debut recitals for young musicians (known at the time as 'coming-out recitals'), in which artists would add weight to their programme by including a new composition. While this targeting of specific performers tended to work within Ireland, his attempts to interest high-profile artists from abroad were less successful. In 1970 he hosted a dinner for the distinguished soprano Rita Streich, who had given a recital at the Royal Dublin Society and took advantage of the situation to ask her if she would be interested in a new composition written for her. Doubtless compelled by the circumstances, she agreed, but the work *Rima* was never performed and Wilson later decided to destroy it before resetting the text in 1988. Another work which almost suffered the same fate was his piano piece *Capricci* from 1969, which finally got a performance in 1979:

> I wrote it for a visiting pianist who turned it down. I forgot about it for some years after that, being more interested in my subsequent work. I remembered it eventually, dusted it off and showed it to Philip Martin, who gave it a superb performance. That made me write my *Symphonic Variations* for Philip.[14]

Capricci is one of two large pieces composed for piano in the late 1960s, the other being *Thermagistris* from 1968. Despite Wilson's own proficiency as a player and the fact that he composed at the piano, he produced few works for the instrument. Discussing his ambivalence about the piano he wrote:

> Though the piano is the only instrument that I have ever been able to play competently, I do not very much like writing for the piano. Other composers I have known, good ones, have said the same. After Debussy, Ravel, Bartók and Ligeti, it is difficult to think of anything else of musical value that can be done on a keyboard. New gimmicky effects can be devised, but music does not consist of gimmicky effects.[15]

Thermagistris had been a self-consciously virtuosic piece for pianist Charles Lynch, who was to give a recital at the Wigmore Hall, London. In the excitement of writing for someone able to surmount any technical challenges flung at him, Wilson seems to have rather lost himself in technical displays, forgetting the necessity for some sort of musical argument on which to hang these, but due to Lynch's advocacy the work received a considerable amount of performances and in 1971 Lynch recorded it for the short-lived New Irish Record Company. In *Capricci*, Wilson attempted to create something new by resorting to extended techniques. A chart at the beginning of the score describes the four methods of playing directly on the strings used: the string can be struck with the fingertip or the nail, a specified number of fingers can be used to play clusters and the fourth sign 'indicates playing on the string with the finger bent, nail scraping the string'. Wilson also asks for glissandi to be played directly by the fingers on the strings. Apart from these, there are frequent conventionally achieved clusters and at several points keys are held down to achieve sympathetic vibrations. The more unusual techniques would probably have been familiar to Wilson via the music of Henry Cowell, who had been invited to Dublin in 1956 by the MAI to give a lecture on contemporary American music. Among the pieces demonstrated was Cowell's *Aeolian Harp*, in which the pianist plays directly on the strings of the piano.[16] Wilson noted of the title:

> Writing *Capricci*, I was interested in extending the sound spectrum of the piano, while respecting the qualities of the instrument. The piece is an attempt to achieve some sort of synthesis between the tonal and the serial, between the lyrical and the percussive. Perhaps it is a foolhardy attempt; hence the title. Musically it combines styles of a toccata with flowing dancelike passages.[17]

The work begins with isolated low notes setting out different irregular patterns and the first instances of the strings being struck by the fingers and nails.

Example 4.1: *Capricci*, bars 1–10

At several points in the piece this idea returns, marking off different sections of the work. The most distinctive idea appears at bar 38 and is accompanied first by clusters which are played by the fingers directly on the strings and then by a syncopated dance-like idea.

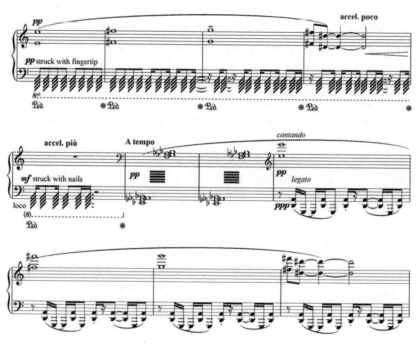

Example 4.2: *Capricci*, bars 38–48

This theme is not developed to any great extent over the course of the piece, instead reappearing in its original form with a different accompaniment each time. For example, the final section (beginning at bar 318) consists of repetitions of this idea, each one gathering force, first by gradually rising in register and then, through the thickening of the texture, bringing the work to an ecstatic and virtuosic conclusion.

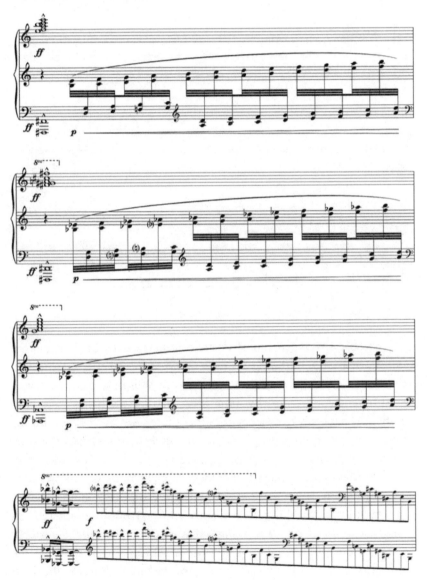

Example 4.3: *Capricci*, bars 340–343

The opening part of the piece alternates between rhythmic chordal passages and toccata passages, with both hands playing in octaves, while the second section is dominated by a single line of music with repeated notes shared between the hands. The repeated notes trace out a number of intervals, at first gradually expanding from thirds to fourths to fifths, later honing solely on fifths before returning to a more variegated grouping of intervals.

Example 4.4: *Capricci*, bars 144–151

The obsessive repetition of these ideas gets interrupted at random intervals by passages utilising Wilson's group of special effects, while in a third, much more diffuse, section of the work Wilson seems to be trying out different conflicting rhythmic ideas in the two hands, one after another. As happens in a number of other places, just as this is beginning to build up some momentum it suddenly dissipates in a haze of on-the-string playing, and in some ways one begins to feel that the title rather than referring to background techniques, might seem to refer to the capricious manner in which Wilson constantly interrupts the momentum of the composition, breaking off suddenly and juxtaposing unlikely ideas beside each other without any sense of transition. The sudden switches to the various quiet rumbles and swishes achieved by playing on the strings is also quite disruptive to the flow of the piece. However, the focus on so few ideas throughout helps to ensure that in a dedicated performance the work hangs together in a convincing manner.

While *Capricci* languished on the shelf, Charles Lynch's 1971 recording of *Thermagistris* received positive reviews in journals such as *Gramophone* and *Records and Recording*. Irish composers were also coming to the attention of some of the London critics via the Dublin Festival of Twentieth Century Music. Founded in 1969, the festival, which was funded by the MAI, RTÉ and the Arts Council, ran annually until 1972 and thereafter became a biennial event. Apart from the exposure to what was happening in the wider world of contemporary music it gave to Irish composers, the festival was attended by critics of the main English papers as well as critics from other parts of Europe. In Wilson's case in the early years he tended to be represented by minor works such as the light *Diversions on a Theme by Handel* for organ in 1970 or oddities such as the *Music for a Temple* for accordion, electric guitar and percussion which featured in the 1971 festival. The premiere of *The Táin* in 1972 was the first time he was represented by a substantial work and it was to be 1978 before he was represented by a large work in an evening concert when *A Woman Young and Old* was performed as part of the opening concert. It seems likely that these events are not unrelated to the fact that Wilson only joined the music committee prior to the 1976 festival.

The publication of his accordion quintet and studies combined with the recording of *Thermagistris* and other domestic successes must have suggested the possibility of getting signed up to a major publishing house in the UK. At this time, while some composers had the occasional work published, no Irish composer had been signed up to a major publishing house, making it very difficult for them to distribute their music and get it performed abroad. Over the next ten years Wilson made a number of efforts to bring his music to the attention of a range of houses. In 1970, he approached Donald Mitchell of Faber Music, but was turned down. An application to Curwen Edition later in the year yielded the news that it was being amalgamated with Faber, who would now take care of any large-scale compositions. He also received a refusal from Novello. In 1974, on the advice of English critic Felix Aprahamian, whom he had met and befriended at the 1970 Dublin Festival of Twentieth Century Music, he approached Josef Weinberger Ltd and Chappell with the score of *Hunting of the Snark*, pointing out that the work was about to receive a revival performance. Chappell turned it down citing economic reasons, but Weinberger responded, asking for a recording of the piece, before deciding against publication. He also wrote to Novello again without success.

Attempting to capture the attention of publishers in the early 1970s, Wilson faced a number of problems. Several publishers wanted to hear recordings of works before committing to anything, but the quality of recordings available was generally poor; many of Wilson's pieces had been recorded in less than ideal circumstances, sometimes by Wilson himself on unsuitable equipment, and frequently with non-professional players. When it came to his larger works, in 1970 he had not got a recording of the revised first symphony and only extracts from *Twelfth Night* had been recorded. The cost of making copies of scores was also extremely high and, until the advent of a fund from the Performing Rights Society, had to be borne by the composer as RTÉ had no budget for copying or the making of parts. This made him reluctant to send out scores unless there was a real chance of their being seriously considered. In general it would seem that UK publishers were reluctant to take on a composer based away from the major musical centres such as London. Music publishing was expensive and it would also seem that many of the English companies were experiencing financial difficulties at this point, making them even more reluctant to take on an unknown composer domiciled in a country with little opportunity for performances of the larger-scaled compositions. One final application, this time to Thames Publishing, was turned down in 1975 as the company was in the process of restructuring.

The various problems and restrictions Wilson faced were, however, sometimes the impetus for creating imaginative alternatives, and in this period Wilson experimented with a different approach to dramatic composition. The catalyst for this was the Irish soprano Veronica Dunne, a singer noted for her thespian abilities. The first work Wilson wrote for her was his set of *Irish Songs* (1970), of which he wrote in his programme note that he hoped he had been able 'to give some sort of picture of the Irish character in its considerable variety – lyrical, magical, enraged, inconsolable, comical'. By this stage he had been living in Ireland for over twenty years and had gradually settled into the rhythm of Irish life, the people both charming and frustrating him by turns. Frequently his remarks about Irish people are wry comments on their informality or inefficiency, such as his comment to his sister-in-aw about an employment possibility: 'In theory it would work, but theories here are awfully theoretical.'[18] His most incisive judgement came from a conversation with Elsa Gress remembered in his memoirs:

> Once she said 'The Danes have a great sense of Law, but no sense of sin.' 'That is the exact opposite of the Irish,' I said. 'They have a great sense of sin and no sense of Law.'[19]

He also described his relationship with the country as a love affair, qualifying this by adding 'like most love affairs [it] is punctuated with bursts of enraged loathing.'[20] However, others commented on his level of assimilation, with Ian Fox noting:

> I think literally he lost his identity. In his head he honestly considered himself Irish, he had been here for so long . . . In the end he sounded more Irish than John [Campbell] who *was* Irish.[21]

As the work was intended as a portrait of his adopted nation it is interesting to see exactly what range of moods and impressions are gathered together in this assortment of verse. The most immediately striking thing about this curious portrait of a nation is the extremes of character it highlights, giving one a sense that this is a result not so much of the temperament of the nation as a reflection of Wilson's own reserve.

In the cycle Wilson followed his strategy of setting poems of the second rank and selected Thomas Moore's 'Music at Night,' 'Sea Ritual' by George Darley, 'A City Shower' by Jonathan Swift, 'Swallows' by Edward Dowden, 'The Widow Malone' by Charles Lever, 'A Glass of Beer' by James Stephens and 'The Black Rose' by Aubrey de Vere. Of the authors chosen, perhaps, the only ones who would be household names in Ireland today would be Swift, though he is certainly not remembered for his poetry, and Moore, whose name is indissolubly wedded to the airs to which a portion of his verse was originally appended rather than as a writer of independent original material; indeed the text by Moore chosen by Wilson is 'Echo' from the eighth volume of his *Irish Melodies*.

The cycle opens on a note of romanticism depicting the echo of lovers' sighs each to the other and several of the songs revolve around loves of different types. At the extreme opposite in terms of character is the setting of Stephens' string of curses directed by one woman to another who has refused her a drink, illustrating a colourful turn of phrase and the passion of the dipsomaniac. A lighter note is created by Lever's tale of a beautiful widow won from a path of modest solitude by a swain from a far part of the country whose ignorance of her decorum makes him more forward than her neighbours. This is set to an insistent 12/8 patter with a touch of music hall delivery about it.[22] The lines selected from Swift's long 'Description of a City Shower' retain a certain amount of Swift's biting tone while depicting the quintessential aspect of the Irish weather. The three verses of Dowden's 'Swallows' set by Wilson again depict an image of the Irish countryside in which the rapid scalic fragments and trills in the accompanying part endeavour to capture something of the images of flight in the text. By contrast Darley's poem demonstrates the

Irish flair for the gothic as the dead man is buried by mermen. The cycle ends with de Vere's poem which, when taken out of its original context within the larger structure of *Inisfail*, as it is here, seems to strike a note of romantic nationalism.[23] This final song begins with a short wordless passage for the singer, which recurs in varied and ever more elaborate forms to punctuate the poem and to conclude the setting.

Idle romanticism, drunkenness, nationalism, grubby cities and small town gossip are all part of this mirror for the Irish, with the extremes of mood traversed over its duration being a reflection of a changeability he felt was evident in the temperament of the people and the landscape. However, against Wilson's declaration that he was recreating the Ireland he knew in these songs needs to be placed his later statement that the cycle varied from lyrical texts 'to others that I had chosen largely because to set them would be a challenge'.[24] This doubtless refers particularly to the Swift and Stephens poems. In the case of the latter, Wilson resorted to a type of dramatic recitative, a lot of which is delivered freely over tremolando chords. Wilson is strikingly successful in recreating the necessary kaleidoscope of feelings in his music, and in many ways this cycle is more successful than others, which on the surface would have a more unified and organic organisation. 'Music at Night', 'Swallows' and 'The Black Rose' are more traditionally melodic and as first, last and central song form a supporting structure for the dramatic songs that are clustered around them. The work, however, places considerable demands on the singer, who needs to be able to dramatise in a short span such a variety of moods and characters from romantic dreamer to scabrous drunkard.

Impressed by Dunne's performance of the cycle Wilson began casting around for further texts he might set specifically for her, and one evening, over the course of a dinner with Ian Fox, Wilson mentioned his hope that he could find something suitably dramatic. Fox was particularly interested in the old Irish story of The Táin, from the Red Book of Leinster and suggested creating a dramatic monologue from the story. He offered to put together a verse rendition of the text in rhyming couplets in a 'nineteenth century style'.[25] Fox sketched out a few paragraphs which he sent to Wilson, noting:

> The original consists of a story told in prose and in a loose sort of verse very similar to Biblical psalmody, interspersed with songs and ballads. I would like to follow this, using a slightly archaic style (which I hope avoids being twee), based on 10 to 15 main songs linked with declamatory recitative written in Biblical style. I think this is consistent with the mood of the original.[26]

With Wilson's approval he then completed the work. Wilson was slightly ambivalent about the source material at first and in a letter grumbled that most Irish legends 'seem to be about one man heroically bashing another man on the head', something that failed to appeal to a man who, with the experience of war behind him, abhorred violence and destruction.[27] As work progressed, however, he began to change his mind, noting 'I started off disliking everyone in the saga, and gradually warmed', and he later described the story as 'a genuine epic with something of the stature of Greek tragedy'.[28]

The work is based on a four-note cell, D, E, B flat and A, and is structured as a series of alternating recitatives and arias for soprano, piano and percussion. It was tailored very specifically to the abilities of Veronica Dunne, who apart from her dramatic abilities had a wide vocal range; while most of the material is notated in the mid to low soprano range, the section depicting the appearance of Feidilm the prophetess is notated in bass clef and descends to a D below middle C. A number of key passages are spoken by the singer, including the opening invocation and the fight of the bulls near the close of the work (of which Wilson declared there was in this scene 'no place for music').[29] The fight between Ferdia and Cuchulainn moves from a type of sprechgesang to speech. The most lyrical passages are Cuchulainn's lament and his address to Ferdia, his foster brother and closest friend whom he has to fight and kill. Unusually a number of passages are written in a simple modal type of style as if Wilson was attempting to imitate the surface sounds of folk music, something he normally avoided.

Example 4.5: *The Táin*, bars 529–549

After the premiere Wilson reported to Clarice Wilson:

> It was done in costume, in a performance I shall find unforget-
> table, by Veronica Dunne (Kathleen Ferrier's Eurydice). The only
> work of mine that ever got more applause was *Twelfth Night*, but
> for this the audience went quite wild with enthusiasm.[30]

Wilson followed this piece in 1974 with another monodrama for
Dunne on an Irish legend, this time the story of Cuchulainn's sickness, his
agreement to fight Fand's foes and his affair with her which lasts until his
wife Emer attempts in her jealousy to attack Fand. The work ends with the
reconciliation of Cuchulainn and Emer and the return of Fand to her
husband Manannán. *Fand*, which includes an important flute part along
with the piano and percussion accompaniment of its predecessor, is a less
dramatic work than *The Táin* and does not have the same impact as the
earlier work. In the same year he also orchestrated his *Irish Songs* to
heighten the dramatic quality of the original work. Particularly notable is
the orchestration of Dowden's poem. Wilson set the vocal part strophi-
cally with the accompaniment altering throughout, though both are
dominated by a simple rhythmic ostinato resulting in a taut, controlled
and powerful setting of the text. With full orchestra, including bells and
tam-tams, Wilson was able to realise in more powerful format the
ominous tolling of the 'dead bells'. In the final song, he decided to alle-
viate the static chordal accompaniment by adding a line for a solo violin
that sometimes follows the vocal line, sometimes intertwines with it and
sometimes develops its own independent counterpoint, giving the song
considerably more weight than it had in its original form.

The work attracted highly positive reviews in both forms, but for Wilson
the orchestral premiere was to be particularly memorable and important:

> My *Irish Songs* had their première with orchestra on Friday, and
> proved a triumph for both Veronica Dunne and me. The audi-
> ence went wild, but, more important, every section of the
> orchestra – flute, oboe, clarinet, bassoon, horn, trumpet, trobone,
> violin, viola, 'cello & bass – came to me with congratulations, and
> said they loved playing the work. RTÉ's director of music said it
> was my best work . . . The conductor, Colman Pearce, wants a
> symphony from me by next June, so that I shall have a hell of a lot
> to write next winter.[31]

In many ways the composition of the two short dramatic pieces and the
songs for Dunne acted as an outlet for Wilson's interest in opera at a time

when he realised it would be impossible to get any company to stage a full-length work. It also demonstrated to him what could be achieved dramatically with just one singer, if a strong enough performer was available.

Despite Wilson's inability to interest any UK publisher in his work he did manage to obtain a number of performances in England, the most exciting for him being a performance on 22 April 1974 of *Le Bateau Ivre*, a twenty-minute orchestral work composed in 1971, in a concert given at the then Collegiate Theatre in Gordon Street by the London Philharmonic Orchestra, conducted by Vernon Handley, under the auspices of the Society for the Promotion of New Music. Wilson noted, 'It will be exciting to have a performance by a really first-class orchestra.'[32] The soprano Jane Manning was appearing in the same concert and Wilson later sent her some of his music. This was to become an important artistic relationship and Manning was to champion Wilson's work both in performance and in her books on contemporary vocal repertoire.

Le Bateau Ivre, originally premiered in 1972 by the RTÉ Symphony Orchestra under the work's dedicatee Albert Rosen, takes its title from the eponymous poem by Arthur Rimbaud. However, while one might assume that the work was a representation of the poem, Wilson's programme note begins by explaining 'My work is not an attempt to translate Rimbaud's *Le Bateau Ivre* into music. The poem was one among several things that motivated the composition.'[33] This is prefaced in the original programme by the words '*Le Bateau Ivre* was composed in the Autumn of 1971 and was inspired by Rimbaud's fantastic poem.' More intriguingly the concluding passage in the programme for the premiere, subsequently dropped from the official programme note, stated:

> There remains the question: why did I write *Le Bateau Ivre*? This music is the nearest I am ever likely to come to an autobiography. But, as with Tchaikovsky's autobiographical Sixth Symphony, the work must stand or fall on its musical merits.[34]

Unfortunately Wilson did not elaborate further here or in his letters about the autobiographical elements in this piece, but in his memoirs he gives one indication of what some of the other motivations behind this commission were:

> Until you have seen it, you cannot imagine how beautiful the Arctic can be. We had to go quite a long way north: latitude 74, above Bear Island. Often at night we saw the Northern

> Lights, and luminous plankton flashing in the bow wave. Later,
> I tried to convey something of this in my orchestral piece *Le
> Bateau Ivre*.[35]

Perhaps the sense of breaking free, which is evident in the poem, however one decides to interpret its meaning, and its rich descriptions of the sea with its phosphorous and delirious open skies, merged with Wilson's memories of his time spent in the navy and made it seem like an apposite title to appropriate.[36] The sense of freedom may link to Wilson's claim that he 'would not have missed the war for anything' because of the experiences he gained and also the social freedom that the war paradoxically gave to people.[37]

For Wilson, the work was also an experiment with different techniques, and he noted in his programme note:

> At the time of writing *Le Bateau Ivre*, I was interested principally in the expressive possibilities of dynamic variation. The score is full of very detailed dynamic instructions, and instead of giving crescendi and diminuendi to the orchestra as a whole I have used a 'fragmented' dynamic technique. Rhythms are fairly straightforward; never irregular, as they are in some of my other works. Harmonically, procedures vary from twelve-note passages to a section in C major without accidentals – something that I had used previously in the first song of my cycle *Another Direction*.[38]

Derek Ball remembers Wilson being very excited by this idea of fragmented dynamics and also by his decision to avoid any overlapping of phrases in the piece and how he demonstrated this in composition classes at the time.[39] The avoidance of overlapping also applies to the moves from one part of the piece to another; there are very distinct breaks as the music moves from one to the next, and as a result the work is highly and clearly sectionalised. However, most of the sections are linked to each other through shared melodic and motivic material, while an interruption at bar 122 of the opening section prefigures the atmospheric second section with low double basses, wind trills, string glissandi and isolated soundings of the sleigh bells.

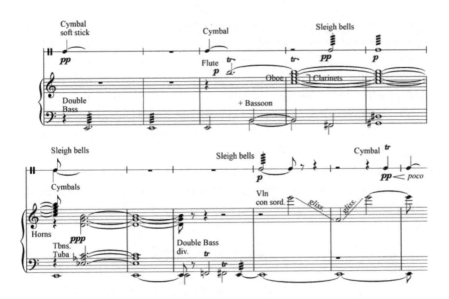

Example 4.6: *Le Bateau Ivre*, bars 122–132

Much of the music is based on the first important theme heard on horn with agitated string accompaniment or on scalic patterns.

Example 4.7: *Le Bateau Ivre*, bars 12–19

The second section of the work marked 'Nocturne' is presumably where Wilson depicts his nocturnal journeys through the Arctic waters. In this section a melody unfolds in the lowest register of the flute, illuminated by splashes of glockenspiel with pianissimo rolls on the bass drum. This section also includes the short passage referred to in Wilson's note where first the basses and then the other instruments all play independent lines using all the notes of a C-major scale. This type of rich sound created with multiple independent lines based on the same harmonic collection of pitches was something that Wilson was to exploit more fully in his later orchestral works. After a short scherzo, which like the opening contains much use of scalic material, the work concludes with a calmer section, starting with solo flute and viola before the other strings enter and the flute drops out. The long ecstatic melodic line is given to the first violins, while the scalic patterns are given to the inner strings, bringing the work to a close.

Example 4.8: *Le Bateau Ivre*, bars 385–389

What must at the time have seemed to be an event of far lesser importance than the London premiere of *Le Bateau Ivre* was a commission in 1973 from a Cambridge student, David Gress, for some incidental music for a play by his mother, Danish writer Elsa Gress, entitled *Ditto Daughter?* Elsa Gress and her husband, the American artist Clifford Wright, lived on the island of Møn in a house and studio in the grounds of Marienborg Castle, home of Count Peter Moltke.[40] Thorkild Harboe, Wilson's friend from the war years, was a close friend of Peter Moltke and a frequent visitor to Elsa Gress' home. He had kept in contact with Wilson since the war and had visited Dublin for the first performances of *The Hunting of the Snark* in 1965, and it would seem, was also a fairly regular visitor in the 1970s. He frequently mentioned Elsa Gress and Clifford Wright in letters to Wilson and it seems also mentioned Wilson's name frequently when visiting Gress. Wilson had also at various times sent him recordings of pieces. The Cambridge students had no money to pay a composer for music for *Ditto Daughter?*, but David Gress, on the basis of what he had heard about Wilson and not knowing any other composers, decided to write to him asking if he would provide some music for flute, viola, mezzo-soprano and tenor for the production. Wilson decided to accept the commission on condition that the music became an integral part of the play and was used in any future productions of the work. Elsa Gress informed Wilson that she was happy with this arrangement for, while she had already asked the theatre director Tom O'Horgan to provide music, he had abandoned the task due to other engagements, and after attending the play in March she wrote again to express her delight, declaring that the music was 'identical with my wishes'.[41]

Wilson was unable to attend the performances due to new commitments in Dublin and also because he was reluctant to leave Campbell, whose health had been deteriorating for some time. Campbell had long suffered from osteoarthritis caused by his early athletic achievements. He occupied himself with a number of different ventures. A keen woodcarver, he made various things ranging from a rocking chair to a drum used in the first performances of *The Hunting of the Snark*. He built a pottery kiln and taught himself how to make ceramics, including the dinner service used for meals. He also made sculptures in stone, lacquer and ceramic, while in 1964 he patented an improved version of a rotary-piston pump.[42] In the early 1970s, he became increasingly delicate, his osteoarthritis being further complicated by a series of accidents and increasing heart trouble.

The uncertainty about the future raised by Campbell's deteriorating health played an important part in Wilson's decision in 1971 to accept the position of composition teacher at the Royal Irish Academy of Music after the retirement of Archie Potter. He started with twelve pupils at two guineas per hour.[43] By the summer he was teaching three days a week and also took on teaching at the Academy's summer school; however, he then cut this down to a single day, teaching from 10am until 8pm.[44] Early pupils included Derek Ball, John Buckley, Brian Beckett, Jerome de Bromhead and Roger

Doyle. Composition lessons were given individually and Wilson based his lessons around whatever work the student brought with him to the lesson. He would slowly read through the student's work making suggestions for possible improvements without being in any sense dogmatic, trying at all times to avoid imposing his own musical voice on the student and ensuring that no matter what was presented to him he could find something to praise.[45] One of his first pupils, John Buckley, recalled:

> I was very unsure of myself, trying out a route to becoming a composer, and he was enormously supportive on a number of fronts, first of all just in assuring me I had some ability and should stay with it. Technical detail was always forthcoming; he had an encyclopaedic knowledge of what instruments were capable of doing, their characteristic styles and their repertoire; he could send you off to listen to four cor anglais sonatas and he would point out what exactly you were to listen to. He would frequently illustrate this with examples from his own music as well . . . Quite often he would lend you a recording or score of a piece and say 'go have a look at that and see how it is done here.' It would mainly be from a technical perspective. In the early days, for example, when I was writing small-scale sonatas I wrote a sonata for cor anglais and piano and he said that the cor anglais part seemed to work very well because I'm a wind player but that the piano writing was a little bit stodgy and he suggested ways of developing figurations. He would send you back to Mozart or Schumann as readily as he would send you to Bartók and Stravinsky. So his perspective on the range of musical history was very broad and one received a very good all round musical education by pursuing the suggestions that he would make.[46]

The election of Erskine Childers as president of Ireland in 1973 was good news for Wilson as he knew Childers socially. Childers was unusual for a prominent Irish politician in that he had a genuine interest in the arts. Apart from attending the revival of *The Hunting of the Snark* in March 1974, Wilson had managed to arrange for his Second Violin Sonata to be premiered in the president's official residence Áras an Uachtaráin, but just weeks before the performance could take place Childers died and the piece was not performed until 1976.[47]

By contrast with the problems posed by piano, the violin was clearly an instrument that appealed to Wilson, and if one discounts his wartime sonata and a fantasy from the early 1960s, both now lost, there are six sonatas and a short piece entitled *Colloquy*. Each sonata was dedicated to a different performer (Therese Timoney, Mary Gallagher, Geraldine O'Grady, Alan Smale, Catherine Leonard and David O'Doherty) while *Colloquy* (1968) was composed for O'Grady. Most of the sonatas are relatively short one movement works and they delineate the shift in Wilson's approach to form, from the more clearly organised early works, including *Colloquy*, which utilises a repeated eleven-quaver ostinato in the bassline of the piano throughout its 153 bars, to the more improvisatory impression given by the late sonatas. For Wilson the string instruments were 'the instruments that sing' and this quality of lyricism is a feature of all the sonatas.[48]

The third sonata, which due to circumstances was premiered two years before the second, is one of the more substantial of these works, lasting approximately twenty minutes and falling into four distinct movements. The first is improvisatory in tone, and although much of the material is based on the opening intervals, the rapid changes of mood give the impression of the composer throwing a disparate range of ideas at the listener in quick succession. By contrast the more focused second movement is based on a ground bass, which gives to the slowly unfurling melody an uneasy tension.

Example 4.9: Violin Sonata no. 3, second movement, bars 1–17

The movement follows the expected trajectory in the first half, building up gradually until it reaches a dramatic climax with rapid scalic passages in the violin part and chords in the piano part at bar 55. After this Wilson begins to move the ground line through the upper registers: it appears in the piano right-hand part as a melody and as the upper part of a series of chords, and appears once in the violin line before the movement ends without either the piano or the ground theme. It is followed by a playful scherzo which Wilson described as 'a whirling affair, occasionally tripping over its own feet in a momentary change of rhythm'.[49] This leads without a pause into the final movement, a slow arietta. A rather unusual effect is achieved here as both hands of the piano part are given an identical slow simple line two octaves apart, over which the violin unfolds another slow moving melody, forming a strangely tender ending to this weighty sonata.

Example 4.10: Violin Sonata no. 3, fourth movement, bars 1–15

By 1975, Campbell's health had declined further and it became clear that he was dying. Wilson described how the composition of the symphony took place against the backdrop of Campbell's final illness:

> He had been failing in health for the first six months of 1975. I occupied myself during that time with my second symphony. I wrote it sitting at my desk, without recourse to my piano, because I did not want to disturb him with thunderous chords. My symphony had its first hearing not long after John's death in July, 1975. I don't know whether or not it is a good work, but the writing of it probably saved me from having a breakdown.[50]

In contrast to his other symphonies, which each perhaps suffer from a certain prolixity, the second symphony is a more coherently argued and sustained work in a taut single movement lasting less than thirty minutes in duration. At its centre stands a setting of Shakespeare's Sonnet no. 55, concerned with memory, time and decay:

> Not marble nor the gilded monuments
> Of princes shall outlive this pow'rful rhyme;
> But you shall shine more bright in these contents
> Than unswept stone, besmear'd with sluttish time.
> When wasteful war shall statues overturn,
> And broils root out the work of masonry,
> Nor Mars his sword nor war's quick fire shall burn
> The living record of your memory.
> 'Gainst death and all-oblivious enmity
> Shall you pace forth; your praise shall still find room,
> Even in the eyes of all posterity
> That wear this world out to the ending doom.
> So, till judgement that yourself arise,
> You live in this, and dwell in lovers' eyes.

The inclusion of this text and the subtitle of the symphony, 'Monumentum', point towards the work's programmatic impulse and indeed this work was of particular autobiographical significance for Wilson, being a monument to his relationship with John Campbell of almost thirty years. The symphony was an attempt to encapsulate something of Campbell in music, an act of memory and homage. But it was also a cathartic act for Wilson to counterbalance the loss of his partner, resulting in a work that has a taut angular ferocity unusual in Wilson's output.

Campbell died on 2 July 1975 and was buried two days later. In place of a religious service there was a short ceremony at which Jim Harkin read some Shakespeare sonnets. Wilson's symphony, with its setting of Sonnet 55 and dedicated to Campbell's memory, was premiered on 23 July of the following year. For the best part of thirty years Campbell had not just been Wilson's partner but had also been fiercely supportive of all Wilson's endeavours, financially and emotionally, even when it seemed as if Wilson would never make the breakthrough into the compositional world. In a letter to his sister-in-law Wilson wrote: 'John was a hero to me too, for thirty years or so, and he ended like a hero. I hope my music will do something to justify his belief in me.'[51]

For his official programme note Wilson discusses the work's relation to the classical concept of the symphony:

> The basis of the classical symphony is tension: tension between related keys, and between different types of theme (a 'masculine' first subject in the tonic, a feminine second subject in the dominant, for example). To be a symphony at all, a similar tension must exist in a work. In the present case, tensions are more fundamental than those in a classical work. For instance two or more keys are used simultaneously, or contrasted with material based on invented scales, or conventional modes or twelve-note passages.[52]

The single movement of the symphony subdivides into five sections, with the third or central section containing the setting of Sonnet 55.[53] The sonnet is the one section which Wilson worked out at the piano.[54] Although there is no direct evidence regarding the sequence of composition of this work the possibility exists that this section was composed first, as the material in other parts of the symphony can be clearly related to both the melodic line and accompaniment of the sonnet. The notes E, F and B form what Wilson described as the 'motto' of the work and they appear in various transpositions and variants throughout, including at the word 'lover's' in the final line of the poem. This cell suffuses the entire work and is first heard at the very opening, which presents a particularly clear example of how Wilson juxtaposes two distinct ideas to create tension. The opening bars contain a strange detached set of dense white-note quaver chords interrupted at uneven intervals by rests.

Example 4.11: Symphony no. 2, bars 1–10

Against this Wilson places a more exotic free-rising pattern in clarinets accompanied by percussion, resulting in the contrast of irregular against regular, free against fixed and chromatic against white notes.

Example 4.12: Symphony no. 2, bars 19–28

Over the course of this introductory section there is a gradual break-down of the first idea, with extra notes added each time it returns, increasing the chromaticism. Additionally, individual lines of the chords are transmuted into melodic fragments until the original texture is eradicated, a moment marked by the first of a series of four-part brass chorales, the upper parts of this one consisting predominantly of parallel fifths. These chorales are again linked to the sonnet setting. Wilson set the octave of the sonnet for brass and voice with distinctive parallel fifths in the lower parts, giving this section with its images of war and pomp a rather austere quality.

He then switched to a rich string threnody in the final part of the poem, underlining the personal nature of the material and giving it extra weight.

Example 4.13: Symphony no. 2, bars 347–363

Flanking the sonnet are two fast sections. The first of these, prefaced by a series of fanfare-type figures for brass and percussion, takes the ideas presented in the introduction and develops them further. However, the fact that Wilson constantly intercuts between ideas, which frequently appear in foreshortened form and contrasting textures, gives the music a strangely fragmentary effect despite its tight links to the previous section. Isolated tonal-sounding chords (usually a combination of two different tonal chords, one in the treble and one in the bass) and short legato melodic passages in the violins are pitted against various modal and artificial scales and trills, giving the music a somewhat hallucinatory quality. Amid the busy string counterpoint, the prominence of short scalic patterns derived from the opening quaver chords is notable and this material returns at the close of the piece. Stability of a sort only arrives near the close of the section with a long unfolding oboe melody which passes to alto flute and percussion, prefiguring the alto-flute counterpoint at the opening of the sonnet.

Mirroring this section is the lengthy fast section that follows the sonnet. The sonnet had ended in a relatively unambiguous D minor, but the flutes suddenly play their closing figure backwards and flutter-tongued, and the music dissolves into rapid semiquavers on clarinet, bass clarinet, tenor saxophone and cellos in piled fifths, like a speeded-up chant *cantus firmus* against which fragments of ideas from earlier parts of the symphony appear, including parts of the introduction and ideas from the fanfare section.

Example 4.14: Symphony no. 2, bars 416–420

As the section progresses, the E, F, B cell becomes increasingly prevalent and we get the tightest integration of two contrasting ideas from the opening interrupted by momentary passages of melodic material on violins doubled by flutes. Paralleling the way in which the end of the first fast section centred on brass, the second part of this section is scored predominantly for strings. Just as the opening of the work centred on the dismantling of a musical idea, the whole work concludes with the disintegration of the entire material of the piece. The section is cut off abruptly and after a short pause the coda commences in which all elements have been filtered out of the music until the only thing left is a series of rising-scale patterns, starting with three notes on the bassoon, an aural reminder of the opening three-quaver motto. Underpinned by quiet strokes on a suspended cymbal, with the E, F, B motto repeated on the vibraphone, the rising scales gradually invade all parts of the orchestra, lasting for different lengths and moving at different speeds until the bass drops out and the music seems to dissipate into the upper atmosphere.

Example 4.15: Symphony no. 2, bars 559–569

The second symphony is a highly cogent work, well sustained throughout its half-hour duration. It contains material that is very striking on first hearing and stands out as one of the most successful works in Wilson's output, a fitting memorial to his partner. However, sluttish time was to have his way with the symphony after all. The work received one inadequate performance; it is clear from the recording of the event that the orchestra was ill-prepared for the challenges in the faster passages of the work and the singer was also somewhat below par. Indeed in writing to a prospective publisher in 1980 enclosing a tape, Wilson noted that the performance was not representative of his intentions.[55] While initially Wilson attempted to get another performance of the work, it was eventually dropped from the lists of his best works that Wilson frequently drew up, superseded by more recent compositions. The comment in his memoirs that he did not know whether or not the work was good but it had helped to prevent him having a breakdown suggests that he eventually came to doubt its quality and almost saw it as a therapeutic experiment of greater biographical than musical interest.

5 Connections with Denmark and return to Opera

The period following Campbell's death saw Wilson involved in several different ventures in Ireland to promote music and develop its infrastructure, but it was also a period in which he began to capitalise on a number of connections he had made outside Ireland in the previous years. This period was very busy as Wilson not only continued to produce compositions at the same rapid rate but he also had a heavy teaching schedule, and in order to supplement his income he took on a considerable amount of radio work. This extended from general programmes on music, talks about composers or specific works and interval talks during broadcasts of concerts to appearances on travel programmes.[1]

In addition to this, shortly before Campbell's death he had got involved in a local venture. The rector of Monkstown, Richard William Maurice Wynne (1919–2000), had wanted for some time to use his church for concerts and in discussion with Wilson they came up with the idea of hosting a short season of concerts in early summer. 'May in Monkstown' was to run from 1975 until 1978, when Wynne left Monkstown, and contained between four and six concerts each year. A number of the concerts were given by colleagues who had worked in the past with Wilson premiering his music, such as Bernadette Greevy, Charles Lynch, Anne Makower, John O'Conor, Geraldine O'Grady and Mary Sheridan. In some of the concerts (and particularly in 1976), music by Wilson was featured, including the premieres of his first string quartet, second violin sonata, seventh canticle and somewhat unseasonaly, his *Canticle for Christmas*. Wilson was to compose his *Nativity Ode* for Wynne in 1978, but due to Wynne's departure from Monkstown this was not premiered until 1985.

This period also saw the beginning of what was to be the most important international collaboration of Wilson's career. Shortly after Campbell's death, Elsa Gress wrote to Wilson with news of a new production of *Ditto Daughter?*, which was to take place in 1976 in the Riddersalen Theatre, Copenhagen with musicians from the Royal Theatre. She hoped he would be able to add some extra music for the performance and rescore it for the new forces. Wilson travelled to Copenhagen to discuss the project with

Gress and they struck up an instant rapport; it would seem her personality was not unlike that of the late Campbell and as with Campbell Wilson was somewhat in awe of her intelligence:

> Elsa was a tough lady. She didn't suffer fools gladly; in fact she didn't suffer them at all. I was accustomed to that: John had had a similar trait of character . . . I once said that talking to Elsa was like playing chess on a trapeze. Sometimes I would be trying to consider some idea that she had thrown out, and realise that Elsa was now on some quite different trapeze. One realised, having taken thought, that there was a correspondence between the two sets of thought. The two trapezes were swinging in opposite directions, which is important, if you are thinking of making the jump.[2]

So successful was the visit that Wilson was to become a regular visitor to Denmark, collaborating on a large number of projects with Gress, her artist husband Clifford Wright and the director of the Riddersalen Theatre, Jytte Abildstrøm. Abildstrøm recalls how Wilson would always ask Gress if she had anything new they could work on when he visited and their surviving correspondence shows them constantly exchanging ideas and proposing collaborations.[3] Indeed in Gress' novel, *The Simurg*, he makes a brief appearance as 'Jack, the Anglo-Irish composer, who was the one person in the company she had worked with, and liked to work with.'[4] Only some of these works made it to the stage; Elsa Gress' writing, with its reputation for intellectual challenges and avoidance of realism, was not always something theatres were willing to take on.[5] However, Wilson's admiration for her work motivated him to write music for any project she proposed.

Ditto Daughter? is set at some point in the future in a world without men and depicts a mother and daughter using the technology of the time to conjure up various figures from the past to explore what use men were and what the concept of love meant. Wilson wrote predominantly percussive music for what he described as the 'cold, clinical manless future', while for the visions of the past he weighted the music in favour of cor anglais, horn, harp and cello. The majority of the music is a set of variations on a theme presented at the outset. The full score was first performed with the play at the Riddersalen Theatre in October 1976, with Jytte Abildstrøm as the mother and the singer Daimi Gentile as the daughter . It ran for fifteen performances and was revived the following year for a further eighteen performances.

This system of uniting the material musically through a variation-based structure was also used for his second collaboration with Gress, a play entitled *Scapegoat*. Here, however, the treatment is more elaborate, partly due to the fact that, unlike the music for *Ditto Daughter?*, which was written on two separate occasions some years apart for different forces, this was written in one go. The play is an examination of the career and cultural afterlife of Lord Byron, given a Faustian twist by framing the play with a debate between God and Satan – while playing badminton – regarding his salvation or damnation, with Byron saved at the end by the intervention of Augusta Leigh and a host of male and female lovers. Swipes are taken at Ernest Hemingway, Allen Ginsberg, Che Guevara and Norman Mailer among others, while the cast includes a range of people from Thomas Moore and Alexander Pope to Mick Jagger and Germaine Greer. The heart of the drama for Wilson was contained in the modal setting of Byron's 'So we'll go no more a roving', which was composed first. This then formed the basis of much of the music for the play. The other elements are a parodistic quote from Tchaikovsky's *Swan Lake* to mark Zeus' appearance as a swan during a lesson in love given by Byron to Lady Caroline Lamb and hidden references to Gluck's *Orfeo*. *Scapegoat* was scored for a larger group of instruments including harpsichord and electric and acoustic guitar as well as flute, horn, strings and percussion. While at various times it seemed as if the work was to be presented in Denmark or New York or even filmed for television, it remains unperformed.

It was enthusiastically followed by more music for a variety of other projects. In 1980, Wilson provided music for Jean Cocteau's *The Wedding on the Eiffel Tower*, though in the event his music was not used for the production which relied instead on recordings of various types of music. In 1983, Wilson quickly put together some music for a production of a cut version of Yeats' play of renunciation *The Only Jealousy of Emer* at Jytte Abildstrøm's suggestion, and this was performed in February of that year. A production of a play entitled *1985*, based on an updated version of Hans Christian Anderson's *Girl who trod on a Loaf*, yielded a considerable amount of music of which only the short *Music for a Mechanical Organ* was used. A collaboration with Clifford Wright and Elsa Gress, based on the temptations of St Anthony, seems to have been related to the same project and may originally have been intended to form part of the performance; it also remains unperformed.

Back in Ireland Wilson's involvement as a juror at the 1976 Cork International Choral Festival led to a further collaboration, this time with the English choral conductor Stephen Wilkinson. Wilson had first made contact with Wilkinson, who also worked with the BBC in the early 1970s, after hearing a programme of music based on the poetry of Hopkins. Wilson submitted his *Carrion Comfort* for consideration and was informed by Wilkinson that the programme only included choral music and that no further Hopkins programmes were planned.[6] When in 1976 both men met as jurors at the Cork Choral Festival, Wilson seems to have taken the opportunity to give Wilkinson a copy of *Burns Night*. Wilkinson spent some time studying the work before deciding to include it in a programme broadcast on Burns Night 1977.

Wilson clearly gave Wilkinson a list of his other choral works and Wilkinson asked if he could also include his other early Burns setting *Tam O'Shanter* in the programme. Wilson had composed this in 1965, inspired by his own time spent in Burns country, where he had seen Alloway Kirk and the avenue down which Tam is depicted as fleeing.[7] However, he had never been entirely happy with the piece and faced with the possibility of a performance and broadcast in England, Wilson decided, against his normal practice, to revise the work, adding parts for piano and percussion to the unaccompanied original in order to match the 'snap and crackle of the poem'.[8] He completed the work by January 1977 and dedicated the piece to Wilkinson. After being accepted by the BBC Reading Panel, this new version was broadcast on Hallowe'en that year with the BBC Northern Singers accompanied by Keith Swallow on the piano and the percussion part played by Peter Donohue, who was later to become better known as a pianist. The revised work is, like the poem it sets, rather episodic in structure, but contains many striking passages, particularly in the first half of the piece. The added instrumental parts are not overloaded, like some of Wilson's accompaniments, and the clear simple textures in a passage such as that describing Tam setting off 'Weel mounted on his grey meare Meg' past Alloway Kirk 'Whare ghaists and houlets nightly cry' coupled with the folk-like vocal lines, make the work immediately engaging and memorable. There is also a strong built-in tension through the various sections leading to the central tarantella and ensuing chase. The ending is unusually abrupt and has a slightly unsettling effect.

In the aftermath of the broadcast Wilkinson asked Wilson to send him any further choral works he had for consideration, but in 1978 he wrote to Wilson turning down *The Pied Piper* due to 'some reservations about it as it stands'.[9] He decided, however, to commission a new work from Wilson for another choir he conducted, the amateur William Byrd Singers of Manchester. The choir was including new works in each of its concerts and Wilkinson was encouraging composers to score the accompaniment for instruments other than the piano. He had evidently been sent recordings of various non-choral works by Wilson and, on the basis of the accordion quintet, proposed to Wilson the idea of writing a piece for choir and accordion. Wilson accepted the suggestion and for his text turned to a work he had been considering setting for some time.

Alexander Pope's poem *The Rape of the Lock* was another of those texts Wilson had first encountered as an uncomprehending schoolboy, which he later became very fond of:

> I can't imagine why twelve-year-olds were given *The Rape of the Lock* to study. We had no earthly idea of what it meant, nor knowledge of the world for which it was written. Of course, nobody told us what the rude bits meant – 'Maids, turned bottles, call aloud for corks.' That was a pity. Had we known, we would have studied with more diligence.[10]

At some point, possibly around the late 1960s, he began toying with the idea of some sort of staged work based on the poem and he divided the poem into two acts with seven scenes:

Act I	Act II
Sc. 1 The Levee	Sc. 5 The Spleen
Sc. 2 The Baron	Sc. 6 The Battle
Sc. 3 The Thames, the sylphs	Sc. 7 The Apotheosis[11]
Sc. 4 Hampton Court, the Rape	

This first plan omits the opening of the work and Wilson decided to draw up a slightly different rough scenario (becoming less detailed as it progressed), including this opening with suggestions for an elaborate staging:

> The singers in tiers surround the stage . . . (on Baroque clouds?)
>
> Canto I: Ariel high up above stage, in a spotlight. Stage otherwise dark (A youth more glittering than a birthright beau). Query: the sylphs are invisible to the mortals – how to indicate this? Ariel descends slowly to stage and dances his invocation . . . Belinda seen asleep with lapdog. Sol thro white curtains shot an opening ray. Enter Betty.
> The levée. Puffs, powders, patches, Bibles, billets-doux. The busy sylphs surround their darling care. Friends (Clarissa, beaux, etc.) enter. Fade to
>
> Canto II: The baron's prayer. The altar; the sacrifice. The Powers give ear and answer half his prayer . . . After which Baron leaves for Hampton Court.

Canto III: Belinda, on arm of Sir Plume, descends staircase to waterside and embarks in barge. Sylphs appear gradually aloft (some to the sun their insect wings unfold) Ariel's second address.

Canto IV: Hampton Court. Singing, laughing, ogling and all that. Card game. The board with cups and spoons is crowned (flunkeys set tables). Clarissa presents scissors. Frantic sylphs. The lock is cut. General consternation. Baron triumphant. End Part I

Part II Canto V
The cave of Spleen. Umbriel's entry and address. Gift of the wondrous bag.

Canto VI
Belinda's Thalestris mourning. Umbriel arrives and opens bag. Sir Plume

Canto VII
Clarissa's address. The battle. Belinda joined by Olympians as the Baron flies.

Canto VIII
Apotheosis.[12]

It is unclear whether Wilson was thinking of creating an opera or a choral ballet in the same mould as his *Pied Piper*. He assigned vocal ranges to the main characters with Belinda as soprano, Clarissa an alto, Ariel a tenor, Sir Plume a baritone and Umbriel a bass, and beside some of these he placed the names of members of the RTÉ Singers who had also taken part in the premiere of *Twelfth Night*.

When trying to find a text suitable for accordion and choir, Pope's text sprang to mind again and Wilson decided that it was 'exactly the thing; a fantastical poem, calling for fantastical treatment'.[13] He felt that the important thing was the 'dichotomy between the surface elegance of fashionable Eighteenth-Century society and the squalor of the back streets – "The hungry judges now the sentence sign/And wretches hang, that jurymen may dine" – which Pope follows immediately with his description of a smart card party at Hampton Court.'[14] This is not perhaps what comes across to an audience and the work as a whole is rather variable in its effect. The choral parts are relatively simple without too many challenges and there are some very effective moments, such as the depiction of the early morning sun at the lines 'Sol through white curtains shot a timorous ray/And oped those eyes that must eclipse the day'. The effectiveness of the accordion varies greatly throughout the work. It is very successful at underpinning the mincing description of waving fans and malicious gossip among fashionable society.

Example 5.1: *The Rape of the Lock*, bars 247–260

However, the longer choral lines show up the inability of the instrument to create effective long sustained lines and its weak tone also fails to achieve the type of apotheosis Wilson had in mind for the closing section of the work:

> Near the end come lines that haunt me. Pope is speaking of the stolen lock of Belinda's hair, that has been transformed into a star – 'Not Bernice's locks first rose so bright/The heavens bespangling

with dishevelled light.' Dishevelled, mark you: *dishevelled.*
Language has found a sudden incandescence.[15]

Two other connections from the past were to result in a series of vocal
works in the ensuing years. The first of these came via his friendship with
accordionist Mogens Ellegaard. In the late 1970s, Wilson wrote to his
sister-in-law to tell her that he had received two letters: 'One from the
Residente Orchestra in The Hague, asking for scores and tapes: the other
from Dorothy Dorow, probably the best singer of modern music in Europe,
asking for songs. A day that made up for a lot of other days.'[16] The
approach from the Hague does not seem to have led anywhere, but the
letter from Dorow was to mark the beginning of a fruitful artistic partner-
ship and close personal friendship. Dorow had heard about Wilson from
Ellegaard when she was working with him and flautist Rien de Reede.
Original works for this particular combination being a little scarce, they
decided to commission a work from Wilson, and the result was his setting
of John Donne's poem *Air and Angels.* By autumn 1979, Wilson was able to
report that Dorow had written to say she liked the piece and was willing to
perform it, adding that they should collaborate again. The work was premiered at the Ijsbreker in Amsterdam in 1980 and was toured to a number
of places, including Hilvershum, where it was recorded and broadcast by
Dutch radio. Wilson had by this stage written a considerable amount of
music for the accordion and relished the chance to use it in a song setting.
For much of the opening of the work the high flute and soprano parts lie
over low wheezing fifths in the accordion. At the end of the first stanza
there is a cadenza-style passage for the accordion in which Wilson highlights its ability to articulate fast staccato passagework and effects peculiar to
the instrument such as the bellows shake. The open textures and curious
sounds achieved by this combination in a slightly unexpected way manage
to match the strangeness of the text chosen, though unfortunately the
scoring does militate against frequent performance.

In 1978, Jane Manning, whom he had met at the London performance
of *Le Bateau Ivre,* travelled to Dublin to perform *A Woman Young and Old*
at the Dublin Festival of Twentieth Century Music. As Wilson reported to
Clarice Wilson:

> The Festival opened in a blaze of glory. My Yeats songs with
> orchestra were sung by Jane Manning, no less. It was marvellous
> to work with a really top-class singer, who could do anything one
> asked, and who, incidentally, had really studied the poems and

111

knew what she was trying to do. After the concert she came back
here to supper, with Felix Aprahamian and various other people.
As yet I haven't got a tape of the performance, but I'll let you
have a copy as soon as I get one.[17]

Manning and Wilson became great friends and undoubtedly Wilson used the
opportunity of the post-concert supper to propose writing a piece for
Manning. In 1979, he composed *The Windhover*, a short cycle for soprano
and clarinet, for her. This utilises the Hopkins poems 'The Windhover',
'Moonrise' and 'As kingfishers catch fire, dragonflies catch flame'. The cycle
forms part of the considerable portion of his vocal output where Wilson
abandons the traditional use of piano as the accompanying instrument for
vocal pieces.

Wilson's first tentative move away from writing a traditional supporting
accompaniment for piano had been in a cycle from 1969 to poems by his
friend, the Belfast baritone James Parr.[18] Appropriately entitled *Another
Direction*, the work is scored for soprano, clarinet and piano. The first song
'Sixth Floor Survey' is scored for voice and clarinet, the second 'The Island'
for voice and piano while the remaining five use all three performers.
Despite the omission of piano in 'Sixth Floor Survey', it is notable that the
clarinet's role in the remaining songs is generally that of a less important
added colour rather than a strong independent part. The exception is the
final song 'Domesday', where the clarinet, varying between parodistic
shrieking of the *Dies Irae*, independent lines and doubling of the vocal line,
is an equal with the other parts. It is also notable that this final song, 'Sixth
Floor Survey', and 'The Island,' where the characteristic Wilson ostinato
right-hand pattern on the piano is enlivened by a bass part that fails to align
with it metrically, are the strongest songs in a particularly memorable cycle.

The idea of using instruments other than piano to accompany the voice,
which is tentatively explored in the first song of *Another Direction* was one
that Wilson explored further at the behest of Anne Makower, who recalled:

> The *Three Vocalise* for cello, horn and soprano arose from a con-
> versation where I said to him that as a singer one is always
> singing with either a piano or an orchestra. I felt that the one
> thing one missed out on was the sort of chamber music where
> instead of being accompanied one is on equal terms with instru-
> mentalists. He immediately went off and wrote these pieces
> without words so that I would *be* an instrumentalist.[19]

These three pieces use a variety of different vowel sounds interspersed with
a few French words and phrases, and present particular challenges to the

singer, both in terms of maintaining pitch in an unusual aural texture and also in their range (which reaches up to a top F).

By the time of *The Windhover*, Wilson had therefore had considerably more experience at writing for voice with an accompanying part that was free of the conventions derived from piano writing. In Manning Wilson had an ideal vocalist with an agility and wide range that could match to a considerable extent these characteristics of the clarinet. While the extrovert setting of the title song places the greatest demands on the vocalist, with its repeated wide leaps, the most affecting setting is the more controlled and spare setting of Hopkins' moonlit ode. Even at points in these three songs, where the parts are to an extent shadowing one another, Wilson creates the impression of two almost independent voices intertwining until the climactic close of the final song, which acquires extra weight as Wilson sets the words to unexpected parallel movement in the two parts, bringing the tightly conceived cycle to an effective conclusion.

Example 5.2: *The Windhover*, 'As kingfishers catch fire, dragonflies catch flame', bars 28–43

The work was premiered by Manning in 1983 in a concert at the Wigmore Hall that also included Messiaen's *Harawi*, the premiere of Birtwistle's *Deowa* and music by Nicola Le Fanu and Tzvi Avni, which elicited a glowing review from Hilary Finch in *The Times* that Wilson was to cherish:

> I enjoyed James Wilson's *The Windhover*, three Hopkins settings written for Jane Manning, more, perhaps, than anything in the evening. Here, Alan Hacker's clarinet extended, lit and suggested, filling out the 'instress' of the wordsetting. It, in turn, was unusually effective in its thrifty virtuosity, its sparing use of pitch and expressive space and its acute ear for the vibration and resonance of each word and poem.[20]

In 1979,Wilson composed a Harpsichord Concerto for Gillian Smith, the daughter of Olive Smith, who had supported Wilson in the earlier part of his career. This was not his first work for Gillian Smith; in 1965, he had composed a short piano concerto entitled *Anna Liffey* for her as a wedding gift, while in 1967 he had composed a cor anglais sonata for Smith and her husband Lindsay Armstrong. Wilson was well aware of the capabilities of the harpsichord having studied it himself, and he had also heard Smith perform the concerto by Manuel de Falla in May 1979. Smith was also at this time playing some of Bartók's pieces from *Mikrokosmos* on the harpsichord, which Wilson may have been aware of.[21]

Wilson described the harpsichord concerto as being 'partly serial, partly atonal' and it demonstrates the looseness with which Wilson approached the serial technique.[22] In general he tends to treat the row as a large motivic cell from which sections can be broken off and developed separately, with much doubling back over portions of the row. The opening chord on the harpsichord also highlights one of the main thematic ideas, which is the group of major thirds C, E, G sharp /A flat, C. The clarity of the instrument and its inability to sustain are exploited effectively in the main idea introduced by the harpsichord and this mood is sustained for the duration of the movement.

Example 5.3: Harpsichord Concerto first movement, bars 27–30

Rapid passagework and repeated notes are also used throughout. The second movement is based on the material from the close of the first and follows without a break. For the final movement Wilson creates a jig-like theme from his row, demonstrating his rejection of actual serial technique while also paying homage to the typical dance finale of the baroque concerto. Again the theme constructed contains note repetitions and other divergences before the full complement of pitches is reached with the B flat in its fifth bar.

Example 5.4: Harpsichord Concerto third movement, bars 401–408

Textures are thin throughout the concerto in order for the harpsichord to be heard, but in this last movement even the harpsichord is restricted to a single line for much of the time. The close of the movement brings a surprise as the tempo slows and the textures change suddenly, and the work ends with a series of mysterious descending figures in the upper strings answered by the harpsichord ruminating in double octaves.

Example 5.5: Harpsichord Concerto third movement, bars 516–529

The concerto was hailed by Charles Acton with laudatory hyperbole:

> If Stravinsky had written a harpsichord concerto this would have
> been it. That is far from an uncomplimentary sentence, for the
> first movement has Stravinsky's allegro drive, his insistent
> repeated quavers and his thoroughgoing classical approach. All
> these movements are expert, precisely judged and true music.

> There are few enough modern harpsichord concertos: this should be an asset to any harpsichord player.[23]

While the concerto is not as Stravinskian as Acton seemed to think, lacking his clarity of form and his rhythmic invention, it is a very effective work demonstrating a clear understanding of the solo instrument's capabilities. Wilson's own response to the work in a letter was more equivocal than that of the critics: 'Glad you like the harpsichord thing. As always I find that I like bits, but that more could have been done. However, if I listen again in a year's time, I will probably like it better.'[24]

During this period Wilson also played an important role in a number of organisations working to create a modern infrastructure for music in Ireland. In the mid-1970s he became secretary of the Association of Irish Composers (AIC), a position he held for eight years until 1983.[25] He remained on the committee until 1986 and in 2001 was made honorary president. During his period of involvement the committee was involved in the plans for the AIC to publish music by Irish composers, and a number of his pieces were copied and bound by the AIC. He also helped oversee the establishment of the Irish Composers Centre in 1983. This centre was set up as a limited company with Wilson and Bernard Harrison as its first directors, and was intended to act as an archive for scores and recordings of Irish composers' music. Later in the 1980s the centre was overtaken by a new organisation set up by the Arts Council, the Contemporary Music Centre. While Wilson never served on the board of this organisation, he kept in close contact with it and would often suggest ideas and bring young composers to its attention.[26] From 1983, Wilson also sat on the Irish Advisory Committee of the Performing Rights Society (PRS), a position he retained when the Irish Music Rights Organisation was founded. This was successful in providing funds for the copying of scores and other issues surrounding copyright. Not all promotional ventures led to success, however. Wilson recalled an AIC reception organised in conjunction with an exhibition of music by Irish composers and held at the premises of the PRS specifically for music teachers. It was also linked to a competition at the Feis Ceoil for the interpretation of contemporary music for which the AIC was providing a prize. On the evening of the reception only one teacher, Deirdre Doyle from the Royal Irish Academy of Music, attended. For Wilson this was indicative of the ignorant and antagonistic approach of Irish music teachers towards twentieth-century music.[27]

Wilson served on the board of the Dublin Festival of Twentieth-Century Music from 1976 and when Seóirse Bodley stepped down he became chairman of the committee presiding over the 1982 festival. Unfortunately this festival coincided with some of the worst winter weather Dublin has experienced. The Kontarsky brothers who were to perform Stockhausen's *Mantra* were unable to get to Ireland due to flight cancellations, while the centrepiece of the festival, a performance of *Inori* conducted by Stockhausen, also fell a victim to the weather. As many of the orchestra had not been able to get to all the rehearsals, Stockhausen decided to cancel the performance and play a recording of *Inori* instead, followed by live performance of 'Aries' from *Sirius* by his son Markus Stockhausen.[28] The 1984 festival featuring Arne Nordheim and Mauricio Kagel took place without any problems, but the 1986 festival was cancelled due to a lack of adequate funding leaving an enormous gap in the Dublin musical scene which has arguably never been filled since.

The move by the AIC into publishing coincided with Wilson's last major attempt to obtain a UK publisher. In May 1980, on the recommendation of the pianist Richard Deering, he wrote to Scotus Music Publications and, after the company had expressed interest, Wilson sent a list of compositions for consideration, commenting that he would be submitting some of his choral works to the AIC for publication as this genre did not interest Scotus. By the following year Scotus had agreed to publish *Le Bateau Ivre*, *Dances for a Festival*, Bagatelles for Orchestra, and the concertos for trumpet, horn and harpsichord. For some reason, towards the end of the year, Wilson suddenly decided to withdraw the works from the publisher.

Around the same time Wilson began to write a column for the music periodical *Soundpost* in which he discussed his approach to composition and other assorted topics. In the summer of 1981, he devoted the column to a defence of the newly established academy of creative artists, Aosdána. Administered by the Irish Arts Council, Aosdána is an affiliation of artists deemed to have made an outstanding contribution in their field, originally limited to a total of 150 members. To artists who need it, the organisation provides a stipend, or *cnuas*, to enable them to concentrate fully on their creative work. The announcement of the scheme prompted a savage attack in *The Times* from Bernard Levin, who wrote that artists were to be put on the state payroll at '4000 jimmy-o'goblins a year':

> The jimmy-o'goblins in question are Irish ones it is true (and should therefore perhaps more appropriately be called jimmy-o'leprechauns) and the punt is at present at a discount; all the

same, considering that the recipients don't actually have to do anything at all for the money, it should not be sneezed at and I don't suppose will be. The first 150 free-loaders, incidentally, are to be selected by the Irish Arts Council, but after that they will select themselves. (I bet they will. Literally, I should think) . . . Certainly my claim is as good as that of any of the drunks, joxers, layabouts, schnorrers, fiddlers, thimble-riggers, touchers – and other members of the fancy who will shortly be jostling to join the queue . . . It can be said with very considerable assurance that from the moment the first of the 150 paid hacks are signed up and nip round the corner to turn a bit of it into liquid assets by courtesy of the good Messrs Jameson, there will not be a single word or note written, not a fragment of marble chipped or a square inch of canvas dabbed with paint, that will be of any artistic value or significance to any human being alive or as yet unborn . . . It will do the recipients quite a bit of good, of course, though even that may be offset over the years by cumulative damage to the liver.[29]

Wilson may have been particularly goaded by the lines:

> For you must not suppose that you have to be Irish of the Irish to qualify for this lovely shamrock-coloured lolly. When it comes to giving other people's money to con-men the Irish Government is plainly as warm hearted as Lambeth Council itself: foreign chancers already living off the fat of the land in the Republic under the scheme that allows 'creative artists' to escape taxation there (a scheme presumably instituted because it was felt that such folk might add a bit of tone to the place) can leap aboard the bandwagon, as can those born in Ireland and living abroad, never mind all those of Irish descent who can bear to visit the old sod long enough to pick up their winnings.[30]

Defending the organisation in *Soundpost* Wilson wrote:

> The composer in the Irish street has in the past devoted his creative thought to what he expects to get performed soon: he needs to hear it (you learn to compose by hearing what you compose) and he wants to collect his royalties. Naturally, he has been on the lookout for commissions from the Arts Council, R.T.É. and other bodies. At the back of his mind there has, I suppose, been a desire to write certain things simply because they need writing: things that are heard, when he wakes in the middle of the night, saying 'Time is running out. Write me, before it is too late.' Perhaps we shall now find that more Irish composers are

following their private vision, at least some of the time, instead of working to a dateline.[31]

Wilson was one of eight composers nominated among the first eighty-nine artists.[32] His appointment at the organisation's foundation meant that he could give up his teaching at the Royal Irish Academy of Music and his radio work. In a 1980 letter he had noted:

> Since writing *Twelfth Night* I have stuck to one character dramatic pieces and things of that ilk: there is no possibility of getting a big piece produced in Ireland, and if I ask anyone abroad about such an idea, they tell me, politely, to get lost.[33]

The stipend he now received meant that he could return to working on large-scale operatic projects rather than concentrating on small-scale commissions and in 1981 he began work on opera *Letters to Theo*.

In 1974, Wilson had read a selection of the letters of Vincent van Gogh and instantly became convinced that they could be used to form the basis of an operatic work. Fired by the drama and pathos of the letters he began work on fashioning a libretto at the end of the year. There is another mention of the opera in a letter from January of the following year, after which it would seem he left it aside, recognising that it would take a considerable amount of time to compose and that there was little chance of a performance. In the gap between this first conception of the work and its composition, Wilson had encountered some of the theatre works of Peter Maxwell Davies at the Dublin Festival of Twentieth Century Music. Ian Fox recalls him being particularly impressed by the power of *Eight Songs for a Mad King*, which Seóirse Bodley conducted at the 1974 festival when ideas for *Theo* were germinating and *Miss Donnithorne's Maggot*, which was performed by the Fires of London in 1978, and there is no doubt that in some ways these influenced his approach to creating his one-man opera.[34]

In the intervening period he had also continued to experiment with the serial technique. Like many Irish composers of his generation Wilson had fairly ambivalent feelings about the music of the Second Viennese School and serialism. Wilson's diaries testify to his interest in hearing performances of works by Schoenberg, and he did express interest in the earlier expressionist works in interview.[35] On the other hand, when asked in his last published interview for his concept of hell, he replied 'Schoenberg's String Trio'.[36] As with other Irish composers who began to experiment in use of twelve-note pitch collections in the 1970s and after, the music of Berg was cited as the main influence, based on a simplistic view of Berg as the composer who used a modified, free form of serialism, diluting his music with tonal chords.[37] For Wilson there was the added attraction of Berg as a supremely accomplished writer for the voice and for the theatre.[38] When it came to post-war developments in European modernism, including integral serialism, Wilson had no real interest and when asked by Gerard Victory if he wished to go to Darmstadt to discover more about what was happening in the music of the European avant-garde, he decided against attending.[39] He had a similar lack of interest in electronic music, stating:

> You can get much weirder new sounds with standard instruments. I get so bored with recitals of electronic music. You can't tell one piece from another. It sounds like a harmonium out of tune.[40]

The slow underlying pulse of much contemporary music was something which tended to irritate him, possibly stemming to some extent from what he realised was his own tendency to write slow music, but also from what he perceived as the lack of movement in music of the post-war avant-garde, especially when compared to the music of the French neoclassical composers or Bartók or Stravinsky.[41] The late music of Stravinsky did, however, demonstrate how the serial technique could be married to a soundworld Wilson was more attuned to.

He seems to have first considered trying to get *Letters to Theo* staged in Denmark at the Riddersalen Theatre and wrote to Elsa Gress outlining his ideas for the work:

> My idea is, roughly that the instrumentalists should be dressed as hospital orderlies and placed on the stage, to one side of the acting area. Vincent's first attack of madness is indicated by the instrumentalists putting down their instruments and chanting gibberish – some sort of obscene travesty of what he had been writing (maybe based on St Paul's 'Whatsoever things are pure' etc.) For the last scene, there is a scarlet blanket on the bed. Vincent, at the end, walks with his gun forward into darkness. Gunshot. The players slowly get up, put the body on a stretcher, cover it with the blanket. Exit – silence. Which of course is not exactly true, because Vincent merely wounded himself and walked back to the inn where he was living: he was left without any attention through a summer's day and night and died from loss of blood.[42]

This idea of using the instrumentalists as protagonists was dropped by Wilson when he decided to utilise a small chorus in the work. In the first production they were clothed in white hospital coats and Wilson explained, 'The chorus are not real people; they are inside Vincent's head. At times they are meant to illustrate a specific painting or even the creative ecstasy.'[43] The chorus also act as barometer of Vincent's mental state; they first 'echo what Van Gogh says, then contradict him and at the end, as he gets madder, anticipate what he says.'[44] Wilson envisaged the singers moving around the performance venue while singing, to give what he called a 'surround sound' effect.

While one friend sent Wilson an article outlining a homoerotic interpretation of the intense relationship between Van Gogh and Gauguin, it would seem that neither this nor the depth of Vincent's relationship with his brother Theo were the key element in Wilson's attraction to the subject.[45] Wilson felt there was an organic unity to the letters and that the gradual manner in which Vincent's character is revealed gave them an innate drama. Most importantly, Vincent was the epitome of the brilliant artist destroyed by public indifference and isolation; a man unable to sell his paintings to a public unable to recognise his genius. In interview he noted, 'Apart from Theo, his woman friend and Theo's wife, who kept the letters, no one treated him well . . . He died because no one bothered about him.'[46] In a later interview he described the opera as 'an act of contrition for the evils of the world'.[47] The letters are also rich in descriptions of Vincent's paintings and his heightened visual response to colours and the scenes he painted. Wilson also saw a parallel between his music and Van Gogh's art, noting in a letter that 'I have, once or twice, tried to do in the music what he did with his brush – those small flecks of colour, almost pointillist.'[48]

For the opera Wilson selected lines from a range of letters from 1875 to just before Vincent's death in 1890 and arranged them roughly in chronological order, dividing the work into five scenes, each representing a particular phase of Van Gogh's life. The first scene covers the 1870s in the Netherlands and England, the second covers the period spent in the Borinage where Van Gogh worked among the miners as a preacher, the third is set in the Netherlands and concerns itself primarily with the creation of paintings. After a short fourth scene of lines from a single letter sent from Paris, the last scene set in Arles, entitled 'The Starry Night', depicts Vincent's committal for insanity and eventual suicide. In Wilson's selection of lines from the letters a number of threads are isolated. The first of these is Van Gogh's interest in religion and his decision to become an evangelical preacher in imitation of his father who was a pastor. Wilson follows this in the third scene with Vincent's rejection of conventional religion, perhaps echoing his own youthful journey towards atheism. From the opening words of the opera describing a walk he had taken in England, which would later be transmuted into a picture, there is an emphasis on descriptions of work, the experience of artistic creation, and the fitful nature of inspiration. The nature of love is dwelt on in a number of scenes; the only line to be repeated is one which appears in the first scene and reappears as the final line of the opera 'Love needs so much more than people imagine'. Throughout the opera Wilson also stresses the fragile nature of Vincent's mental state. Within minutes of the opening he tells how his head sometimes aches and his thoughts get confused. The overall trajectory of the libretto is unremittingly tragic, the darkness only illuminated by moments of 'creative ecstasy' when a work of art is described. To achieve this Wilson sometimes carefully cuts passages and paraphrases sections of the letters. A clear example of this occurs in the short fourth scene where the libretto states:

> If you fall in love and get married, you will rise to a country house. Enjoy life. It's better than killing yourself.[49]

The darkness of this line is heightened by being coupled with other lines where Vincent states that he feels 'old and broken'. However, when the original context of the lines is examined, the tone is not so unrelentingly bleak:

> I know that these big long canvases are difficult to sell, but later on people will see that there is open air in them and that they are good-humoured. So now the whole lot would do for decorations for a dining room or a country house. And if you fall very much in love, and then get married, it doesn't seem to me out of the question that you will rise to a country house yourself some day, like so many other picture dealers. If you live well you spend more, but you gain more ground that way, and perhaps one gets on better these days by looking rich than by looking shabby. It's better to have a gay life of it than commit suicide. Remember me to all at home.[50]

This unvaried darkness coupled with Wilson's decision to have the chorus wandering through the hall singing, chanting, sobbing and laughing caused one critic to dismiss the work as an example of 'overkill', but most critics reacted to it favourably, while Charles Acton declared it 'the outstanding Irish opera'.[51] The opera also won an Independent Arts Award in 1984.[52] Wilson himself noted, 'God knows, Theo isn't exactly entertainment. It tears your heart out. It even hurts me to listen to it. There were times when I wanted to stand up and say stop, that's enough.'[53]

The music is based on a twelve-note pitch collection.

Example 5.6: *Letters to Theo*, pitch collection

Each scene is based on a cell drawn from this collection, derived using different permutations of numbers. The first scene simply takes the first four notes of the row to form a motif which is particularly important throughout the opera. The mining interlude, which leads into the second scene in the Borinage, marks a shift to the next four pitches of the row, but, as the opera progresses, more complex combinations of numbers are utilised. The full collection is only heard at the close of the opera when Vincent's penultimate letter is set to these pitches, with a retrograde form in canon in the accompanying instruments. The second scene also introduces a rhythmic figure which dominates this part of the work, consisting of two quavers, a quaver rest, a crotchet and three quavers. The syncopation caused by the rest and the fact that it always appears on a single pitch make this idea stand out clearly throughout as a strong musical motif and helps give unity to a scene which could easily have become a series of fragmented pictures of unrelated topics. It also underlines the obsessive nature of Vincent's preoccupation with both his own failings and how he might be viewed by his family. Wilson reuses the motif at a number of points in the opera, such as at the close of the third scene when Vincent falsely imagines that he has made the breakthrough he desires with his art, declaring 'My palette is thawing – the early coldness is leaving. I never knew before that colour and modelling come so easily.' This is then juxtaposed with the despair of the following scene, accompanied only by repetitive figures on the harp.

In the first half of the opera Wilson balances out the bleakness of much of his material with passages of warmth to accompany meditations on light, relationships and the creative act. Typical is the passage where Vincent tells of the woman he has met, the singer's line accompanied by parallel triads in the upper string and marimba.

Example 5.7: *Letters to Theo*, Scene iii, bars 130–137

As the piece progresses, there are less of these passages and Wilson also thins out the instrumentation. In particular the strings are used more sparingly in the final two scenes before dropping out altogether for the final pages of the opera. Set against this comparative regularity and strictness of musical organisation is the vocal line for Vincent, which is highly irregular in its attempts to capture the rhythms of speech. Wilson was particularly pleased when Czech conductor Albert Rosen compared the vocal line to those of Leoš Janáček. Indeed, it is not just the vocal line but also the use of short motifs which are repeated unaltered to create larger musical paragraphs, that is reminiscent of Janáček's approach.

The work was premiered in a concert in St Stephen's Church in Mount Street, Dublin on 26 November 1984, directed by Anne Makower, conducted by Colman Pearce and with John Cashmore singing the role of Vincent. Wilson had strong ideas about what he wanted his ideal production to look like and hoped to utilise projections of Van Gogh images and laser lights, but these proved prohibitively expensive; even with Arts Council funding, Wilson had to provide £2000 towards the cost of performance himself.[54] Two years later the work was filmed by RTÉ with the same director, conductor and soloist, and was broadcast on 28 December 1986. Wilson was delighted with the result though once again it proved too expensive to use any of Van Gogh's paintings, except for *Sunflowers*, for the opening titles. While he usually avoided spending too much time at rehearsals of his stage works, being happy to trust the production team with his work, he attended almost all of the television rehearsals out of curiosity to see how the whole process worked.[55]

A work which is closely linked to *Theo* is Wilson's song cycle *Emily Singing* (1985), a commission from the soprano Virginia Kerr. It was Kerr who suggested the use of Emily Brontë's poetry for the work. Wilson chose not to set any complete poems, but rather to select lines from a variety of poems to create what he described as a portrait of the author. These he grouped by theme, noting:

> *Emily Singing* falls into three main sections. The first is an expression of Emily's fascination with the wild and mysterious Yorkshire country where she lived. This leads to a meditation on the creative process; Emily was no Victorian prude, and the sexual overtones are clear. In the final sequence, the poet expresses her pantheistic creed.[56]

Wilson's decision to construct his own text from fragments of Brontë's poetry is perhaps appropriate, considering the convoluted publication history of many of these poems. Apart from the twenty-one poems published in Emily's lifetime, her reputation rested for many years on an edition prepared by Charlotte Brontë, in which texts were silently edited, amended and in some cases rewritten. It is only since the 1940s that relatively reliable editions of the poems, as written by Emily, have been available. It took Wilson some time to settle on which lines he would use and what form the work would take, as is evidenced by a series of sheets among his papers containing various extracts from poems, some of which he later set, some of which he discarded. At one point, the three sections of the work were to fall into a fast-slow-fast pattern dealing with nature in winter, summer and finally 'metaphysical matters'.[57]

As the work stands, it is not just Emily who sings through the lines but also her sister and in a very real sense Wilson himself. Only one Emily Brontë poem is set complete, the three-stanza 'High waving heather 'neath stormy blasts bending'. This is prefaced by four of the eight stanzas of 'How still, how happy! those are words/That once would scarce agree together'. Third comes the first six lines of 'Come, walk with me', of which Wilson had originally intended setting the first full stanza. This is followed by a Charlotte concoction of lines from one of Emily's longer poems coupled with a number of her own that alter the meaning of the text from a romance of a captive to a musing on the nature of inspiration, a change reinforced by Charlotte's title 'The Visionary'. Charlotte's modified meaning, describing the long wait through the night before the rustling air brings the 'Strange Power' of insight is presumably the very thing that attracted Wilson to the text. Wilson follows it with further lines from Emily's original poem, though this may be a coincidence as these lines also appear in her published poem drawn from the same source, 'The Prisoner'.

> He comes with western winds, with evening's wandering airs,
> With that clear dusk of heaven that brings the thickest stars;
> Winds take a pensive tone, and stars a tender fire
> And visions rise and change which kill me with desire.
> Then dawns the Invisible, the Unseen its truth reveals;
> My outward sense is gone, my inward essence feels –
> Its wings are almost free, its home, its harbour found;
> Measuring the gulf it stoops and dares the final bound.

By placing these beside Charlotte's revisions, Wilson similarly alters the meaning to give them a charge of what he perceived as Emily's (and perhaps by extension his own) erotic view of the nature of creativity. Three pantheistic stanzas from 'No coward soul is mine' are linked to two stanzas depicting the natural surroundings from 'A little while, a little while' by four and a half lines extracted from the middle of 'Plead for me' asking 'why I have persevered to shun the common paths that others run', again highlighting Wilson's vision of the lonely artist. The work concludes with the final eight lines from 'Stanzas' believed by some to be by Charlotte rather than Emily, beginning 'I'll walk where my own nature would lead'.[58]

In several ways this song cycle builds on Wilson's experience of writing *Letters to Theo*. It centres on similar themes; the nature of creativity and inspiration, the nature of belief and faith and the colours of the countryside coupled with their evocation in an art form. As with *Theo* the work also utilises a twelve-note pitch collection used in a variety of ways, some of which are relatively strict. The row is heard at its simplest when it appears in melodic guise on the cello before the final text and is then taken up by the voice for the first line (see Example 5.8), but derivations from it underpin the music from the very opening of the piece where the first eight notes act as the opening motto. In some sections, a characteristic feature is isolated, as in the setting of 'High waving heather 'neath stormy blasts bending', which focuses on the row's distinctive groups of thirds. In other sections Wilson uses permutations of the full row, such as in his setting of 'Come, walk with me'.

Example 5.8: *Emily Singing*, bars 418–426

The subtle doubling of the voice by various instruments is reminiscent of the later music of Berg which Wilson claimed to base his pitch technique upon, but the delicacy of the scoring throughout is closer to songs by Ravel and other French composers.

By contrast with the Brontë texts with which Wilson felt a strong affinity, the centenary of James Joyce's birth in 1982 encouraged Wilson to grapple with Joyce's most challenging work. The two resultant pieces were *Nighttown*, which did not receive its first performance from the Dublin Sinfonia until 1983, and *Plurabelle*, composed for the ensemble Cadenza. *Nighttown* was commissioned for the same instrumental formation that is used by Kurt Weill in his *Berliner Requiem*, with which it shared a pro-gramme.[59] Towards the end of the work, Wilson specifies in the score that various instruments should improvise for about thirty seconds.

> For a classically-trained composer, this is dangerous ground. And
> for classically-trained performers too. There was an occasion
> when, in a work for chamber orchestra, I asked the trombonist to
> improvise on a particular phrase for thirty seconds or so. At
> rehearsal, the result was not brilliant, but when we had discussed
> the piece together, his playing coruscated. I said to him: 'If I had
> known you could play like that I would have written it.' 'If you
> had written it' he answered, 'I couldn't have played it'. From then
> on I realised that, if you want performers to improvise, make sure
> that they know how to do it before asking them. Otherwise you
> will fall at the first fence.[60]

Wilson had included a short passage towards the end of his *Symphonic
Variations* (1980) in which the percussion and harp are asked to improvise
in a fast tempo while the horns play the (fully notated) main theme; but
after the experience of rehearsing *Nighttown* he was to be much more
restrictive in his use of aleatoric elements in his work.

Writing *Plurabelle* was, Wilson stated, a way of getting to understand
Joyce's *Finnegans Wake*. The work sets a selection of lines from the final
section of part one; Joyce himself had recorded the final eight minutes of
this 'Anna Livia Plurabelle' section. Wilson's approach was not to set a
large continuous passage of text, but rather to gather together a rather disparate collection of lines from across this section of the work, in some
places only setting part of the chosen sentence. The work opens with the
call of one of the two washerwomen, and concludes with a selection of
lines from the last four pages (the pages recorded by Joyce), in which the
onset of night is described along with the metamorphosis of the washerwomen to tree and stone respectively. In every sense this is a work of two
halves. The first is very disparate and shifts quickly from one bit of material to another, in a bizarre way reflecting the patchwork manner in which
the text has been constructed. Much of the text whizzes past in rapid syllabic patter, relieved only by an all too brief moment of lyrical expansion
for the lines 'she daren't catch a winkle of sleep, purling around like a chit
of a child, Wendawanda, a finger-thick, in a Lapsummer skirt and
damazon cheeks for to ishim bonzour to her dear Dubber Dan'. Of all
the texts set by Wilson this one threatens to submerge the added sounds
with its own music, and the 12/8 section that ensues heightens the sense
of a composer uncomfortable with the text, syllabically processing it as
fast as possible, even if the mood could be justified to a degree by some of
Joyce's punning references to nonsense rhymes. At the midpoint, however,
there is a complete change in the music as Wilson turns to text drawn

from the closing pages, starting at 'Look, look, the dusk is growing! My branches lofty are taking root.' Here the picture drawn by Joyce of the gradual descent of darkness, with the sounds of the river and nature forming a backdrop to the magical transformation of the women, inspires a more sensitive engagement from Wilson and the result is a very evocative aural depiction of the night. Scraps of sound in varying registers, based on the intervals prevalent in the opening of the work, appear around the slow-moving vocal line.

Example 5.9: *Plurabelle*, bars 248–256

The work garnered an enthusiastic response from Charles Acton, who compared Wilson's work with Joyce's own recitation, though in fact Wilson does not follow the pacing or word emphasis Joyce uses:

> Considering Joyce's own reading of the end of 'Anna Livia Plurabelle', I was alarmed at the prospect of hearing James Wilson's setting . . . In fact, I enjoyed the depths of the work very greatly indeed, and felt that Mr Wilson had written exactly the music implied by Joyce's words and suggested by his own voice. Could one say fairer than that?[61]

While the work may be uneven in quality, the long atmospheric closing section ensures that the work remains in the memory long after it has concluded.

While this period marked a return to large-scale composition, it did not mark an end to Wilson's teaching, but rather the beginning of a new phase. In 1982 the regional arts office in Limerick, Mid-west Arts, invited composers to spend a month in Clare to meet with local musical organisations with a view to establishing a way in which some sort of creative work or activities could be developed within the region. John Buckley attended and put forward a series of proposals at the end of the period, one of which was the establishment of a composition summer school. This idea was approved and the following year Buckley led a school for a week in Coláiste Mhuire in Ennis with a small group of students, modelled on a course he had attended in Guildford University run by John Cage and Merce Cunningham. Buckley felt at the end of the first course that it needed to be expanded if it was to operate on the scale he originally envisaged, and that he would need assistance.[62] He invited Wilson to join him as course director and Wilson remained involved, after Buckley had himself left the course in 1993, gradually reducing his involvement after 2000.[63]

From 1984 the course took place over two weeks. Coursework would be divided between the directors beforehand, with variation from year to year in who covered which topic. As the course became more established, visiting composers were invited, at first mainly Irish composers and then increasingly composers from abroad. Students over the years included Elaine Agnew, Rhona Clarke, Siobhán Cleary, Stephen Gardner, Marian Ingoldsby and Gráinne Mulvey.[64] Works completed by the students during the course would be performed and recorded at its conclusion, something in which they were greatly aided when Michael Alcorn, who first attended as a student, joined the directors to give classes in music technology. They also began to invite professional performers, something that was particularly interesting for Wilson as well as the students, and he kept copious notes for reference of the various extended techniques he heard from performers at the summer school. John Buckley recalled:

> Jim wrote several pieces incorporating unusual or non-standard performance techniques that the musicians had spoken about. You'll find that for example in the works that he wrote for Alan Smale after the period of the Ennis Summer School; these new effects suddenly appear, such as harmonic glissandi . . . after these lectures Jim would say 'My God that's a lovely sound; I think I'm

going to try that,' and lo and behold in the next composition you'd find an example of some technical development.[65]

Wilson also continued to teach selected people privately during this period. Curiously, while he was a strong supporter of younger Irish composers, not just as a teacher but also as a member of the main musical and artistic bodies in the country, it is notable that he seems to have had little interest in the work of his immediate Irish contemporaries. Nowhere in his private correspondence does the name of any of his Irish contemporaries appear, nor is there any mention of their work. Once he had established a certain security and confidence in what he was doing he became less concerned with examining what his compatriots were doing and was content to 'plough his own furrow'.[66] It seems indicative, however, of the tense relationship between the composers of this generation that he does not seem to have included them in his social gatherings.

One of the artists he invited to the summer school was Dorothy Dorow and the 1980s and 90s saw Wilson compose several other works for her. In February 1985, Dorow wrote to Wilson asking him to write something for a new duo she had formed with the cellist Aage Kvalbein after working on a piece by Nordheim for this combination. She also suggested that he might consider using an 'ancient' text.[67] It would seem that Wilson first wanted to set D.H. Lawrence's poem *Snake*, and by April he had received permission to set the text. However, at some point, whether for reasons of time or because of Dorow's suggestion, he set instead three short texts to form a five-minute cycle entitled *Runes*. They appear in chronological order in the cycle. The first is the anonymous fourteenth-century Irish verse 'I am of Ireland'. This is followed by lines from *The Old Wives' Tale* of 1595 by George Peele. The cycle concludes with another anonymous verse, this time from the seventeenth-century, 'If all the world were paper'. Wilson gave the title *Runes* to the work as he felt there was 'a fantastic, near-magical quality to the poems'.[68] The weightiest of the three settings is the central one, which is composed as a dramatic scena, with the stage for a conjuring set by the cello's line, which tends to alternate between tremolandi and rapid repeated semiquavers, while the soprano has an incantatory line with slow moving melismas. The nonsensical final poem is set in a very simple manner, with the vocal line deliberately placing stresses on the 'wrong' words of each line (*If* all the world were paper *and* all the sea were ink *and* all the trees were bread and cheese), while the first song is for the most part set to a rhythmic ostinato in 7/8 which makes its way into the vocal line at the words 'Come and dance with me.' The repetitions of the word 'in Ireland' finally bring the song back to the point where it started, with the voice singing the words to the same pitches as had been used for the opening statement, 'I am of Ireland'. The work was premiered in Stockholm in October 1985 and subsequently toured by Dorow and Kvalbein. In 1988, they recorded it for Simax.

The period from the mid-1980s to the end of the decade was dominated, however, by the composition and attempts to mount a production of a two act opera, *Grinning at the Devil*, to a libretto by Elsa Gress. Gress had originally asked her then regular collaborator, Tom O'Horgan, to write the music and so much of 1982 and 1983 was spent encouraging Wilson to get to know more about Karen Blixen, on whose life the opera is based, while trying to definitively disengage O'Horgan from the project. Blixen, who had published under the nom de plume Isak Dinesen, was in fact no stranger to Wilson. In 1963, he had written to Clarice Wilson:

> Have you read Isak Dinesen's *Seven Gothic Tales*? They were printed in Penguin recently, and I had to read them, especially as they were banned here. She is one of the writers I like most, not just admire, but like, as a friend.[69]

In 1982 he had written the music for Virginia Campbell's production of Blixen's puppet play *The Revenge of Truth*.[70] He had also known Henrik Stahl, who had been a friend of Blixen's husband Baron Bror Blixen-Finecke. He quickly wrote to Gress indicating his interest:

> Yes I've been through it several times and I can do it if you want me to. It gives fine opportunities for music, and music of a kind that would be new for me: it would stretch me, which is what composition is all about. So if you want me to go ahead, let me know. I estimate that I could let you have a finished score within a year from now.
>
> As I said I imagine a chamber orchestra rather than a full symphony orchestra, which would, I think over-weight the voices. And a chamber orchestra would be more practical . . . I think it could be a major work. I like the libretto greatly.[71]

Gress finally gave Wilson the go-ahead in the second half of 1983 and she got a verbal agreement from the then director of the Royal Theatre to premiere the work as part of the celebrations of Blixen's centenary in 1985. With this in mind, Wilson dropped his ideas for a simple chamber opera and decided to score the work for an orchestra with double wind, four horns, two each of the other brass instruments, a wide array of percussion including marimba, vibraphone and xylophone, harp and strings. By January of 1984 Wilson was working on the second act, and by April Gress had received copies of the complete score and brought one of them to the Royal Theatre.

At this point the plans for production began to unravel rapidly. In the interim, the Royal Theatre had been closed for renovations and a new director of the opera had been appointed. As no written agreement had been made, the new director was free to turn the work down and Gress was only able to arrange for the mezzo-soprano Edith Guillaume to sing some extracts from the work at public celebrations to mark Blixen's birthday. In the hope of mounting a production somehow, and with the tiny Riddersalen Theatre in mind, Wilson began the arduous task of making a reduced scoring of the work, this time for horn, percussion, piano, string quartet and synthesiser. The synthesiser was used throughout to distinguish between scenes of fantasy and scenes of reality and could also provide imitations of larger percussion instruments that would not fit into the small theatre. This was completed in 1986, but before any staging could take place the authors got embroiled in a legal argument with the estate of Karen Blixen, which claimed the work was in breach of the copyright laws by appropriating Blixen's intellectual property. Bizarrely, the Rungstedlund Foundation claimed that the work was a dramatisation of Blixen's *Out of Africa,* to which the libretto bears only a tangential relationship, but there was the added complication of the enactments of passages of various other Blixen tales in both acts. The dispute, which in retrospect seems to have been caused more by Gress' sometimes abrasive personality rather than anything in the libretto, was eventually settled, but it was not until 1989 that the opera was finally premiered in the Riddersalen Theatre ,with Edith Guillaume and John Cashmore as the two primary protagonists and Verner Nicolet, a flautist from the Royal Theatre, conducting the group of musicians.[72] Anne Makower directed the production.

The title of the opera is drawn from a phrase that appears in 'The Deluge of Norderney' from *Seven Gothic Tales* ,where one character declares:

> For I have lived long enough, by now, to have learned, when the devil grins at me, to grin back. And what now if this – to grin back when the devil grins at you – be in reality the highest, the only true fun in all the world? And what if everything else, which people have named fun, be only a presentiment, a foreshadowing, of it? It is an art worth learning, then.[73]

This art of grinning back at any adversity cast in her path was a key to Gress' understanding of Blixen's character. As Gress wrote of a later novel, it is 'composed of fiction, fact, observation and imagination. Plus something else.'[74]

The first act of the opera depicts the stormy relationship between Blixen – who is referred to throughout as Tania, the name her friends knew her by – and Denys Finch Hatton, who is leaving her house at the foot of the Ngong Hills in Kenya to go on safari with friends. The act is prefaced by an overture which includes fragments of spoken dialogue relating to the first scene of the second act. The audience is then addressed by the figure of Tania, who explains:

> We'll tell you of love and life, turned into stories,
> And of storytelling turned into love and life.
> We lived these lives, we died these deaths.
> But facts speak things, not truth. What here you see
> Is minding truth by what its mockery be.[75]

The scene changes to a drawing room and Tania sings her 'Aria to Ariel', which was also the original title of the opera. The Ariel Tania sings of is Denys, who was killed when his two-seat Gipsy Moth plane crashed. The climactic moments are underpinned by a chorus singing music which suggests the African setting of their affair.

Example 5.10: *Grinning at the Devil*, Act I, bars 397–406

This music returns at the end of the act when Denys leaves and the audience hears the sound of the plane crash. We then move back in time for the remainder of the act, which is essentially a long duet of love and bitterness for Denys and Tania. During the course of their arguments Tania and Denys improvise parts of different fantastical tales in imitation of the way the real Blixen conceived the stories she later published. For the libretto Gress draws on stories published in the collection *Seven Gothic Tales*: sections of 'The Deluge at Norderney', 'The Roads round Pisa' and 'The Dreamers' are enacted by Denys and Tania as she Scheherazade-like attempts to prevent his leaving. Denys in return offers her the tale of the mythical Simurgh Bird, drawn from Sufi writings, a symbol that recurs in Gress' other writings.

The second act is set about thirty years later and depicts Tania's visit to US; we see her meet Marilyn Monroe, Arthur Miller and Carson McCullers among others.[76] After most of the characters have left and McCullers has fallen into a drunken slumber, the final guest asks Tania about Africa. After he leaves she conjures up the spirit of Denys, Ariel to her Prospero. She tries to prolong the vision by telling him one last story, Blixen's final tale 'Second Meeting'.[77] Denys gradually withdraws, telling her that she will soon join him in death.

The dramatic challenge for Wilson was to create musical tension strong enough to hold attention throughout a first act in which little happens in terms of dramatic action, while ensuring that the second act did not seem like a slightly frivolous appendix to the passions displayed in the first. Musically the work is based around three ideas. The first is a four-note cell consisting of a minor second, a tritone and a major second. The second idea is a scale that is the basis of the majority of the harmony throughout the opera. The third idea is a collection of superimposed minor triads. The first cell is contained within the other collections.

Example 5.11: *Grinning at the Devil*, Act I, cells

Particular difficulty for Wilson was caused by two specifications of pre-existing music in the libretto. First, Tania asks Denys to sing 'the aria I love so well' and he responds with a performance of 'Where'er you walk' from Handel's *Semele*. Following this there is the enactment of the singer Pellegrina Leoni's tragic final performance in *Don Giovanni* signalled by a quotation from the Mozart-da Ponte opera, 'Crudele? Ah nò, mio bene!' It would seem, however, that, as with the structural challenges the libretto presented, Wilson was unwilling to let Gress know he had any problems with her work or to ask her to change anything and so he had to try and find a musical solution himself.[78] References to Mozart's opera gradually emerge from the orchestral textures just before the relevant quotation and it also has the advantage of occurring during one of the fantasy sections of the scene, but the Handel is a much larger and potentially more disruptive element. Wilson's approach is to try and work elements of the Handel into his music to make the final appearance seem less like a foreign object suddenly dropped in the middle of his music. While Denys' performance of the Handel is unaccompanied, the figuration from the original Handel accompaniment appears repeatedly throughout the scene, though this is unlikely to be noticed by the audience. The sections of each verse are also separated by instrumental interjections linking the work to Wilson's surrounding material. Ground for the appearance is also to a certain extent prepared by Denys' previous aria 'Ah, the sweet sickness, love, you fight in vain', which is described in the libretto as 'a Purcellian air'. Wilson sets it in a vein not far removed from the English neo-Renaissance mode of his student songs, in an attempt to bridge the gap of centuries between his music and the music of Denys.

Example 5.12: *Grinning at the Devil*, Act I, bars 600–615

This music reappears in the second act when Tania, in response to a question about the possibility of 'a seraphic love set to a tune', tells the man who asks her that it is possible to love seraphically to a tune but also quite impossible. Each of the fantasy scenes is given distinctive music, frequently with a neoclassical edge in keeping with the varying settings of Dinesen's stories, resulting in a very heterogeneous score. There is also a setting of the 'Corpus Christi Carol' for Tania in the first act, which Wilson sets in the manner of a folksong based entirely on the four-note cell mentioned above. With its elemental quality it makes a suitably dramatic return in the second act as Tania conjures up the dead spirit of her lover. Throughout the final pages of the opera this music is dominant, with Wilson deriving various chordal transformations of the song's distinctive intervallic structure, until the four basic pitches from the cell upon which it is based are filtered out to saturate the texture of the closing bars.

Grinning at the Devil was to remain Wilson's favourite of his operas. The work was given twenty performances at the Riddersalen to full houses and the queen of Denmark attended one of them. The work was very well received by the Danish press, and Poul Erik Pind writing for *Opera* finished his review stating 'I hope this opera will soon have a chance to be seen on a larger stage. It deserves it.'[79] There was also some coverage in the Irish press, with Pat O'Kelly and Ian Fox travelling to Denmark to review it. Both called for Irish performances, with Fox noting 'It is a creation which would suit the Gate, the Wexford fringe or the Opera Theatre Company excellently and would appeal to non-operatic audiences as much as to those who are regular attendees.'[80] Wilson himself in interview said:

> The opera is big news in Denmark and Sweden at the present time
> ... and now I'm hoping that perhaps it can be seen in Ireland with
> the two main principals of the Copenhagen production. Yes, I'd

love to have it presented here and I cannot see this posing any problems in the matter of transporting the costumes and sets. There is interest in it here already.[81]

Despite Wilson's optimism the work has never been performed in Ireland and he never heard the work in its original orchestral garb. The success of the work was also clouded by the fact that Gress had died in summer 1988 before the work was premiered. Reflecting on her death Wilson wrote:

> Better, I suppose, to die when you are looking forward to something than when it is over. To travel hopefully, as they say. I can see her, walking past Tivoli, hugging the score of *Grinning at the Devil*. To have known her was an immense and undeserved privilege. It was an epiphany.[82]

6 Late Works

The later years of Wilson's career saw a number of changes to his style. The experience of rescoring *Grinning at the Devil* for chamber forces had made him think seriously about how to get the widest range of sonorities from a small ensemble, and the combination of keyboard with strings and horn was one he returned to in his final opera, the unfinished *Stuffed Raspberries*, and which he used in a modified form in another late opera, *A Passionate Man*, in both cases adding that most flexible of wind instruments, the clarinet.[1] His belief that he had managed with this combination to achieve the maximum effect with minimal means was strengthened when Verner Nicolet, who conducted the premiere, told him 'everything that was in the original version is in the reduced version'.[2] Indeed in all Wilson's later music there is a move towards increased clarity of sound resulting in thinner textures. This is reflected in his admiration of the music of two contemporaries whose music is noted for its clarity of texture and instrumental finesse, Witold Lutosławski, who had appeared in the Dublin Festival of Twentieth Century Music in 1978, and Henri Dutilleux, whose *Metaboles* had been featured in the 1980 festival:

> What I love in music is economy and clarity. I want to hear everything that is going on, which is why, to my mind, one of the best twentieth century composers was Henri Dutilleux, in whose music – may it be for an enormous force – you'll hear every note. He's been an inspiration.[3]

He summed up his shift in approach by talking of how his admiration for the orchestration of Elgar's violin concerto was gradually replaced by a preference for the leaner scoring found in the cello concerto.[4] His interest in the operas of Janáček, which in *Letters to Theo* had already resulted in less lyrically oriented melodic lines as the speech rhythms of the text determined the nature of their setting, was extended during these later years to works by the next generation of Czech composers, many of whom died in the Holocaust. In addition to this, Wilson's approach to form became more abstruse, particularly in the extreme economy and concision of the late sonatas. He still, however, strived for elements of lyricism and tonality in some of his vocal music stating:

> And God help me, I still believe in a tune. I know they're not fashionable, but it's one of my constant preoccupations, not to be old-fashioned and at the same time to preserve the viability of tunes. Especially of course for the voice, because the voice works on intervals. And if you're writing minor ninths and augmented fourths all the time, the poor singer can't cope. It's worst for a singer because a singer is his own instrument. If he or she is anxious about getting it right, the voice goes. I've heard the best singers there are trying to cope with wildly difficult vocal lines, and they usually end up swearing.[5]

The late years also saw the composition of a number of substantial orchestral works of which *Angel One* for strings holds an important position in his output both as one of his most attractive and texturally striking works and as his first work for strings since the early divertimento and the multi-movement *Ceremonies* from 1963, which he later withdrew and destroyed. Commenting on this in his memoirs Wilson recalled:

> In 1987 I faced the fact that I had never written a proper work for string orchestra. There had been the Divertimento, but that was a student piece. The main thing that had stopped me, since that time, was the quality of the competition. If the idea of writing something entered my head, an admonitory voice said: *Eine Kleine Nachtmusik*, Dvořák Serenade in E, Introduction and Allegro, *Tallis Fantasia*. Therefore I settled on something else to write. But that same admonitory voice now went on to say: "You are no chicken. If you're ever going to write a string work, isn't it time you got down to it?" So at long last I wrote *Angel One*, for fourteen solo strings.[6]

Clifford Wright had given Wilson a painting entitled *Angel and Harlequin* and this was one of the inspirations behind the work, as he noted in a letter: 'It is called *Angel One*, because it is about painters who painted angels. One is Paul Klee, and the other is Clifford Wright, who was married to Elsa Gress, and the piece is dedicated to him.'[7] It is clear that Wilson approached this task with an extra degree of care and seriousness of intent, and from his correspondence it is also evident that the composition of this fifteen minute work took an unusually long time. Writing to a friend he noted, 'I am fathoms deep in my work for fourteen strings, started about two years ago, and many times interrupted for the best possible reasons.'[8] The extended time for gestation of the ideas doubtless helped to make this a particularly strong composition in Wilson's output. The work is scored for fourteen solo strings: three each of first and second violins, three violas, three celli and two double basses.

Apart from the visual impulses behind this work the influence of Lutosławski's music is also evident in his limited adoption of the controlled aleatoric writing found in Lutosławski's later works. In certain passages of these works pitches are strictly notated, but the speed and amount of time spent on each one is left to the performer, with the conductor indicating the end of each section. As the pitches are carefully selected the harmonic possibilities for each section are predetermined and the aleatoric element gives a certain iridescence to the texture. Wilson begins *Angel One* with a restricted form of this technique, which he was also to use in a number of other later works. The upper strings gradually enter with short figures that are repeated and the length of each section is indicated by second timings measured by the conductor. The pitch material in this example is limited to C, D, G and A flat. This cell plays an important role in the first part of the piece, while one of the pitch collections that controls the later sections of the work also contains this intervallic cell.

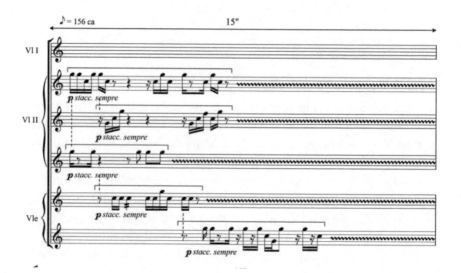

Example 6.1: *Angel One*, bars 1–8

The entry of the lower instruments leads to a return to normal barring and there are no further aleatoric passages in the work. The following bars begin the process of integrating these aleatoric ideas into measured music, with the motif being stated in various permutations and rhythmic arrangements. A series of chords starting at bar 13 adds most of the rest of the pitches of the chromatic scale, the only note missing being F natural, which finally appears in bar 33. After this introductory material the work proper begins with a *più mosso* section in which various scalic ideas are drawn from the full chromatic spectrum. A series of glissandi which returns later in the piece lead into a slow section marked *cantando*, again based on all twelve pitches, the main melody of which begins with rising fifths reminiscent of the opening. For this section the interest lies almost solely in the upper parts.

Example 6.2: *Angel One*, bars 87–101

At bar 185 a solo viola launches a rapid dance-like section, with the rising fifths of the previous section now found in the harmony provided by the lower instruments. After a passage in which harmonic glissandi move through the various instruments the upper strings detach themselves to play a slower-moving melody in which the tensions between the fifths and tri-tones of the initial cell are explored in linear form.

Example 6.3: *Angel One*, bars 241–251

The sense of increasing empty space in the texture between the top and bottom parts is emphasised by a passage for increasingly high-lying violin lines over low double-bass chords. A hint of the texture to follow is given as a high solo violin is first joined by a second and then a third, each playing individual material. After a further quiet hesitation the final section bursts forth in an explosion of sweet fourteen-part counterpoint, in which the pitches are restricted to C, D, E, F sharp, G sharp, A and B.

Example 6.4: *Angel One*, bars 272–276

As the upper parts climb ever higher, the basses and celli at first drop out before returning with dramatic pizzicato statements of the contrasting cell D, E, F natural, G natural, A, B, C sharp. One by one each instrument drops out until only the first violin is left holding a high E. *Angel One* is a highly successful work by Wilson and the closing section is perhaps the most radiant example of this dense polyphony also found in *Le Bateau Ivre* and his later third symphony. Wilson's ear for different colours and textures enlivens the work considerably and it is a striking demonstration of the range of possibilities available when working with strings.

Over the next two years Wilson composed two string concerti; a violin concerto for Alan Smale entitled *Pearl and Unicorn* and a viola concerto. The genesis of the latter is reminiscent of the origins of his accordion quintet and demonstrates Wilson's ability to pick up on any opportunity to get a piece taken up by a prominent performer. On 5 May 1988, an interview with viola player Rivka Golani appeared in *The Irish Times* to publicise a concert given by the BBC Philharmonic in which Golani would be soloist in a performance of Hector Berlioz's *Harold en Italie*. It outlined her career and her interest in the visual arts and mathematics, but the line that caught Wilson's eye came at the end of an account of the many new concertos she had recently premiered where Golani stated 'I intend to go on looking for new works and if there are Irish composers reading this, I'd be more than delighted to hear from them.'[9] As he had been away at the time of the performance in Dublin, Wilson purchased a recording of Golani playing a transcription of the Elgar Cello Concerto to get some sense of what her playing was like. He then wrote to her enclosing some of his music including *Angel One*, suggesting that if she was interested in his music he was willing to write a concerto for her. She invited him to visit her in London to discuss the project and while there she demonstrated the qualities of the viola which her husband Otto Erdesz had built for her. One of the features Golani had perfected on this asymmetrical instrument was completely accurate intonation up to the highest register, where some instruments can sound decidedly thin, and so Wilson decided to include some passages in this register in his concerto.[10]

Shortly after this visit Wilson travelled to Israel. The fact that Golani was an Israeli had possibly already triggered associations between this journey and the piece he was yet to compose. However, the catalyst for the work as it finally emerged was a visit on a bright, hot afternoon to the memorial to children who died in the Holocaust at Yad Vashem in Jerusalem. The effect of walking into this dark chamber, where a single candle is reflected in thousands of mirrors and a voice recites the names of the dead children, was for Wilson 'one of the most moving experiences of my life'.[11] He decided to name the work after the seven-branched candlestick that symbolises Israel, while the third movement was designed as a threnody for the children of the Holocaust.

It was presumably Golani's interest in mathematics that gave Wilson the idea to construct his first movement on what he described as 'a complex mathematical basis'.[12] Axel Klein has pointed out the importance of the number three and its multiples in this movement for the metre, phrase lengths, instrument groupings, pauses and intervallic construction.[13] The overall structure was inspired by Stravinsky's *Symphonies of Wind Instruments*, a textbook example of Stravinsky's technique of intercutting different material: short snatches of the final chorale appear throughout the earlier parts of the piece as short sudden interjections, disrupting the linear flow of the music. Wilson's movement is made up of a series of different blocks of material, each with its own distinctive scoring, which are then interleaved following his numerical plan. It is launched by a three-note figure in the brass which belongs to material heard later in the movement, and music for violins at the top of their register, divided into six parts to create what Wilson described as 'a sort of aural cloud' which then 'drifts . . . over the music of the first movement'.[14] (see example 6.5)

After nine bars violas join the violins and then a slow melody is heard on the cellos and bass clarinet which dovetails into the solo viola's entry in bar 18. After twenty-four bars the strings disappear and a new block of material is heard scored for wind instruments. This in turn is followed by a section in which the brass are dominant, and it is to this block that the opening three-note figure belongs. Throughout these altering blocks of sound the viola has a long unfolding melodic line, which avoids virtuosic passagework and remains independent of the changes taking place around it. The pattern continues throughout the movement, though the next twenty-four-bar string section is not the same as the opening 'cloud', eschewing the higher register and, after the first three bars, the six-part part-writing. The 'cloud' in fact only reappears once, at bar 220, with different pitches, but rather than appearing in a single block as before we hear first a single bar of it, then after three bars' rest follow three bars of the cloud. After a further two bars' rest, six bars of the material are heard and finally after seven bars' rest a longer section of nine bars is heard. In a similar way, isolated brass chords are spread throughout the concluding passages of the movement until it fades into silence.

Example 6.5: *Memorah*, 1st movement, bars 1–11

The second movement is a short scherzo in which the viola is accompanied by brass and percussion only. In this movement Wilson makes explicit the link between the brass and militarism which was implied in the first movement and he noted that in this movement the voice of humanity threatens to fall silent in the face of the 'machinery of death'.[15] It is a dark and shadowy movement which mostly utilises quieter dynamics with the occasional sudden, short, loud outburst. Towards the end there is a sudden change as the viola plays a melody marked dolce in double stops; this is a foreshadowing of the Brahms palimpsest of the final movement. However, this is cut off by a short passage of interplay between pizzicato viola and percussion which forms a sort of dark, failed reprise of the opening.

Example 6.6: *Menorah*, second movement, bars 71–77

The third movement is the kernel of the work and is the movement most directly inspired by the children's memorial at Yad Vashem. The dark chamber with its flickering lights is evoked by the opening bars. Over the pianissimo roll of a bass drum the notes A flat and E flat (and their enharmonic equivalents) shimmer through the orchestra from a low A flat on the double basses and harp upwards. Disturbance occurs in the fifth bar with the appearance of a tritone in the horn parts. This tension between perfect fifths and tritones threads its way throughout the melodic material of the movement.

Example 6.7: *Menorah*, third movement, bars 1–9

Gareth Cox has pointed out the superficial resemblance between this passage and the opening of *Das Rheingold*, where the notes E-flat and B flat form a primeval fifth from which stem chains of E-flat arpeggios depicting the River Rhine before the theft of its gold sets in motion the train of events that drags the various characters away from a state of innocence to corruption and ultimately destruction. Considering Wagner's notorious anti-Semitism it is possible that Wilson was making a slightly awkward intertextual point, but he himself never alluded to any relationship with the Wagner opera.[16] It is more likely that the resemblance is an unintentional result of his attempt to depict the atmosphere of the dark interior of the Holocaust memorial, the differently coloured E flats echoing through the orchestra representing the flickering candle reflected endlessly through the surrounding mirrors.

Wilson constructed the movement as a palimpsest, in which traces of Brahms' lullaby *Guten Abend, gute Nacht* can be discerned with varying degrees of clarity throughout. On the opening page the repeated D-sharp quavers on the timpani are the first small hint at this tune, and by bar 20 an F-sharp crotchet is added to them, making their origin clear. The repeated quaver on a single pitch and the rising minor third recur throughout the movement, while a further elongation clearly linked to the Brahms melody is also important, first appearing in the wind parts at bar 11 and developed further by the viola from bar 40 onwards.[17]

Example 6.8: *Menorah*, third movement, bars 11–12

By contrast with this music of lament, at bar 56 there is a short passage of seven bars based on lighter textures and short-note values among the higher string and wind instruments underpinned by harp.

Example 6.9: *Menorah*, third movement, bars 57–59

This breaks through a second time for a longer period at bar 83 in which Wilson couples limited aleatoric devices to the short repeated figures. At bar 92 violins are asked to repeat a four-note figure, the leader of each section starting it, with each other player beginning it as they hear the nearest player beginning it. Two bars later the vibraphone is given a series of boxes, each containing pitches on which the player must improvise and this idea is then carried over to the string section. The section concludes with a very quiet fanfare figure for the trumpets, marked dolce, incorporating the Brahms idea and the ambiguous play of fifths, fourths and tritones that has dominated the movement, giving a sense that the instruments have been removed from the warlike sphere of the second movement and incorporated into the more human world of the third. A long solo passage for viola with sparse occasional underpinning from the orchestra brings the concerto to a close. Wilson in later years regarded this as his greatest work and while a certain restraint may have resulted in the finale being less emotionally involving for the listener than he originally intended, *Menorah* is a well-argued and convincing musical structure. Gareth Cox hailed it as 'one of the finest Irish works of the last ten years'[18] and it was an obvious first choice for Wilson when a CD recording of some of his orchestral works was proposed.

As usual Wilson quickly followed this piece with more music intended for the same performer, in this case a song cycle *Wildwood* with Golani and the singer Maureen Forrester in mind.[19] Three years later, with no performance in sight, he transposed the work for soprano and violin to suit Dorothy Dorow's vocal range, but Dorow was unable to give the premiere of the work in 1995 due to unforeseen circumstances and the first performance was given by Tina Verbecke with Alan Smale. The original version had meanwhile received its premiere in 1994 with Aylish Kerrigan and violist Naomi Ogina. Utilising deeply religious poems by Mgr Kevin Nichols, using the image of trees to reflect on issues of time, virtue and death, the cycle could hardly form a greater contrast with Wilson's final cycle for Dorow written in 1990. The three poems by Leland Bardwell set in *Undesirables* are wryly humorous, focusing on a fly, a bedbug and finally the contrast between a group of amorous Hell's Angels and the mothers who, in the bedroom, 'embrace the gin in the freezer'. The element Wilson highlights in his short programme note is the element of compassion he discerned for these various forlorn creatures in the texts. Whereas the vocal line in *Wildwood* is a lyrical counterpart to a more virtuosic instrumental role, in *Undesirables* there is a mild flirtation with the sort of avant-garde techniques with which Dorow has long been associated. Toneless consonant prolongations, short improvisatory passages based on the syllables of the word 'bedbug' and a line that leaps across a wide range are matched in the cello part by the appearance of a variety of harmonics and pizzicati and passages played beyond the bridge. *Undesirables* also gives the impression of a much freer use of pitch than *Wildwood,* though it is the lyrical melancholy of the final song that stands out in this cycle, being less reliant than its predecessors on the extra-musical skills of the performer to create an impression.

Undesirables was premiered by Dorow with David James as part of Wilson's seventieth-birthday celebrations in 1992, with Wilson noting that it would probably be Dorow's final recital as she was retiring.[20] The retrospective concert also included *Runes*, his third violin sonata, *Explorations* for piano and *Breeze and Calm* for violin and dancer. Wilson gave a number of interviews to mark his birthday and used them to highlight the problems he still faced, noting 'You get just as big knocks when you're seventy as you do when you're twenty.' In particular he highlighted the problems created by the lack of performances and recordings:

> I would like a huge sum of money to make CDs of contemporary Irish music; properly done, with very good, beautifully-designed booklets to go with them. Hundreds and hundreds of these things would have to be given away to conductors and performers to show them what is available. Unless you can go abroad armed with a library of CDs which you are prepared to give away, it is very difficult to do much. Even in countries which have no money, they shower you with CDs. Another thing I would do is to send the National Symphony Orchestra abroad with a programme entirely of modern music.
>
> One of the worst things we composers labour under is that if you get a second performance of anything you're very surprised. You've worked for seven or eight months on a big orchestral work and it's given one hearing, quite often not a public performance, just a recording for broadcast . . . Everybody says, 'oh yes that was nice. Now what are you going to write?' If you're in, say, Germany the piece would be taken all around the country.[21]

In private he was more frank about the increased problems with the demise of the Twentieth Century Music Festival and the increasingly provincial attitude of many in positions of importance in Ireland who felt that there was no need to have non-Irish performers invited to Ireland for performances of contemporary music whether it be Irish or not:

> I wish I could do more to encourage performances of your work here. But it is the same for me in England; I am always met with

'We've got problems of our own, please go away.' And English performers who want to perform Irish music over here are met with 'We've got our own performers,' which is great for preventing the popularising of Irish music abroad.[22]

As Wilson was to find, the establishment position of seniority given to him by age did not necessarily translate into performance opportunities.

In another birthday interview Wilson noted that he was 'determined now not to embark on writing anything that is not guaranteed a performance'.[23] Yet at this time he was in the midst of putting together a libretto for an opera with no prospect of a commission or performance, noting 'It won't be done before I die, and probably not at all. But it needs to be written.'[24] The opera *Virata* marked a return to full-scale opera with chorus and standard orchestra and Wilson realised that this meant the chances of it ever receiving a performance were extremely low. The opera is based on a short story by Stefan Zweig entitled 'Virata or the Eyes of the Dying Brother' published in English translation in a volume of Jewish-themed stories by Zweig which also contained 'The Legend of the Third Dove', set by Wilson in 1991. It was Jytte Abildstrøm who first drew Wilson's attention to the story. Abildstrøm, as a result of growing up during the Second World War, has strong pacifist views and Wilson shared her abhorrence of the horrors of war having experienced something of this at first hand.[25] *Virata* examines the role of the individual in the wider world and the inability of anyone to disengage from their surroundings to achieve personal ethical perfection – one's inaction can have consequences every bit as bad as one's actions.

Wilson wrote the libretto himself and compiled a large file of pictures which he hoped could be used as a basis for a stage production. He began work on the libretto in the early 1990s, completing a draft of it by 1992, but it was left aside when he decided to compose *A Passionate Man*. It was taken up again around 1996 and completed in 1999. The work is divided into four scenes linked by interludes. The libretto stipulates that the set must incorporate a gauze screen to enable Indonesian *wayans* or shadow puppets, to be used during the interludes. The plot tells of a warrior who finds he has killed his own brother in battle and, in an attempt to atone and to find truth and an ethical lifestyle, rejects war to become first a judge, then a sage and finally the keeper of the king's hounds. The piece is rather different from Wilson's other operas. The chorus is given an unusually important role throughout the opera, accompanying the shadow plays with reflections on the action and Virata's development, but it also interjects commentaries from offstage during each scene. The work also unfolds in a series of semi-static tableaux and this lack of action, combined with the role of the chorus and the importance of the shadow plays, gives the work something of the feel of oratorio. Abildstrøm attempted to get the opera houses in Copenhagen and Århus interested in the project, but as Wilson suspected the work was not performed during his lifetime.

The opera for which he shelved *Virata*, *A Passionate Man*, owes its existence to author Bruce Arnold, who approached Wilson in either late 1991 or early 1992 with a play he had written about Jonathan Swift entitled *A Most Confounded Tory*.[26] In his play Arnold concentrated on two aspects of Swift's life. The first and dominant thread in the play is the political role played by Swift over a four-year period in London, when he wrote essays and pamphlets for the Tories, resulting in the disgrace of the Duke and Duchess of Marlborough and the ending of the twenty-one-year war with France. The second aspect, which Arnold felt made the play particularly suitable for musical treatment, is the relationship between Swift and Hester Vanhomrigh, known to posterity by Swift's name for her, 'Vanessa'. For Arnold the simple tale of a man falling in love with a young girl he taught to read and write had been lost through speculation about his relationship with Esther Johnson ('Stella') and his attitude towards women generally. Wilson read the play and felt that rather than providing incidental music, this work, which he likened to *Don Carlos*, needed to be turned into an opera.[27] The focus on Swift as the man who attacked the Duke of Marlborough on account of his propagation of war and, who ended up 'discrediting war itself' in particular appealed to Wilson, linking the work to the anti-war sentiments that form a part of the temporarily abandoned *Virata*. Arnold was sure that if the work was completed on time it would be possible to find the funding to mount it in 1995 as part of the celebrations surrounding the 200th anniversary of the founding of St Patrick's Hospital, the psychiatric hospital built with money bequeathed by Swift. Two members of the board gave their support in principle, but it was not until 1994, long after composition had begun, that a definite commitment from the board of the hospital was received. Anne Makower agreed to direct the finished work and Colman Pearce agreed to conduct it.

Wilson began work by fashioning a libretto from the play Arnold had given him. His first concern was the length of the play; when a text is set in the traditional manner favoured by Wilson it takes considerably longer to sing than to say it, therefore the text had to be substantially reduced. However, the changes made to the play were more substantial than mere pruning and the result was, as Arnold himself described it, quite different from his original while still fully representing the ideas of the play. Wilson prefaced each act with the voice of Swift reading from Part One of *Gulliver's Travels*; the first passage is from the opening chapter depicting the moment when Gulliver wakes to find himself a prisoner in Lilliput, and the second passage, from the seventh chapter, depicts the sentencing of Gulliver to have his eyes removed with sharp arrows. These are read to a little girl, another of Wilson's additions to the opera, whom he describes as being 'a cousin perhaps of those three boys in *The Magic Flute*'.[28] Wilson felt that the readings from Gulliver helped to 'emphasise the savagery that is constantly simmering away under the whole opera.' One scene was added to each act depicting Stella in Ireland with her companion Rebecca Dingley, passing the time by reading Swift's letters to them and commenting on his affairs. To make the final scene of the opera, in which Vanessa confronts Swift, having discovered that he is leaving London, more dramatic, Wilson added a scene set in Ireland in which Dingley and Stella receive news of Swift's imminent return. This is played simultaneously with the London scene. At the close the silent girl from the Gulliver readings moves to the front of the stage and utters the words 'A kind of victory?', an enigmatic ending to a potentially confusing scene.

It is curious just how many of Wilson's ideas about how to construct an opera *A Passionate Man* contravenes. In his *Soundpost* articles and in various articles and interviews Wilson had discussed these, in particular focusing on what makes a suitable libretto:

> A good opera is even harder to write than a good string quartet. In comparison, something like a symphony or a concerto is easy. For instance, the composer may choose a libretto that is undramatic, or too complex, or too abstruse. He may fail to differentiate musically between the characters. He may write music that is fine according to his theory of composition, but which is inappropriate to the particular story. His sense of musical timing may be good, but it may not coincide with the necessary dramatic timing: think, for instance of those Richard Strauss operas where the action finishes five minutes before the curtain comes down, and everyone is left standing around like lemons while the orchestra floods the theatre with sumptuous but dramatically irrelevant sound. Or a composer may destroy a telling effect with an inappropriate sequel.
>
> Of all the pitfalls, the biggest is to choose the wrong libretto. An operatic story needs to be clear, fairly simple, and preferably already familiar to the listener. Because, after a first hearing, your audience will not have picked up the finer details: they know that if the heroine has fallen down dead in Act Three they have seen a

tragedy, and that if, like Gounod's Mireille, she has got up again and burst into a waltz, it was a comedy. And they know that the baritone in the black cloak was the villain. And that's about it. Attempts at abstract philosophy go for nothing. If you write an opera on, say, *Titus Andronicus* (I hope you won't) or *Our Mutual Friend* or *The Mayor of Casterbridge*, the chances are that anyone who is laying out good money for a seat will take the trouble to do a bit of homework before coming.[29]

In similar vein he noted in interview:

A short story is usually about the right length for an opera; in the average novel there's far too much material. On the stage a story has got to be comparatively simple; if it isn't, no one's going to know what's going on. This is why I think, if you're looking for a subject, you should choose a story that people already know.[30]

For Wilson it did not matter whether the plot was nonsensical or not. For him operas such as *Lucia di Lammermoor, Così fan tutte* or even *Il Trovatore* were successful despite having what he felt were ridiculous plots because most importantly the characters evoked the sympathy of the audience, whereas in his view, operas such as *Turandot, Lady Macbeth of Mtsensk* and *The Fiery Angel* failed, as identification with the central characters became impossible for the audience.[31] Similarly there had to be coherence about the thrust of the plot with no sudden changes like the volte-face that forms the basis of the second act of *Die Zauberflöte*.[32] One could of course argue that despite all these clearly outlined ideas about the nature of a perfect libretto Wilson generally ignored them in practice; of the seven operas completed before he died, possibly only *Twelfth Night* could claim to utilise a well-known plot, *The Hunting of the Snark* being the only other one to take a relatively well-known work of literature as its basis. In part this can be attributed to circumstance: if a project was suggested to Wilson with the possibility of performance, unless his reservations were particularly grave he was willing to leave them aside and work with whatever libretto was presented to him. However, the problems are significantly more acute in *A Passionate Man*, of which one can say that simplicity is not its defining feature.

A Passionate Man focuses on the complicated political manoeuvrings which took place in the last years of Queen Anne's reign, an episode of Swift's life far less well known than the events which took place during his tenure as Dean of St Patrick's cathedral. The result of an attempt to retain some sense of the fast-moving intrigue of the political scene is an intensely wordy libretto, but one which, when sung, is difficult for the audience to follow. This is not helped by the fact that several key people mentioned in the text, such as Abigail Masham, make no appearance and the most dramatic events of the work, such as the attempted assassination of Robert Harley and the dismissal of the Duchess of Marlborough, are merely described. The operatic love story of Swift and Vanessa can get lost in the welter of political intrigue and speculation that comprises most of the text, and the cuts make it difficult for the characters to stand out as rounded figures; too often they are more like news reporters than real people involved in the turmoil. In this respect, the comparison with Wilson's model, Schiller's *Don Carlos* as set by Verdi, is rather telling. In *Don Carlos*, the personal and political are completely intertwined, but the gradual destruction of the central character dominates. In *A Passionate Man*, the story of Vanessa is not linked to the greater events occurring in court, and the domestic and political dramas fail to combine to impact on the audience; the personal tragedy of Vanessa does not stand out to a great enough extent.

Musically the work also suffers from problems. Wilson wrote that he wished to 'give the feeling of an impending explosion; a boiling pot with the lid jammed tightly on'. The result is a work which relies to a great extent on much repetition of short, jagged fragments of material, while the vocal lines tend to be quite unrewarding also. From Swift's reputed connection with John Gay's *The Beggar's Opera*, Wilson got the idea of making his work a type of modern-day equivalent of Gay's work, though at a somewhat remote distance.[33] As Gay had based his work around the popular songs of the day, Wilson decided to incorporate popular songs contemporaneous with the action of the opera. Some of these, such as *Lillibulero* and *Over the Hills and Far Away*, appear in Gay's work. Others include *Lavender's Blue*, the sea-shanty *Lowlands*, which is sung by a chorus during the final scene, and *Marlbrough s'en va-t-en guerre*. All of these tunes are simple in construction and fail to blend into their new atonal surroundings. Wilson further compounds this problem by using the tunes at key moments of the work, such as when Swift, in despair, sings to Vanessa of the impossibility of their marrying due to the age difference between them, using lines from *Cadenus and Vanessa*:

> What planter will attempt to yoke
> A sapling with a fallen oak?
> As years increase, she brighter shines;
> Her lover, with each day, declines.
> And he must fall a prey to time,
> While she continues in her prime.

As frequently happens in Wilson's later operas, this significant moment is set unaccompanied to underline the importance of the words.[34] However, in this case it is set to the tune of *Over the Hills and Far Away*, which rather undermines its sense of tragedy and trivialises the emotions of the scene.

The most striking passage of this opera is the opening of this scene between Swift and Vanessa, the fifth scene of Act Two. It begins with Swift and Vanessa entering from the bedroom in a state of undress, and Wilson set the scene with a rare passage of lyricism. The passage is based on conflicting adjacent tonalities, in this case D and E flat, a sound which is used throughout the opera to represent Swift.

Example 6.10: *A Passionate Man*, Act II Scene v, bars 22–40

It is the only point in the opera at which Wilson allows the music to open out; for the rest of the opera it is constrained by the necessity of delivering the large amount of text. Had Wilson provided more moments where the music responds to the specific alterations of situations and moods of his cast, it is possible the work would have been more dramatically successful and could have assisted audiences in identifying with the characters rather than viewing it as a display of obscure passions on the part of unsympathetic people. The other musical problem with this work stemmed from the performance circumstances at the premiere and the reduced orchestration. It is clear that while Wilson had successfully worked with smaller groups he felt that this opera really needed something on a larger scale, with a more varied palette than can be provided by string quartet, clarinet and horn to respond adequately to the action. He therefore gave a considerable amount of material to the synthesiser, specifying what instrument it should imitate at each point. The use of synthesised sound as a substitute for trumpets and other orchestral instruments is very unsatisfactory and can have almost risible results (particularly with the technology of the time). Apart from these musical and dramatic problems, rehearsals were particularly fraught as some of the singers had difficulty learning and remembering their parts and extensive cuts were made to make the work tauter and to increase the dramatic pacing.[35] Indeed Jane Manning, who was performing the role of Rebecca Dingley, felt that Wilson himself was not happy with the opera.[36] The reviews of the work were generally poor, which greatly upset Wilson, though he claimed in his memoirs that he had not been perturbed by the 'one' review which had panned the opera as 'its author had no conception of the requirements of theatre'.[37]

Wilson's next major work after the opera was his triple concerto *For Sarajevo* inspired by a photograph which had appeared in many newspapers during the siege of Sarajevo in 1992 showing the cellist Vedran Smailovič playing his cello in the ruins of the National Library. Wilson had seen the picture at the time but does not seem to have immediately responded to it. In 1994, after the death of his brother, his sister-in-law wrote enclosing a recording of the funeral and also the photograph of Smailovič, saying, 'Finally there is the picture of the musician in Sarajevo which I mentioned to you. Maybe it will inspire another masterpiece.'[38] Two things struck Wilson about the photograph. The first was that it represented, unlike most war imagery, a figure of hope rather than despair. He also wondered what the cellist could be playing in this situation.[39] The decision to write for three solo instruments rather than just solo cello may have been inspired by Michael Tippett's concerto (1978–79), which Wilson particularly admired. A small orchestra is used to counteract the inevitable problems of balance, with important parts given to the harp and the timpani. The music is lyrical, almost romantic in places, something it has in common with the Tippett concerto.

The first soloist to enter after the opening timpani motivic figure is naturally the cellist and the other instruments take it in turn to open the subsequent movements. The first movement ends with the viola which then starts the fast dance-like scherzo. This contains a contrasting grazioso section which returns to conclude the movement. Towards the end there is a short violin cadenza and it is a long violin solo that opens the final movement. This movement, which begins with slow-moving quavers in the bass, almost has a ceremonial quality and the movement in general favours the upper voices while the cello recedes into the background, in contrast to the first movement where a careful balance between the three soloists is maintained. At the close we return to the timpani figures with which the work opened. Apart from the lyricism of the work, it is notable that the second movement is one of Wilson's most successful scherzo movements, with a genuine forward-moving impetus.

Describing the work to Maria Balfour, who designed a cover for the score, Wilson noted, 'The last (slow) movement of the concerto has the direction "serioso ma non mesto" – serious but not sad – which could apply to the whole work.'[40] It was written with three specific performers in mind: Alan Smale, Constantin Zanidache and Aisling Drury Byrne. He had already written solo concerti for Smale and Drury Byrne and Zanidache had performed Wilson's *Menorah*. The main problem for Wilson was obtaining a commission for the work, not just in order to acquire a fee but in order to ensure it would be performed. To a friend he noted:

> Have been shamelessly propositioning RTÉ to commission my triple concerto for violin, viola, 'cello and orchestra. Yesterday they said YES! I hate hawking myself around but unless I do, nobody reacts. The concerto is already sketched, but much remains to be done.[41]

Wilson managed to persuade RTÉ to commission it as a way of marking his seventy-fifth birthday and so it was premiered in December 1997. Considering the subject matter of the work RTÉ decided to invite members of the Bosnian Community Development Project to the concert and through them discovered, to everyone's surprise, that Smailovič was living near Warrenpoint in County Down. A surprise meeting between Wilson and Smailovič was arranged and took place at the rehearsals for the concert. After the performance, which Smailovič also attended, he presented Wilson with a copy of the picture that had inspired his work, with a dedication to the composer.[42] Interestingly the following year Wilson provided music, scored for solo cello, for Jimmy Murphy's play *Aceldama* which depicts the emotional journey of a sniper on the hills above Sarajevo.

While Wilson still faced problems obtaining performances, it seemed in the late 1990s as if one of his longstanding wishes was to be fulfilled. In 1995 the Contemporary Music Centre produced the first of a series of ten free promotional CDs featuring short samples of music by living composers and Wilson's cello piece *For Cliodhna* was included on the second CD in 1997. More importantly the Naxos/Marco Polo company began a short-lived project to record works by Irish composers and in 1996 recorded a CD of Wilson's orchestral works performed by the National Symphony Orchestra under Colman Pearce. The works chosen for the CD were his violin concerto *Pearl and Unicorn* played by Alan Smale, *Menorah* performed by Constantin Zanidache and a short piece for orchestra entitled Concertino which had been premiered by Pearce and the orchestra in 1994.

Wilson described Concertino as a study in colour and texture:

> The starting point of the music was an autumn sunset over the Wicklow hills. I asked myself what were the equivalents in music of these particular colours and shapes? These matters decided, the music itself took over, as it always does.[43]

The work is written for a large orchestra with a considerable array of percussion instruments including wind chimes and flexatone. However, as with much of his late music there are very few passages where the full forces are employed and the emphasis is on small, transparent groups of instruments. The piece is almost like a study in orchestral colour, with the texture constantly varying over its thirteen-minute duration. A number of different effects, which as Wilson notes on the score he obtained from the writings of Carlos Salzedo, are specified for the harp, while the string parts also use a variety of techniques, including playing on the bridge. Taking into consideration some of the surface features of the work and its structure, it is possible that Debussy's *Jeux* was at the back of Wilson's mind when working on this piece.

The opening of the work is the part most clearly related to Wilson's starting idea. A mysterious atmosphere is created with harp chords accompanied by a low trill on the timpani, with isolated sounds from a suspended cymbal and wind chimes. Gradually various string instruments enter, muted and playing tremolandi, with glissandi on the harp and timpani. Very quietly the trumpets announce a simple idea, a chord of B and C sharp with the top part playing an E which shifts to an F sharp. At this point the flute enters with the first melodic idea, however this soon tails off and fragments of melody are heard passing through all registers of the orchestra.

This idea of colouristic fragmentation of melodic ideas corresponds with what is happening in the work on the larger structural level. While behind the harmony of the work hover the various types of constructed scales Wilson used as the basis of his later work, the piece as a whole is built using a series of very short ideas which recur unpredictably in various guises. Some of these are instantly recognisable: a short arpeggiated figure outlined in staccato semiquavers stands out clearly in the wind parts at bar 69 and so is identifiable in its dramatic reappearance on solo violin in the gaps between large chords for full orchestra at bar 94 and again when it appears in the middle strings at bar 120. Visually this idea is also present in the passages at bars 72 and 160 where the strings are asked to play on the bridge though the aural effect is radically different. Some of these individual threads are momentary, like the descending ornamented flute figure in bar 47 that reappears in amplified form in the violins in bar 154. Others have more long-ranging impact, such as the three-note figure that emerges in the tom-toms and xylophone at bar 149. This drops out after a bar or two and re-merges briefly at bar 162, before returning as the basis of a longer canonic passage for percussion and bassoons starting at bar 217.

In contrast to this kaleidoscope of constantly changing colour, a long and stable central section presents a gradual unfolding of a sprawling romantic melody on solo cello, accompanied by clarinet and quiet chords from the bass instruments. The cello is joined by a solo violin as the bass gravitates to a chord of E-flat, giving it some sense of rootedness.

Example 6.11: Concertino, bars 166–183

The work closes with reminiscences of the central section on solo violin and cello, an implied resolution on to an E-flat-major chord and a character-istic contradiction of this by a dissonant chord for wind and vibraphone. The cutting between ideas can lead to a sense of disjunction as one idea trails off and is followed by what seems to be a completely unrelated idea and this also makes the piece challenging to grasp on first hearing. Unusually, however, and thanks to the Naxos project, the work did get a second public performance from the National Symphony Orchestra prior to the recording session in 1996.

Consolidating the sense of Wilson finally becoming an establishment figure with advancing age, he was awarded the Marten Toonder Award in 1997, an award from the Irish Arts Council which honours established artists in music, literature and the visual arts. The following year he began the process of applying for Irish citizenship. His application was approved in July 1999 and he received his certificate of naturalisation on 14 September. His decision to take Irish nationality in 1998 was not for any practical reason but more because he felt he had been assimilated into the country by this time.[44] He remained highly dismissive of attempts to classify him as either an 'Irish' or 'English' composer or to link national ideas with music, a notion he tended to associate with the use of folksongs or a folk tone:

> When people say, 'Are you an Irish composer? Are you an English composer?' I'm just a composer. I try very hard to steer clear of that kind of attitude. I am not in the least interested in incorporating folksy stuff in my music. But I think a composer is, in a way, like a thing in natural history which we studied as children called a caddis-worm. It lives in a stream and makes itself a shell out of bits of sand and broken up other shells and bottle tops and goodness knows what. And I think a composer does that.[45]

Like most Irish composers he avoided any references to the political situation in Northern Ireland in his music and restricted his public comments to withering scorn about politicians who placed no value on the arts. He wrote many letters to the papers and to various lobby groups, particularly in the 1980s when Arts Council funding was cut, but only one comment regarding the political situation in Ireland seems to have survived in his correspondence from the early 1970s:

> As you say, the business in Ulster is worrying. Fortunately, Lynch here is a sensible man. But the heartbreaking thing is that nobody in England has the least idea of what is happening in Belfast and Derry, and never will understand.[46]

In the absence of any further evidence it would be speculative to link his decision to take Irish citizenship in 1998 with the changes in the political life of Northern Ireland after the signing of the Good Friday Agreement by the British and Irish governments in April of that year. On the other hand international political events clearly did impact on him, particularly due to his strong anti-war feelings as is demonstrated by the concerti *Menorah* and *For Sarajevo* and his unperformed opera *Virata*. In 2001, he wrote a short political piece called *Trio* for Jytte Abildstrøm, Daimi Gentile and Edith Guillaume (who had all been involved in the premiere of *Grinning at the Devil*) which touches on ecological issues and political corruption in the planning process, while the same year he was one of the few composer members of Aosdána to sign a letter written by Raymond Deane which condemned the US attack on Afghanistan.[47]

In 2000 Wilson embarked on one of his last big orchestral pieces, his third symphony. The idea of writing the symphony came from Colman Pearce and the impetus was Wilson's dissatisfaction at his tendency to avoid writing fast music in favour of what he called a 'melancholic jog-trot':[48]

> My third symphony is a fairly recent work, and as an exercise I made myself write for a larger orchestra than usual. I am prone to write slow music, and in this I made myself write a lot of fast music. But the slow movement is more thinly textured than the other movements, and I like it the best.[49]

What Wilson does not mention in his programme note for the piece is that this slow movement is inspired by memories of being on watch during his time sailing with Campbell around the Mediterranean in the 1950s.[50] It is interesting that the compositional approach he used to depict this experience echoes the short C-major passage from his other autobiographical orchestral piece *Le Bateau Ivre*. The movement begins with an eighteen-bar passage for solo violin. After a brief discordant interruption from the brass the violin continues, this time in the company of a solo viola. This process continues, throughout the movement with string passages interrupted by wind, brass and percussion. Extra string players are added after each interruption until there are thirteen independent parts, with a vibraphone adding colour to the texture. This is probably the most successful movement of a work which is too long for its rather sparse material. While it is scored for a large orchestra with triple wind, including alto flute and double bassoon, four horns, three each of trumpets and trombones, tuba, timpani and a wide array of percussion requiring four players and piano as well as strings, there is no lack of clarity as Wilson rarely requires anything remotely resembling full forces throughout the work, with the last movement being particularly sparse in its scoring. The work was premiered in 2003. Bruce Arnold recalled that when he congratulated Wilson after the performance, Wilson replied 'I will probably never hear the work played again, in my lifetime.'[51]

The new millennium saw some further recordings of Wilson's music. Since the 1980s he had collaborated directly with Jytte Abildstrøm, their production of Hans Christian Andersen's *The Little Mermaid* touring successfully to Ireland for performances during the Dublin Theatre Festival in 1992. This was followed by a series of works for narrator and instruments, some originally designed for live performance. Stories set included *The Christmas Rose* by Selma Lagerlöf, *The Legend of the Third Dove* by Stefan Zweig and *The Fisherman and his Wife* by the Brothers Grimm. In 2001, Jytte Abildstrøm recorded in Danish her readings of Zweig's *The Legend of the Third Dove* and the Grimm tale *The Fisherman and his Wife* accompanied by Wilson's music for the Focus Production label. In 2002, to mark Wilson's eightieth birthday, a celebratory concert and CD recording were organised with funding provided by the Arts Council and production and distribution organised by the Contemporary Music Centre.[52] Wilson organised the recording sessions and chose the programme which was built around the singer Jane Manning and the contemporary ensemble Concorde. The works featured were the song cycles *The Windhover* (1979) for soprano and clarinet, *Enjoying* (2001) for soprano and flute and *Upon Silence* for unaccompanied soprano. The flautist and clarinettist contributed *Arlecchino* for flute (1979) and *Three Playthings* for clarinet (1983). The disc opened with the Sonatina for clarinet, violin, cello and accordion opus 149 (1998), which had been composed for Concorde, and concluded with a cycle written in 1997 for Jane Manning and her group Jane's Minstrels entitled *Calico Pie*.

This takes lines from three Edward Lear poems: the opening stanza of 'The Yonghy Bonghy Bo', and selected lines from 'The Quangle Wangle's Hat' and 'The Akond of Swat'. Although scored for a small ensemble of piano, violin and horn, the texture in this cycle is also relatively sparse for much of its short duration. Lurking in the shadows cast by the Quangle Wangle's hat is the memory of William Walton's *Façade*, particularly overt in the jazzy tone of the final song. Some of the familiar Wilson fingerprints are there, such as the ostinato figure that underlies the opening of 'The Akond of Swat' and the repeated swaying figure that suggests the mysterious Coast of Coromandel in the opening song. Much of the cycle pokes gentle fun at the conventions of vocal music, such as in the ridiculous melismatic flights of fancy the singer indulges in for the words 'all his worldly goods' in 'The Yonghy Bonghy Bo' or the sudden burst of romanticism in 'The Akond of Swat' for the lines:

> Does he like to lie on his back in a boat
> Like the lady who lived in that isle remote,
> SHALLOTT,
> The Akond of Swat?

The work is one of Wilson's more successful ventures into musical comedy, which sometimes could end up too arch for a modern audience. For the cover of the CD he used Clifford Wright's painting, *Angel and Harlequin*, thus tying the project to another of his important collaborators.

The years 2002–03 were mostly taken up with composition of chamber works, including a third string quartet and fifth violin sonata. The CD he had made with Jytte Abildstrøm had been so successful that they recorded a second CD, this time in English as well as Danish. For this CD Abildstrøm selected three of her favourite tales by Hans Christian Anderson, three that are little known in English-speaking countries. The sharp character studies found in *The Teapot* and *The Snail and the Rosetree* are underlined by Wilson's music with, for example, the snail represented by gruff bassoon writing pitted against more lyrical writing for the harp to represent the rose in the latter. The unchanging mental attitude of the generations of snails is mirrored in the non-developmental nature of the musical material given to the bassoon. In this way the story is gently underlined without the music becoming too dominant. In the mysterious tale of *The Bell*, Wilson provides a more expansive score for a larger group of violin, harp, bassoon and piano. The recording made of the works is an attractive and unusual disc, appealing not just to children but also to adults. In a 2002 interview, Wilson had stated that he was 'naturally not as lively as I was. The odd bit of arthritis and so on . . . I've had nothing much wrong with me since I was about twenty.'[53] However, in 2003, his heart was beginning to give him trouble and during the recording sessions for the disc he fell ill. He insisted, however, that he was fine and did not need medical attention.[54]

As a 2002 interview noted Wilson felt his age entitled him to feel even less bound to expected forms or methods in his music:

> Forms, procedures and genres are all subject to an element of late recklessness from which he clearly derives a mischievous pleasure. 'For instance, I wrote a piece for the theatre at the beginning of the year, for three performers and about three or four instrumentalists. And only in the last ten minutes did I introduce the cello for the first time – which will annoy the cellist – and it finishes with dialogue without music. So that all the academicians will say that this is thoroughly badly written. And I don't give a damn.'[55]

Wilson's later style is clearly demonstrated by his last violin sonata, a one-movement work lasting approximately seven to eight minutes. The first main idea of the piece is announced by the violin in the opening bars, and if one leaves aside the G-sharp grace note it begins by outlining a simple chromatic descending line: E, [G sharp], D sharp, C sharp, C natural, B flat, G flat with a leap up to the previously missing D natural. This is answered by the piano moving in parallel fourths, and these parallel fourths and fifths play an important role in the piano part through the first section, while the violin explores more expansive material above this. A quick glance demonstrates Wilson's rapid filling in of the chromatic space; the missing pitches from the piano's scale in fourths are provided in the ensuing crotchets (E flat, B flat, A flat and D flat).

Example 6.12: Violin Sonata no. 6, bars 1–6

In terms of the wider structure one can divide it according to the changes in tempi, with a second section marked 'Vivace' beginning at bar 34 and a further section marked 'Presto' at bar 116. To a certain degree one also notices changes in the treatment of material at the opening of each of these sections, but all three are essentially dealing with exactly the same motivic material. The material is not 'developed' in a traditional nineteenth-century Germanic way, but the main motives reappear with intervals altered in various ways through expansion and contraction. Textures are constantly altering, something which is particularly noticeable in the central section. A particular rhythmic figure may be set up and repeated but will suddenly be replaced by something different, diffusing the tension that had been built up. At the centre of the work the piano is restricted to short interventions and the violin double stops over long-held notes giving this point a highly static quality. The final presto (which has a metronome mark which is not that fast) is more focused and becomes increasingly dominated by the opening violin figure, played in rhythmic augmentation. It is this figure which, merely transposed up an octave from its first appearance, brings the work to a close. There is no sense of teleological arrival, but instead we have explored a figure from various angles within a loose framework, before the figure returns in its original form, unscathed by the processes it has undergone. Rhapsodic in its approach to form and lyrically restrained in approach it is a successful example of Wilson's late style.

Although the situation regarding opera performance had not altered in Ireland, Wilson was considering the possibility of writing another opera, this time based on Shakespeare's *As You Like It*. Like *Twelfth Night* this is a comedy of disguises with its scenes of Orlando 'wooing' the disguised Rosalind/Ganymede, who also manages in her man's garb to captivate the shepherdess Phebe, and it was doubtless an interest in these erotic ambiguities that made Wilson consider the work. However, all that emerged from this idea is a setting of 'It was a lover and his lass' which forms part of the choral work *Almanac* from 2004. This *a capella* work gathers together a series of poems by different authors to trace a journey through the seasons of the year. It begins with Coleridge's 'Frost at midnight', spring is represented by 'It was a lover and his lass', summer by 'Now welcome summer' from Chaucer's *The Parliament of Fowls* and the work ends in the autumnal twilight of Yeats' 'The wild swans at Coole'. The Shakespeare setting gives the bulk of the text to a solo soprano and solo tenor, while the lower voices are confined to repeated hey-ho-hey noninos and other Morley-esque lines; this splitting of the text perhaps results from Wilson's aborted operatic plans and might ultimately have been incorporated into an opera.

The Shakespeare opera was, however, abandoned when Wilson heard that if he composed a comedy for no more than four singers and small ensemble there was a chance it might be performed in the Riddersalen Theatre. He contacted Anne Makower to see if she could identify a suitable play, one that would fit the performance restrictions. She tried without success to identify anything appropriate:

> Comedy almost always has a lot of characters and the only plays I could think of with four characters or less were the ones by Noel Coward which I felt were not in a style that would be suitable for Wilson. Besides, there would be terrible problems with copyright. So I got an idea and sent it to him, telling him that if he did not like it to say so. He did like it so I then wrote a more

detailed plotline, indicating how it broke into scenes and where there might be arias and so on.[56]

The four characters in this two-act farce entitled *Stuffed Raspberries* are a rich elderly spinster called Jenny Goldworthy and three people with designs on her money: her companion/nurse Sprockett, her nephew and a man who claims to be one of Miss Goldworthy's brothers but who is in fact an imposter. Miss Goldworthy varies from being perfectly rational to imagining she is a variety of famous people from history, such as Florence Nightingale and Marie Antoinette. The plot also includes standard features of farce, such as various characters chasing each other through various doors in the set.

Once again the touchstone for Wilson was Mozart, in this case the Mozart of *Così fan tutte*:

> The music that I have written is, in general, not comic, but I hope beautiful: the humour is in the words. In this I am copying *Così fan Tutte*, which sets frivolous words to ravishing music. And most of my music is quite serious. The text is, of course, broad farce, dealing in a fantastical way with impossible situations. The actions of the characters could not possibly be taken seriously.[57]

Wilson tends throughout to avoid detachable set pieces in order to try and match the fast-moving text. He does use quotation in his setting to underline the comedy of the situation and he commented on this to Abildstrøm:

> When Sprockett is opening the letters with a paper knife, there is a reference to 'Vissi d'arte,' Callas in full throttle. And when Henry talks of his female conquests you are reminded of Leperello's catalogue aria and of 'Largo al Factotum.'[58]

Due to the imminent possibility of performance Wilson once again abandoned his preferred method of composing into full score and instead worked on a vocal score, completing the first act in the summer of 2005. He planned to finish composition by the autumn and then begin scoring the work for string quartet, horn, clarinet and piano.[59] Before he could start work on the second act, however, he suffered a stroke and two days later died on the morning of 6 August. He had left his body to the Royal College of Surgeons, but due to the delays with the post-mortem he was cremated after a simple ceremony organised by Anne Makower at Mount Jerome crematorium on 19 August at which recordings of music including Mozart's Oboe Quartet and his own *Almanac* were played.

7 Conclusion

> I wonder if, in your work, you know when you have produced
> something good; something better than usual. I never have the
> least idea. All I feel is the relief that the job is done and I can get
> on with something else.[1]

The tussle between diffidence about his life's work and the urgent constant drive to create new compositions underpins Wilson's career. It is
interesting to speculate how many of Wilson's traits were formed by the
life-changing decision to relocate to Dublin. He certainly had an unshake-
able core belief that composition was what he was born to do. Had he
remained in London, he would undoubtedly have undergone formal study
for a much longer period with Rowley and possibly also others both in
England and Europe, mastering larger forms and forces before he would
have been in a position to attempt a breakthrough onto the professional
scene. The insecurity that was bred by his circumstances cut in two direc-
tions: it was the thing that spurred him to master all technical matters to
do with scoring, but also for some left him rather too open to deferring to
the wishes of performers.

It is impossible to tell how earlier exposure to more modern trends
from Europe would have affected his style or whether a greater amount of
formal training would have brought his music more into line with that of
his English contemporaries. Instead Wilson was forced to forge his style
by himself, at first largely through composing works which he never got to
test in performance. The process of uncovering his own voice therefore
took longer than would normally be the case. He may have relied in early
years on using rhythmic ideas derived from his experience in the
Mediterranean to give impetus to music which lacked strong structural
focus due to his inexperience at handling larger forms and this can be seen
in some of the surviving early music. In terms of melodic line, Britten's
strictures about the lack of melodic warmth in *The Hunting of the Snark*
could be applied to most of his work; Wilson often joked that 'he could
not write a tune' and was often described by critics as primarily a rhythmic
rather than melodic composer.[2]

When asked in later years to define his style, Wilson would use the world 'eclectic', gleefully pointing out that it was a term frequently used in a pejorative sense by academics and critics. He was not interested in following any particular school of thought and instead adopted a variety of ideas, tonality, polytonality, atonality, twelve-note cells or synthetic scales, and married them to a self-taught technique of variation and expansion. His lack of formal training particularly as regards large-scale forms fed into his own teaching where he did not feel the need for the sort of technical exercises most institutions would have taught:

> The whole essence of the [Ennis Summer] school is that we are trying to teach them how music is being written now, not how it was written fifty years ago. It's no good writing strict sonata forms and fugues these days, no professional is interested in playing that kind of music.[3]

The experience of reworking his first symphony and of composing the three-act *Twelfth Night* were crucial in developing Wilson's technique and this process enabled him to shed the most obvious debts to the soundworld of earlier composers. He was, however, almost fifty at this stage, which makes direct comparisons with English contemporaries difficult; they had all forged their own individual style much earlier in their careers before the arrival of a native modernism in Britain, whereas Wilson's development at the beginning of the 1970s coincides with the arrival of the Dublin Festival of Twentieth Century Music.

The result of this combination of late development and the belated arrival of modernism in Ireland can perhaps be traced to the fact that while he could refer in a letter to Felix Aprahamian as 'an agreeable man, who hates Schönberg thank goodness' and towards the end of his life referred to the same composer's string trio as his idea of hell, Wilson also began to toy with the idea of writing serial music.[4] In the wider picture of music in Ireland at the time this becomes rather more interesting as so many other Irish composers of his generation in the 1970s felt the need to write using some form of serialism. Gareth Cox has noted varying degrees of use of serialism in music by A.J. Potter (1918–80), Gerard Victory (1921–95), Seóirse Bodley (b. 1933) and John Kinsella (b. 1932) as well as a number of composers born after the Second World War.[5] One gets less of a sense of mass conversion while Schoenberg's *Dance around the Golden Calf* plays in the background, but rather that the composers felt the need to prove themselves in a medium for which they themselves may not have had much innate sympathy. Whether, as I have suggested elsewhere, they were particularly influenced by the critic Charles Acton's loud trumpeting of serialism and any evidence of it in works by Irish composers – particularly the alleged serialism of Seán Ó Riada's compositions – is hard to tell at this point.[6] The advent of the Festival of Twentieth Century Music in Dublin featuring works of the European avant-garde and more importantly exposing Irish composers to international critics may have also persuaded some of the necessity of abandoning their customary approach to composition to prove their ability to be as *au fait* with current trends as any foreigner – the anxiety of critical influence. In Wilson's case the move to twelve-note groups was not such a huge one as, rather than adopting any orthodox form of the technique, he continued to compose much as before, splitting the row into motifs which could be worked in his customary fashion. From this point it was a small step to the use of the synthetic scales that underpin much of his later music. However, Wilson was never to feel sympathy for the avant-garde of his own generation (such composers as Xenakis, Boulez and Nono were all born within a few years of Wilson) or the new direction represented by composers associated with New Simplicity and minimalism which were establishing themselves in central Europe in the 1970s as Ireland was beginning to catch up with modernism. In this sense he felt more in sympathy with the traditional approach of the Nordic symphonists and the refined colouristic approach of composers such as Dutilleux and Lutosławski whose music he could relate back to that of his favourite early-twentieth-century composers, Debussy, Ravel and Stravinsky, despite the differences in style. His music therefore falls outside the camp of the avant-garde which he rejected, but on the other hand, also avoids the uncomplicated melodic approach of someone like Malcolm Arnold or the direct expression of a composer like Benjamin Britten.

It is undoubtedly the case that Wilson was predominantly interested in dramatic writing and he responded instantly to any opportunity that arose. The extent of his engagement with the stage was determined by external factors, the main determinant again being Wilson's decision to move to a country lacking in the infrastructure necessary for a serious attempt to create a stage-centred output. As a result the surprising thing is, not that a fairly high percentage of this part of Wilson's output has remained unperformed, but that such a considerable amount of these works made it to at least one production in his lifetime. Had he lived in a country with a better musical infrastructure, it is possible that, like Britten, he would have concentrated almost exclusively on writing for the stage. At any time he had in mind a number of other operatic projects that were never written. Some, such as *Julius Caesar,* got as far as inspiring a complete libretto. Occasionally a work progressed further before being abandoned. In the early 1980s, Wilson wrote a libretto based on G.K. Chesterton's tale *The Man who was Thursday* and began to sketch out musical ideas for it which were later incorporated into the orchestral piece *Angel 2* (1988).[7] Others seem to have remained as vague ideas: Ian Balfour recalled Wilson discussing the possibilities for dramatic treatment in the life stories of soprano Maria Callas and yachtsman Donald Crowhurst.[8] For most of his life, however, Wilson had to forgo the dramatic ideas in his head and subsume his love of the theatrical and of literature in his song cycles and short choral works.

The decision to move to Ireland had, however, even more fundamental effects on his output. As this book was written after the death of its subject I was totally dependent on written sources and the memories of people who knew and worked with Wilson. Several things were rather striking as I spoke to people; not just those whose interviews were used for the book, but also a wide variety of friends and colleagues whom I encountered over the time I was writing it. Wilson's kindness and generosity were widely attested to and anyone who had been invited to his house spoke volubly about his cooking. However, commentary about the actual music he composed was far more difficult to entice from people ,making one think of a letter fragment in which he wrote:

> I'd always imagined, previously, that most of my friends were waiting, as I was, on the day when I would have a big work played. When it happened I found that most of my friends were indifferent, and one of them was most annoyed and broke off . . . [contact?].[9]

While it would be easy to jump to the conclusion that, for some at least, his music was the least interesting thing about him, in reality it would seem to be symptomatic of a wider problem in Ireland, namely the transitory nature of composition. By this I mean the fact that so few compositions, particularly large-scale ones, receive a second performance, and performing groups fulfil their obligation to new music with a stream of 'world premieres' which for most works will be both first and last performances. The lack of recordings also militates against people getting to know this music and so the inability of many to remember anything detailed about Wilson's music can be accounted for.

This one-performance culture had a negative impact on Wilson's own output. He had a natural disinclination towards revision, which is understandable; a new idea is far more attractive than mulling over how to improve an old one. Writing to Aloys Fleischmann in 1969 he noted:

> Yes, I agree with you about the pruning of my Burns cycle. The
> fieldmouse has much too long a tail, and the cycle needs a vig-
> orous song near the end . . . My trouble, or one of my troubles,
> is that once a work is written I lose interest in it.[10]

The fact that a second performance of a work was highly unlikely would only
have encouraged Wilson to move on to the next piece rather than wasting
time fixing something that would never be performed. The important thing
is the new composition with the commissioning fee and thus the music
becomes disposable. On only two occasions did he undertake major revisions
of a work and in each case the driving force was a musician who wanted to
give the piece a second performance, Colman Pearce in the case of the First
Symphony and Stephen Wilkinson in the case of *Tam O'Shanter*. There were
plenty of other works that Wilson felt needed revision; letters attest to his
plans to cut or edit works should another performance arise, but as this never
happened there clearly seemed to be no point in spending any time on this
type of work.

Although it took Wilson a considerable time to break through as a composer one can argue that it was easier to do in Dublin than it would have been
in, for example, his native London. In the 1960s and particularly the 1970s,
there were a lot of performance opportunities for established figures and considerable press coverage, even if this was frequently poor in quality. The
centrality of RTÉ to music making did of course mean that a small group of
people had inordinate say over what large-scale music was performed in
Ireland. One has also to remember that regionally based and community-
based arts projects have only found favour with government funding bodies
in Ireland in more recent years and the variety of opportunities available to
composers today was not available to Wilson as he was establishing his career.
His Monkstown concerts in the 1970s were in some respects an early attempt
at creating a locally based music event, though it was one for local spectators
rather than local participants; the performers were in the main artists he had
already collaborated with elsewhere. Later in life Wilson was to find that, with
greater access to educational opportunities, in Ireland and abroad, there was a
rapid increase in the amount of composers based in Ireland, resulting in
greater competition for the traditional performance opportunities such as
those provided by RTÉ. In a similar fashion the Contemporary Music Centre
which promotes and disseminates Irish music had to divide its efforts among
an ever greater amount of composers. At points where such competition
became particularly acute, such as in the early 1970s and 2000s, it was
younger composers who were quick to adapt, founding collectives and

creating alternative performance platforms. In general Wilson remained faithful to his strategy of writing for specific performers from within the established concert circuit in the hope of persuading them to perform the works. For composers of his generation who relied to a great extent on the traditional institutes and agencies, it was to become more difficult as they got older to obtain performances.

The standard of performance Wilson's music received varied greatly as he wrote for performers of diverse ability. The qualities of musical understanding and technical security that he highlights when working with performers such as Jane Manning or when the London Philharmonic played *Le Bateau Ivre* indicate what he missed in the majority of performances. It is clear, for example, from archive recordings that the RTÉ Symphony Orchestra has had an uneven history compounded for most of Wilson's career by the fact that it was not until 1990 that a decision was taken to increase the size of the orchestra to ninety-three players.[11] While under particular conductors such as Tibor Paul or Albert Rosen the orchestra could rise to impressive and highly committed performances, at other times poor direction and lack of rehearsal time could impact adversely on the quality of performances.

When it came to the performances of his operas the issue of expense frequently impacted adversely on the form in which they were performed and it is clear that both in Ireland and abroad very few of Wilson's stage works were mounted in anything resembling optimum circumstances. He made constant attempts throughout his career to break into the international scene, but like other composers of his generation he was severely hampered in his attempts by the fact that he could not get representation with an international publisher for his output. While many works were performed around the world, they tended to be small scale or in the case of a work like *Grinning at the Devil*, the performances took place in venues away from the prestigious centres associated with performance of art music. Had *Grinning at the Devil* been premiered at the Royal Danish Theatre as originally envisaged, it would probably have raised Wilson's profile internationally to a far greater extent. Perhaps it is not so surprising then that this mild mannered, reserved gentleman frequently attributed his career to constant anger:

> And what is it, someone may ask, that makes him continue to write? Certainly it is not the hope of a huge income or the adoration of the world: very early in life, you discover that, frankly, most of your friends would be more comfortable if you gave up

music and settled down to a real job of work. No. What makes him go on is unadulterated rage: the fact that the last thing he wrote is only partially successful, and that much more could have been said on the subject, and that it could have been much better expressed. The next work, he says, is going to be that entire and perfect chrysolite of the imagination for which he has been striving. Of course he's going to be wrong again.[12]

Wilson was of course noteworthy for other reasons. The part he played in developing the structures that support composers and musicians in Ireland today and his presence as a composition teacher both in the Royal Irish Academy of Music and at the Association of Irish Composers' summer school in themselves make him a significant figure in the history of Irish twentieth-century music, particularly as at this time third-level Irish institutes did not teach composition. However, there is a discrepancy between how Wilson is viewed even today as teacher and composer.

One of the most common responses I heard from people was that he 'was of course an amateur'. While it was clear from discussions with people such as Mary Boydell that this had been the view in the 1950s and 60s (and in one sense, as Wilson had little in the way of performances or even completed works to demonstrate, it was an understandable view at this time), that it was still a widely held belief, despite his output and the fact that he had taught many of the next generation of Irish composers, was surprising. As already discussed, Wilson was by no means alone in his limited formal training as a composer in Ireland and over the years he gathered a formidable armoury of technical knowledge which he was then able to pass on to his pupils. Surveying his mature work I would suggest that the only way in which his lack of training could be seen as evident is in his unorthodox approach to formal structures, particularly evident in larger works. In some cases constant motivic manipulation replaces any other form of larger structural framework. But in this he is again not alone and many other examples could be taken from other Irish composers of the period. In this sense comparison with a figure such as Brian Boydell, who tends to be identified unquestioningly as one of Ireland's most important composers, throws up a curious sort of double standard. Boydell was in many ways symptomatic of the state of music in Ireland in the first half of the twentieth century, being able to set himself up quickly in Dublin as a conductor, composer, oboist, singer and singing teacher without any difficulty despite his lack of experience. He had briefly studied organ at the Evangelisches Kirchenmusikalisches Institut, before studying natural sciences at Cambridge. He then spent some months in London studying composition with Patrick Hadley at the Royal College of Music before returning to Ireland with the outbreak of the Second World War.[13] In 1942 he obtained a MusB and officially launched himself as a composer with a concert of his own works in January 1944. He consolidated his position as a leading figure in music, taking a MusD in 1959 which enabled him to take the position of professor of music at Trinity College in 1962. His wealthy background and anglicised accent did not seem to have any adverse effect on the way he was perceived (unlike Wilson) and in 1961 he was commissioned to provide an arrangement of the national anthem by the state broadcaster, while in 1966 he was commissioned by the state to provide a work to mark the fiftieth anniversary of the 1916 Rising. As with Wilson, his sporadic and unconventional training meant that Boydell's approach to form was quite unorthodox and in early works such as his first string quartet (1949) the intended teleological impetus of the music is impeded by his technical limitations. Later music tends to favour repetition of motives over any real development, but unlike Wilson, in terms of overall musical language, after the 1940s it would seem that Boydell's music did not alter much; his piano work *The Maiden and the Seven Devils* from 1992 can easily accommodate the grafting in of a passage from his 1953 Violin Concerto. There is no doubting the important role Boydell played in music in Ireland, as conductor of the Dublin Orchestral Players, founding member of the Music Association of Ireland, guest conductor in the early years of the RTÉ Symphony Orchestra, member of the Arts Council for over twenty years and as educator and campaigner, but the curious disparity in the way his music is evaluated as opposed to how Wilson is viewed does raise questions. It would seem that some element of outsider status still clings to Wilson even after his death.

Boydell of course had a more ebullient public persona and his music was not as challenging on the surface as Wilson's music could be. Even when aiming for a more relaxed style, Wilson did not make his music any simpler. It is notable that when he composed a joke concerto for a New Year's Eve celebration, *Umbrage for Orchestra and Six Music Critics*, in which the music critics had to play a number of percussion instruments, Anne Makower, who commissioned it, noted that 'It didn't work a hundred percent because Jim actually made it a little too difficult for one rehearsal.'[14] There is nothing in his output to compare with the lighter orchestral works of Archie Potter or Gerard Victory and unlike many of his contemporaries he never undertook any arranging of Irish melodies as a way of making money or raising his profile, as he had no interest in this type of work and his 'heart wasn't in it'.[15] He also placed no value on music other than art music which he preferred to term 'real' music. For him other music did not deserve the exposure it tended to get: 'I get fed up to the back teeth with hearing people on RTÉ staff interviewing pop singers or folk singers and there is never anything about real music.'[16] Originality was the most important thing in music for Wilson; as early as 1944, in the midst of a diatribe against artists such as Richard Tauber (and presumably by implication the operetta repertoire he was often associated with) and music such as Addinsell's *Warsaw Concerto*, he wrote, 'I have absolutely no time for any creation that does not add something new to the total of artistic experience, and when a work fails to do that, however clever it is, it is useless',[17] while in a later interview he noted 'If something has been said before there's no point in saying it again. Composing doesn't make sense unless you can contribute something new.'[18] Art was what made life worthwhile as he noted in a letter protesting against government cuts to the arts:

> It is the high arts, not possessions or television soap operas or spectator sports, that are truly life-enhancing features of a civilisation, and by which that civilisation will be judged when its politics are forgotten . . . Art is the best therapy for a sick civilisation, and guidance in creative artistic activity would provide our children with an alternative to glue-sniffing, vandalism and mugging.[19]

Wilson's decision to move to Ireland was also to affect the afterlife of his compositions. In Britain there is a wider knowledge among music lovers of works by native composers, and orchestras will frequently feature work by past composers of second and third rank as well as by the most established names. In Ireland the situation is different, with lack of performance and recordings adding to a knowledge vacuum regarding an art form that exists outside the general cultural discourse of the country. In earlier years the RTÉ orchestras would occasionally repeat particularly shorter works, but in recent years the obligation towards 'new' music has almost entirely been given over to premieres. An examination of the lists kept by the Contemporary Music Centre of performances of works by Potter, Fleischmann, Victory, Boydell and Wilson since their deaths is revealing. Although the lists are incomplete the general trends are clear. Potter and Victory have had the least amount of performances, though unusually these include performances by the RTÉ Symphony Orchestra of short and occasional pieces.[20] However, it is notable that these performances have almost all been as part of the summer lunchtime concerts rather than the Friday-night-season concerts. While the amount of individual performances ranges from just over ten for Victory to over thirty for Boydell and Wilson and a remarkable figure of more than sixty for Fleischmann, when one counts the number of different pieces performed, the numbers level out somewhat, with none of the composers reaching figures of over twenty pieces. Fleischmann's higher figure for performances is due to two factors; a family which is highly active in promoting his work and centenary celebrations in 2010 which were used as means of persuading performing groups and individuals to revive his work. In fact approximately sixty per cent of the performances of his work since his death took place in 2010. The Fleischmann family have also launched an important digitisation project, the aim of which is to have free downloads available of all Fleischmann's scores, making his work far more accessible than any other Irish composer of his generation.[21] Of course not every work by these composers deserves to be revived and there are plenty of pieces in the archive of the Contemporary Music Centre that are best left undisturbed. However, a major task of critical evaluation of all composers, while challenging, is surely preferable in the longer term to the current solution which seems to be the complete abandonment of the past. Perhaps such critical engagement will not occur until art music has established itself as part of Ireland's cultural discourse.

In Wilson's case his death was followed by a number of memorial concerts featuring his chamber music and there were also posthumous premieres of a number of pieces which he had composed in his final years. If one omits these from the list of performances that have taken place since his death, it comprises almost entirely of chamber music (*Arlecchino*, Two Pieces for Bass Clarinet, *Donizetti Variations*, Sonatina for alto flute, *three Playthings* for clarinet, *Spanish Arch*, Sonatina, Accordion Quintet, *Grimoire* and Violin Sonata no. 6) with some vocal works (*Almanac*, *Witches Ballad*, *Wildwood* and *Undesirables*). Many of these were performed by artists directly associated with Wilson, with members of the ensemble Concorde responsible for approximately half of these performances. A similar inbalance exists in the recordings commercially available of Wilson's work. *Arlecchino* is an attractive if slight addition to the solo-flute repertoire, its simple triadic opening soon clouded by more chromatic developments. Composed for Verner Nicolet in 1979, Wilson probably never imagined that this occasional piece was to become his most recorded work, with three recordings to date. By contrast a major work such as the Second Symphony has yet to receive an adequate performance, let alone a recording.

While Wilson's music and that of other twentieth-century Irish composers has received scant critical attention to date, there is a growing sense of the need to create a more thorough history of the development of Irish composition and Wilson's compositions form a sizeable part of this. Admittedly Wilson was, partly due to the sheer size of his output, an uneven composer. At its least inspired it can sound fairly anonymous and certain mannerisms – static ostinato figures, repeated scalic figurations and endless tremolos – take the place of musical substance. Wilson was, however, the first to recognise this and understood that any study of his work needed to be selective. In a more congenial musical environment he would undoubtedly have written less and revised more in the light of performances of works. Perhaps the most striking thing about Wilson was his extraordinary resilience in the face of obstacles and his utter determination, despite all the odds, to create a career as a composer. This book is just one possible pathway through the labyrinth of Wilson's surviving scores, but if it helps to steer interested performers on their own journey through the Wilson archive and heightens awareness of even one corner of Ireland's musical past, then it has achieved its aim.

Appendix One
Catalogue of Surviving
Works by Genre

A. OPERAS

The Hunting of the Snark opus 8 (1963)
Twelfth Night opus 30 (1969)
Letters to Theo opus 92 (1982)
Grinning at the Devil opus 101 (1984)
The King of the Golden River opus 111 (1987)
A Passionate Man opus 139 (1995)
Virata opus 153 (1999)
Stuffed Raspberries [opus 176] (2005, unfinished)

B. BALLETS

Divertimento for flute, piano, violin and cello with extra prelude and finale (1957/
    arr. 1965)
Arachne opus 82 (1980)
The Cat that Walked by Himself opus 100 (1983)
Breeze and Calm opus 109 (1985)
In Remembrance (*Dance Ritual*) opus 121 (1989)
Les Sylphides opus 146 (1998) [orchestration of pieces by Chopin]
Dance Pieces (*Ballet Suite*) opus 155 (1999)
Impromptu (*Games*) for violin and piano opus 155A (1999)

C. STAGE MUSIC AND STORIES WITH ACCOMPANIMENT

The Pied Piper of Hamelin – A Masque, opus 25 (1967)
Ditto Daughter? (incidental music) (1973)
Ditto Daughter? (incidental music) opus 66 (1976)
Scapegoat (*Donny Johnny*) (incidental music) opus 69 (1977)
The Wedding on the Eiffel Tower (incidental music) opus 83 (1980)
The Revenge of Truth (incidental music) opus 91 (1982)
The Only Jealousy of Emer (incidental music) (1983)
1985 opus 104/*Music for a Mechanical Organ/The Temptations of Saint Anthony*
    (incidental music) (1984)
The Little Mermaid (incidental music) opus 107 (1985)
The Wonderful Stone for speaker, clarinet and piano opus 113 (1987)
The Christmas Rose for speaker and viola opus 122 (1989)
The Legend of the Third Dove (incidental music) opus 127 (1991)

Aceldama (incidental music) opus 147 (1998)
The Fisherman and his Wife for speaker, clarinet, violin and piano opus 154 (1999)
Trio opus 159 (2001)
The Teapot for speaker, violin and piano opus 165a (2003)
The Snail and the Rose Tree for speaker, bassoon and harp opus 165b (2003)
The Bell for speaker, bassoon, harp, violin and piano opus 165c (2003)
The Lion Tamer's Night Off for speaker and orchestra opus 174 (2005)

D. MUSIC FOR ORCHESTRA/CHAMBER ORCHESTRA/LARGE ENSEMBLE

Divertimento for strings opus 1 (1957)
Suite for Brass Band (1958)
Poema Sarda opus 6 (1959)
Symphony No. 1 opus 4 (1960 revised 1967)
Bagatelles for chamber orchestra opus 45 (1970)
Le Bateau Ivre opus 49 (1971)
Dances for a Festival opus 57 (1973)
Symphony No. 2 'Monumentum' opus 64 (1975)
Nighttown for clarinet, bass clarinet, two saxophones, two bassoons, two trumpets, two trombones, percussion, harmonium and guitar opus 86 (1982)
Angel One for strings opus 112 (1987)
Angel Two opus 95 (1988)
Concertino opus 137 (1993)
Symphony No. 3 opus 157 (2000)
Weathercock opus 160 (2001)

E. CONCERTANTE MUSIC

Violin Concerto opus 5 (*c.* 1962)
Anna Liffey opus 11 for piano and orchestra (1965)
Horn Concerto opus 23 (1967)
Double Concerto for 2 accordions and chamber orchestra opus 34 (1969)
Concerto for Four Flutes and String Orchestra opus 73 (1978)
Concerto for Harpsichord and Chamber Orchestra opus 76 (1979)
Symphonic Variations for piano and orchestra opus 81 (1980)
Concerto Grosso 'Umbrage for Orchestra and Six Music Critics,' opus 88 (1982)
Concerto for Cello and Orchestra opus 102 (1984)
Pearl and Unicorn for violin and orchestra opus 120 (1989)
Menorah for viola and orchestra opus 123 (1989)
Concerto 'For Sarajevo' for violin, viola and cello opus 143 (1996)
Concerto for five wind instruments and orchestra 'Concerto Giocoso' opus 145 (1998)
Concerto for Clarinet and Orchestra opus 151 (1999)

F. PIANO MUSIC

Alla Marcia (1950s?)
Piano Sonata opus 7 (1962)

Thermagistris opus 29 (1968)
Capricci opus 33 (1969)
Five Preludes opus 87 (1982)
Explorations opus 103 (1984)
Ostinato opus 114 (1987)
Tree and Moon opus 148 (1999)
Grimoire for 2 pianos, 8 hands opus 156 (1999)
Orison opus 167 (2003–2005)

G. OTHER SOLO INSTRUMENTAL MUSIC

Tempo di valse for harp (1962)
Jeu des Tierces for organ (1966)
Donizetti Variations for accordion opus 29A (1969)
Diversion on a Theme by Handel for organ opus 35 (1969)
14 Rhythmic Studies for accordion opus 36 (1969)
Fantasia for solo cello opus 63 (1974)
Arlecchino for solo flute opus 75A (1979)
Variations on a French Tune for harp opus 90 (1982)
Solitaire for guitar opus 96 (1983)
Three Playthings for clarinet opus 97 (1983)
Shadow Play for viola opus 115A (1988)
Libberton Moonrise for oboe opus 118 (1988)
Boreas: Sonata for electronically amplified flute opus 119 (1989)
For Cliodhna for cello opus 132 (1992)
Sonata for harp opus 150 (1998, revised 2001)
For Constantin for viola (2001)
Chiaroscuro for cello opus 168 (2003 or 2004)

H. CHAMBER MUSIC

Sonatina for B flat clarinet and piano (1964)
Trio for recorder, harp and cello opus 9 (1964)
Spanish Arch for 2 harps (1966)
Quintet for accordion and strings opus 22 (1967)
Sonata for cor anglais and piano opus 27 (1967)
Colloquy for violin and piano opus 31 (1968)
Music for a Temple for accordion, electric guitar and percussion opus 37 (1969)
Sonata de Valldemosa for violin and piano opus 42 (1970)
Violin Sonata No. 2 opus 50 (1972)
Violin Sonata No. 3 opus 52 (1972)
String Quartet opus 53 (1972)
Sonatina for alto flute and piano opus 56 (1973)
Trio for violin, cello and piano opus 58 (1973)
Divisions for four trombones opus 61 (1974)
Alarums and Excursions for alto saxophone and piano opus 65 (1975)
Prelude for Brass Quintet opus 67 (1976)

Epithalamion for one free bass accordion and one piano accordion opus 77 (1979)
Three Pieces for descant recorder and piano (1981)
Duo for treble recorder and piano opus 85 (1982)
Brass Quintet No. 1 opus 93 (1983)
Two by Four by Two for bass clarinet/tenor saxophone and vibraphone/marimba opus 94 (1983)
Wind Quintet opus 98 (1983)
Monkey for 2 accordions opus 99 (1983)
Duet for Ten for double wind quintet opus 110 (1986)
String Quartet No. 2 opus 126 (1991)
Quintet for Clarinet and Strings opus 134 (1993)
Violin Sonata No. 4 opus 138 (1993)
Cloud Music for 2 oboes, 2 clarinets, 2 horns and 2 bassoons opus 140 (1995)
House of Cards for bassoon and piano opus 141 (1995)
Mr Dwyer's Fancy for 3 guitars opus 142 (1995)
Sonatina for clarinet, accordion, violin and cello opus 149 (1998)
Piano Trio No. 2 opus 152 (1999)
Fanfare for 2 trumpets, 2 horns and trombone (2001)
String Quartet No. 3 opus 162 (2002)
Violin Sonata No. 5 opus 163 (2002)
Serenade for violin, cello and harp opus 164 (2002)
Consequences for flute, harp and viola opus 169 (2004)
Contrariwise for violin and harp opus 170 (2004)
Cello Sonata in one movement opus 172 (2004)
Violin Sonata no. 6 opus 173
Two Pieces for bass clarinet and piano opus 175 (2005)

I. Vocal with Piano, Other Single Instrument or Unaccompanied

Six Chansons de Ronsard pour des voix divers (1950) and '*Au Coeur d'un vol*' (1958)
Après Trois Ans for soprano and piano (1962)
Carrion Comfort for baritone and piano opus 17 (1966)
Three Birds for mezzo-soprano and piano opus 19 (1966)
A Woman Young and Old for soprano and Irish harp opus 20 (1966)
Trefoil for mezzo-soprano, baritone and piano opus 21 (1966–67)
The Solitary Reaper for soprano and piano (1968)
Bucolics for tenor and piano opus 28 (1968)
Amoretti for contralto, baritone and harpsichord opus 32 (1969)
Three Yeats Songs for soprano and piano opus 39a (1970)
Sixth Canticle for contralto and piano opus 39c (1970)
Irish Songs for soprano and piano opus 40 (1970)
When icicles hang by the wall for soprano and piano (1970)
The Wax Banana for mezzo-soprano and piano opus 51 (1972)
Upon Silence for unaccompanied soprano opus 54 (1972)
Seventh Canticle for mezzo-soprano and piano (1972)
Les Fiançailles for soprano and piano opus 74 (1978)

The Windhover for soprano and clarinet opus 78 (1979)
The Witches' Ballad for mezzo-soprano and piano opus 79 (1979)
Good Friday Journey for soprano and piano opus 105 (1985)
Runes for soprano and cello opus 106 (1985)
First Frost for bass and piano opus 115 (1988)
Stirabout for soprano and DX7 synthesizer opus 116 (1988)
Wildwood for soprano and viola opus 124 (1990 rearranged for soprano and
     violin, 1993)
Undesirables for soprano and cello opus 125 (1990)
The Leaden Echo and the Golden Echo for soprano and piano opus 128 (1991)
Three Poems by Susan Connolly for mezzo-soprano and Irish harp opus 129 (1991)
Dublin Spring for baritone and piano opus 158 (2001)
Enjoying for soprano and flute opus 161 (2001)

J. Vocal with Chamber Ensemble

Ode to Autumn for soprano, flute and piano (1968)
Another Direction for soprano, clarinet and piano opus 38 (1969)
Trois Vocalises for soprano, horn and cello opus 39b (1970)
Bestiary for mezzo-soprano, treble recorder, harpsichord and cello opus 46 (1971)
The Táin for soprano, percussion and piano opus 48 (1971)
Fand for soprano, flute and percussion opus 62 (1974)
Songs of Welcome for soprano, tenor, guitar, violin, cello and piano opus 70 (1978)
Air and Angels for soprano, flute and free bass accordion opus 80 (1979)
Plurabelle for soprano, flute, clarinet, harp, piano, guitar, violin, viola and cello
     opus 89 (1982)
Endymion for mezzo-soprano, guitar and piano (1982)
Rima for soprano, flute, clarinet, bassoon, guitar, harp, piano, violin, viola and
     cello opus 117 (1988, revised for soprano, flute, clarinet, horn, guitar, harp,
     piano, violin, viola and cello 1990)
Nine Very Small Songs for soprano, flute/piccolo, clarinet/bass clarinet, horn, vio-
     lin and cello opus 130 (1991)
Vigil for mezzo-soprano, oboe, clarinet, horn, trumpet, violin, cello and double
     bass opus 135 (1993)
Maze for mezzo-soprano, baritone, flute, cor anglais, piano, percussion, violin and
     cello opus 136 (1993)
Calico Pie for soprano, horn, violin and piano opus 144 (1998)

K. Vocal with Orchestra

Après Trois Ans for baritone and orchestra (1962)
A Woman Young and Old for soprano and orchestra opus 20 (1970)
Trefoil for mezzo-soprano, baritone and orchestra opus 21 (1968)
Fourth Canticle for contralto and orchestra opus 24 (1967)
Irish Songs for soprano and orchestra opus 40 (1974)
Emily Singing for soprano and chamber orchestra opus 108 (1985)

L. CHORAL MUSIC

Easter Procession, cantata for tenor, SSAATTBB, 2 pianos (late 1950s?)

Tom O'Bedlam opus 10 for SATB, percussion, harp and piano (1965)

Tam O'Shanter for SATB opus 12 (1965)

Tam O'Shanter for SATB, piano and percussion opus 12A (1977)

Burns Night for SATB opus 13 (1965)

Elegy on a favourite cat drowned in a tub of gold fishes for SA and piano (1966)

The Bailey Beareth the Bell Away for SATB and string quartet opus 15 (1966)

Idle Winds for SATB, B-flat clarinet, percussion and piano opus 16 (1966)

Three Canticles for soprano, contralto, SA and strings opus 14 (1966)

A Song of Light for SATB (1967)

A Canticle for Christmas for SA[children's voices], piano 4 hands, percussion, 2 tre-
    ble instruments, 1 bass instrument, organ /harmonium opus 26 (1967)

Xanadu for SATB [10 solo voices] and celeste opus 43 (1970)

Carmen Carmeliticum for mezzo-soprano, SATB, violin, viola, cello and piano opus
    47 (1971)

Missa Brevis for SA, optional T, organ or harmonium opus 55 (1973)

Nativity Ode for treble voices, SATB, trumpet, percussion, harp, organ and dancers
    opus 71 (1978)

The Rape of the Lock for SATB and accordion opus 72 (1978)

Two Little Choral Pieces opus 75B (1979)

Carol in Thanks for SATB (1979)

Animalphabet for SATB and piano opus 131 (1992)

Keats on Keats for SATB opus 133 (1993)

Utter Nonsense for soprano contralto, tenor, bass, SATB and orchestra opus 166
    (2004)

Almanac for SATB opus 171 (2004)

Appendix Two
Work List

Works Composed Before 1960

A partial list of Wilson's work pre-1960 can be reconstructed from his correspondence, but most of these scores have not survived. In some cases it is not clear whether or not a work was actually completed.

Song cycle on Edith Sitwell's Street Songs (1940s)
Soprano, flute and piano. Referred to in *From the Top*

Piano Sonata (1944)
Piano. Composition of this mentioned in a letter dated 15 October 1944

Violin Sonata (1944)
Violin and piano. Composition of this discussed in a letter dated 15 October and a play-through of it mentioned in a letter dated 3 November 1944

The Waste Land (1944)
Orchestra. The opening of the work is described in a letter dated 29 December 1944 but this may not have been completed

Jenny Kissed Me (late 1940s)
Text: Leigh Hunt
Ronsard Sonnets (late 1940s–1958)
Text: Pierre de Ronsard.
Wilson refers to settings of Hunt's text and the Ronsard poems as being written under the tutelage of Alec Rowley. A manuscript of *Six Chansons de Ronsard pour des voix divers* (with piano) dated 26 September 1950 and dedicated to Isla Morante has survived, which may be a copy of those written while studying with Rowley. A further setting of 'Au Coeur d'un vol' (Ronsard) has also survived in a manuscript dated 28 May 1958.

Esther (1952)
Ballet in three acts. Scenario by Eric Horsbrugh Porter.
Two dances performed: 18 June 1953, Dublin Orchestral Players, Brian Boydell, Abbey Lecture Hall Dublin. Lost/destroyed

Gösta Berling Saga (1950s)
Projected opera on the novel by Selma Lagerlöf. Unclear how much was actually written

Alla Marcia for Piano (1950s?)
Manuscript survives

190

Le Roi de l'Ille opus 2 (1955)
Orchestra. Ballet in two acts. Scenario by Isla Morante. Lost/destroyed

Variations for brass band (1956)
Reference to these in Wilson's diary. Lost/destroyed

Easter Procession (late 1950s?)
Cantata for Tenor, SSAATTBB, 2 pianos. Text: Anon. The manuscript of this setting of *Tomorrow shall be my dancing day* survives

Divertimento opus 1 (1957)
Strings. Dedicated to Boyd Neel.
First broadcast performance: 23 July 1957, BBC Midland Orchestra, Leo Wurmser. Manuscript survives
Divertimento – arrangement of opus 1 for flute, piano, violin and cello with extra prelude and finale (1965)
Flute, violin, cello and piano. Ballet in one act. Scenario by Donald McAlpine. Manuscript survives
First performance: 22 February 1965, Harlequin Ballet, Gaiety Theatre, Dublin

Cynara (1957)
Orchestra. Fifteen-minute ballet in one act. Scenario by Donald McAlpine. A pastorale was extracted from this, but like the rest of the ballet it is now lost

Suite for Brass Band (1958)
The manuscript has survived

Piano Concerto opus 3 (c.1957–59)
Piano solo and orchestra. Written for Gina Bachauer. Wilson first invited Bachauer to dinner in November 1957 and the work must have been complete by the time she returned to perform the Brahms concerto in June 1959 as Wilson recalled them talking through the detail of the score at this time. Destroyed by Wilson

Poema Sarda opus 6 (1959)
Orchestra.
The manuscript of this work has survived

WORKS FROM 1960–2005

The majority of Wilson's manuscripts are held at Trinity College, Dublin Library and copies are held by the Contemporary Music Centre. Where there is no copy of a score at either location I have described the work as 'lost'. It is possible that copies may exist in private collections or in the archive of RTÉ. In a small amount of cases it is clear that Wilson himself destroyed the score.

Works With Opus Number

Symphony No. 1 opus 4 (1960)
Recorded performance: 3 January 1967, RTÉSO, Colman Pearce, Francis Xavier Hall, Dublin. Broadcast on 21 February 1967. Revised in 1967 after the first performance. First performance of revised version: 4 June 1971, RTÉSO, Colman Pearce

Violin Concerto opus 5 (*c.* 1962)
Violin and Orchestra. Dedicated to Michel Chauveton. Wilson heard Chauveton play the Berg concerto in March 1962. He sent Chauveton his concerto in September 1962

Piano Sonata opus 7 (1962)
Piano. Dedicated to Gina Bachauer

The Hunting of the Snark opus 8 (1963)
4 trebles, 4 altos, Tenor solo, Baritone solo, children's choir, piano [4 hands], percussion, string quartet. Text: Wilson after Lewis Carroll
First performance: 5 January 1965, Victor Leeson (Baker, tenor), Herbert Moulton (Bellman, baritone), Nadia Stiven (Bonnet Maker, dancer), pupils of Sandford Park School, John O'Sullivan (piano), Nuala Tweddle (piano), Janos Keszei (percussion – programme gives Stanislaus Stack as percussionist), Audrey Parke (violin), David Lillis (violin), Tania Crichton (violin), Stephanie Groocock (viola), Barbara Barklie (viola), Richard Groocock (cello), Elizabeth Barrett (cello), conductor Brian Grimson, Dagg Hall, Royal Irish Academy of Music, Dublin

Trio opus 9 (1964)
Recorder, harp and cello

Tom O'Bedlam opus 10 (1965)
SATB, percussion, harp and piano. Text: Anon.
First broadcast performance 13 January 1966. First public performance at Radio Éireann Invitation Concert 2 September 1966, Veronica McSweeney (piano), Sheila Cuthbert (harp), James Wilson (percussion), RTÉ Singers, Hans Waldemar Rosen

Anna Liffey opus 11, Movement for piano and orchestra (1965)
Piano and orchestra. Dedicated to Brian Boydell
First performance: 26 November 1966, Gillian Smith (piano), Dublin Orchestral Players, Brian Grimson, Cavan, Ireland

Tam O'Shanter opus 12 (1965)
SATB. Text: Robert Burns
First performance: 1 June 1976, RTÉ Singers, Eric Sweeney, Francis Xavier Hall, Dublin

Tam O'Shanter opus 12A (1977)
Revised version. SATB, piano, percussion. Text: Robert Burns
First broadcast performance: 31 October 1977 (BBC 3), BBC Northern Singers, Keith Swallow (piano), Peter Donohue (percussion), Stephen Wilkinson

Burns Night opus 13 (1965)
SATB. Dedicated to JHPC (John Campbell), Text: Robert Burns
First performance: 24 January 1967, RTÉ Singers, Hans Waldemar Rosen. A radiophonic version called *Rab* was broadcast in 1972

Three Canticles opus 14 (1966)
Soprano, Contralto, SA and strings. Originally called *Bells, Beasts and Stars*. Texts: Thomas Traherne, Christina Rosetti and Gerard Manley Hopkins

The Bailey Beareth the Bell Away opus 15 (1966)
SATB and string quartet. Texts: Anon, Thomas Campion, John Donne, Charles Elton, George Peele, Percy Bysshe Shelley, Sir Philip Sydney and Sir Thomas Wyatt

Idle Winds opus 16 (1966)
SATB, B-flat clarinet, percussion and piano. Text: Eric Porter
Recorded: 12 December 1967, Rhoda Coghill (piano), James Daly (clarinet), John Daly (percussion), RTÉ Singers, Colman Pearce. MS in a private collection

Carrion Comfort opus 17 (1966)
Baritone and piano. Text: Gerard Manley Hopkins. Dedicated to Herbert Moulton. First performance: 21 November 1968, Herbert Moulton (baritone), Havelock Nelson (piano), Belfast Festival

Songs Eternity – motet for double choir, opus 18 (1966)
SSAATTBB. Text: John Clare
Dedicated to the Pananjoti Choir. Lost

Three Birds opus 19 (1966)
mezzo-soprano and piano. Text: Percy Bysshe Shelley, Lord Alfred Tennyson and John Clare.
First performance: 14 March 1967, Bernadette Greevy (mezzo), Jeannie Reddin (piano), Trinity College, Dublin

A Woman Young and Old opus 20 (1966)
Soprano, Irish harp. Text: William Butler Yeats. Dedicated to Gráinne Yeats
First broadcast performances of three songs from the cycle 17 May 1968 Gráinne Yeats RTÉ.
Six songs from the cycle performed 23 November 1968, Gráinne Yeats, Belfast Festival

A Woman Young and Old opus 20 (1970)
Soprano and orchestra. Text: William Butler Yeats
First performance: 16 October 1970, Gráinne Yeats, RTÉSO, Hans Waldemar Rosen
A reduction for soprano and piano was also made in 1970

Trefoil opus 21 (1966–67)
Mezzo-soprano, baritone and piano. Text: William Blake. Dedicated to Herbert Moulton and Gun Knouzell.
First performance of 'Night' 19 April 1967, Hanover. First performance of the full cycle November 1967, Hanover, Herbert Moulton (baritone) and Gun Knouzell (mezzo-soprano)

Trefoil opus 21 (1968)
Mezzo-soprano, baritone and orchestra. Text: William Blake
First performance: 25 October 1968, Herbert Moulton (baritone), Gun Knouzell (mezzo-soprano), members of the RTÉSO and RTÉLO, Hans Waldemar Rosen, Francis Xavier Hall, Dublin. Score in the possession of RTÉ

Quintet for Accordion and Strings opus 22 (1967)
Free-bass accordion and string quartet
First performance: May 1968, Mogens Ellegaard (accordion), Copenhagen Quartet, Brussels, Belgium
Published by Waterloo Music Company Ltd, Ontario, Canada

Horn Concerto opus 23 (1967)
Horn and orchestra. Dedicated to Patrick McElwee
Recorded RTÉ 14 May 1968, broadcast 27 August 1968, Patrick McElwee, RTÉSO, Colman Pearce

Fourth Canticle opus 24 (1967)
Contralto and orchestra. Text: Gerard Manley Hopkins. Dedicated to Bernadette Greevy

The Pied Piper of Hamelin – A Masque, opus 25 (1967)
Soprano, tenor, bass, SATB, flute, horn, percussion, 2 violins, viola, cello, harp
Text: Robert Browning. Dedicated to its first performers
First broadcast performance: Friday 18 October 1968, RTÉ Singers, members of the RTÉSO, Hans Waldemar Rosen.
First public performance using tape of the RTÉ broadcast, Wexford Festival, White's Hotel, Wexford, October 1969

A Canticle for Christmas opus 26 (1967)
Text: Anon. Robert Herrick, Algernon Charles Swinburne and Henry Vaughan. Dedicated to Ruth Jameson
SA [children's voices], piano 4 hands, percussion, 2 treble instruments, 1 bass instrument, organ /harmonium
First performance of five movements from the Canticle: 20 December 1974, Young Lindsay Singers, Ethna Barror, RTÉ Light Orchestra, Eimar O'Broin, St Patrick's Cathedral, Dublin
First complete performance: 27 May 1975, Cecilian Singers, Capriol Consort, Mercedes Bolger, William Ebbs, Clive Shannon, Colman Pearce, Monkstown parish church, Dublin

Sonata for Cor Anglais and Piano opus 27 (1967)
Cor anglais and piano. Dedicated to Lindsay Armstrong and Gillian Smith
First performance: November 1968, Lindsay Armstrong (cor anglais), Gillian Smith (piano), Belfast Festival

Bucolics opus 28 (1968)
Tenor and piano. Text: John Clare
First performance: 20 July 1982, Royal Irish Academy of Music, Dublin, Paul Deegan (tenor), John O'Sullivan (piano)

Thermagistris opus 29 (1968)
Piano. Dedicated to Charles Lynch
First performance: 8 July 1968, Charles Lynch, Wigmore Hall, London

Donizetti Variations opus 29A (1969)
Accordion. Dedicated to Mogens Ellegaard

First performance: 8 July 1969, Mogens Ellegaard, Music School of Lapland
Published by Musikverlag Josef Preissler

Twelfth Night opus 30 (1969)
Libretto: Herbert Moulton after William Shakespeare. Dedicated to John Campbell
First performance: 1 November 1969, Mary Sheridan (Viola, soprano), Anne
Makower (Olivia, soprano), Gerry Duffy (Sir Toby Belch, bass), Brendan
Cavanagh (Feste, tenor), Peter McBrien (Orsino, baritone), Brian Kissane
(Malvolio, baritone), Patrick Ring (Sir Andrew Aguecheek, tenor), Richard
Cooper (Sebastian, tenor), Mabel McGrath (Maria, soprano), members of the
RTÉSO, Hans Waldemar Rosen

Colloquy opus 31 (1968)
Violin and piano. Dedicated to Geraldine O'Grady
First performance: 29 March 1969, Geraldine O'Grady (violin), Veronica
McSwiney (piano), Shelbourne Hotel, Dublin

Amoretti opus 32 (1969)
Contralto, baritone and harpsichord. Text: John Skelton. Dedicated to Herbert
Moulton and Gun Knouzell

Capricci opus 33 (1969)
Piano. Dedicated to Philip Martin
First broadcast performance: 27 August 1979, Philip Martin

Double Concerto opus 34 (1969)
Two accordions and chamber orchestra. Dedicated to Mogens Ellegaard
First performance: Anny van Wanrooy (accordion), Paula van Wanrooy (accordion),
RTÉCO, conductor Proinnsías Ó Duinn

Diversion on a Theme by Handel opus 35 (1969)
Organ. Dedicated to Gerard Gillen
First performance: 9 January 1970, Gerard Gillen, Chapel of Trinity College,
Dublin

14 Rhythmic Studies opus 36 (1969)
Accordion. Dedicated to Joseph Marcello
First performance: 1969, Joseph Marcello, Toronto Conservatoire
Published by Peter McKee Music Company Ltd, Ontario, (subsidiary of Waterloo
Music Company Ltd) and Musikverlag Josef Preissler

Music for a Temple opus 37 (1969)
Accordion, electric guitar and percussion. Dedicated to Mogens Ellegaard
First performance: 1970, Trio Mobile (Mogens Ellegaard, Ingolf Olsen, Bent
Lyloff), Vejle, Jutland, Denmark

Another Direction opus 38 (1969)
Soprano, clarinet and piano. Text: James Parr
First performance: 29 September 1972, Violet Twomey (soprano), Gillian Smith
(piano), Brian O'Rourke (clarinet), Dublin

Three Yeats Songs opus 39a (1970)
Soprano and piano. Texts: William Butler Yeats. Dedicated to Gráinne Yeats
'Sweet Dancer' and 'Lullaby' from opus 39a also arranged for soprano and harp

Trois Vocalises opus 39b (1970)
Soprano, horn, cello. Dedicated to Anne Makower
First broadcast performance: 1972, Anne Makower (soprano), Patrick McElwee
(horn) and Vincenzo Caminiti (cello)

Sixth Canticle opus 39c (1970)
Contralto and piano. Text: John Donne. Dedicated to Anne Woodworth
First performance: 3 June 1971, Anne Woodworth (contralto), Jeannie Reddin
(piano), Royal Irish Academy of Music, Dublin

Irish Songs opus 40 (1970)
Soprano and piano. Text: Thomas Moore, George Darley, Jonathan Swift, Edward
Dowden, Charles Lever, James Stephens and Aubery de Vere. Dedicated to Veronica
Dunne and Havelock Nelson
First performance: 4 March 1971, Veronica Dunne (soprano), John O'Conor
(piano), Goethe Institute, Dublin

Irish Songs opus 40 (1974)
Soprano and orchestra. Text: Thomas Moore, George Darley, Jonathan Swift,
Edward Dowden, Charles Lever, James Stephens and Aubery de Vere
First performance: 30 August 1974, Veronica Dunne, RTÉSO, Colman Pearce,
Francis Xavier Hall Dublin

Rima – vocalise, opus 41 (1970)
Soprano and Orchestra. Dedicated to Rita Streich
Destroyed by Wilson

Sonata de Valldemosa opus 42 (1970)
Violin and piano. Dedicated to Therese Timoney and John O'Conor
First performance: 12 March 1971, Therese Timoney (violin), John O'Conor
(piano), Trinity College, Dublin

Xanadu opus 43 (1970)
SATB (10 solo voices) and celeste. Text: Samuel Taylor Coleridge. Dedicated to Charles
Acton
First performance: 29 April 1971, RTÉ Singers, conductor Hans Waldemar Rosen,
Cork International Choral Festival

Serenade opus 44 (1970)
Oboe, clarinet, horn, bassoon
First broadcast performance: 1972, Jupiter Ensemble. Lost

Bagatelles opus 45 (1970)
Flute, 2 oboes/cor anglais, 2 bassoons, 2 horns, strings. Based on 14 Rhythmic
Studies opus 36
First performance: 10 November 1972, New Irish Chamber Orchestra, André
Prieur, Metropolitan Hall, Dublin

Bestiary opus 46 (1971)
Mezzo-soprano, treble recorder, harpsichord and cello. Text: Walt Whitman, Richard Lovelace, Marjory Fleming, John Keats, Samuel Rogers
First Performance: 1973, Minnie Clancy (mezzo-soprano), Douglas Gunn Ensemble, Christchurch cathedral, Dublin

Carmen Carmeliticum opus 47 (1971)
Mezzo-soprano, SATB, violin, viola, cello and piano. Text: Anon., St John of the Cross
First performance: 15 August 1971, Mary Sheridan (soprano), RTÉ Singers, William Shanahan (violin), Archie Collins (viola), Peter Worrell (cello) and Colman Pearce (piano)

The Táin opus 48 (1971)
Soprano, percussion and piano. Text: Ian Fox. Dedicated to Veronica Dunne
First performance: 29 June 1972, Veronica Dunne (soprano), Courtney Kenny (piano), Jeffrey Cosser (percussion), Examination Hall, Trinity College Dublin
The Táin opus 48A Radiophonic version (1974)
Soprano and 2 pianos
First broadcast performance: 1976, Veronica Dunne (soprano), Veronica McSwiney (piano), James Wilson (piano effects)

Le Bateau Ivre opus 49 (1971)
Orchestra. Dedicated to Albert Rosen
First performance: 15 October 1972, RTÉSO, Albert Rosen

Violin Sonata No. 2 opus 50 (1972)
Violin and piano. Dedicated to Mary Gallagher
First performance: 28 May 1976, Mary Gallagher (violin), Veronica McSwiney (piano), Monkstown parish church, Dublin

The Wax Banana opus 51 (1972)
Mezzo-soprano and piano. Text: extracts from *Bab Ballads, Mrs A.B. Marshall's Cookery Book, Hints on Etiquette for Ladies and Gentlemen* and the *General Catalogue of the Army and Navy Stores*. Dedicated to Ruth Maher
First performance: 12 March 1974, Ruth Maher (soprano), John Beckett (piano), Mount Temple School, Dublin

Violin Sonata No. 3 opus 52 (1972)
Violin and piano. Dedicated to Geraldine O'Grady
First performance: 11 September 1974, Geraldine O'Grady (violin), Eily O'Grady (piano), Town Hall, Dún Laoghaire

String Quartet opus 53 (1972)
Two violins, viola and cello. Dedicated to the RTÉ Quartet. Rededicated to the Testore Quartet
First performance: 11 May 1976, Testore String Quartet, Monkstown parish church, Dublin

Upon Silence opus 54 (1972)
Soprano. Text: William Butler Yeats. Dedicated to Gráinne Yeats

First performance: 20 June 1989, Penelope Price-Jones (soprano), Marlborough Festival, Wiltshire, England

Missa Brevis opus 55 (1973)
SA unison voices (optional Tenor solo), organ/harmonium
First broadcast performance: 1979, Lindsay Singers, Gerard Gillen (organ), Eithne Barror

Sonatina opus 56 (1973)
Alto flute and piano. Dedicated to Patricia Dunkerley
First performance: October 1975, Val Keogh (flute), Clive Shannon (piano), Monkstown parish church, Dublin

Dances for a Festival opus 57 (1973)
Orchestra
First performance: 24 November 1974, RTÉSO, Albert Rosen, Gaiety Theatre, Dublin

Trio opus 58 (1973)
Violin, cello and piano. Dedicated to the Bureau Trio
First performance: 6 January 1974, Bureau Trio, Examination Hall, Trinity College, Dublin

Pentecost opus 59 (1973 or 1974)
Treble voices, oboe, bass clarinet, trumpet, harp and percussion. Dedicated to the Finchley Children's Group. Lost

Trumpet Concerto opus 60 (1974)
Trumpet and orchestra. Dedicated to Josef Csibi
Destroyed by Wilson

Divisions for Four Trombones opus 61 (1974)
4 trombones. Dedicated to Seán Cahill
First broadcast performance: February 1977, Seán Cahill, David Weekley Philip Daly, Hartmut Pritzel

Fand opus 62 (1974)
Soprano, flute, piano and percussion. Text: Anon translated by John MacDonald. Dedicated to Veronica Dunne
First performance: August 1975, Veronica Dunne (soprano), Doris Keogh (flute), Veronica McSwiney (piano), J. Fennessy (percussion), St Canice's cathedral, Kilkenny

Fantasia for Solo Cello opus 63 (1974)
Cello. Dedicated to Gayle Smith
First performance: Aisling Drury-Byrne, St Catherine's church, Dublin
Score later used for the ballet *Conversations* (premiered at the Abbey Theatre 19 March 1978)

Symphony No. 2 'Monumentum' opus 64 (1975)
Mezzo-soprano and orchestra. Text: William Shakespeare
First performance: 23 July 1976, Ruth Maher, RTÉSO, Colman Pearce, Francis Xavier Hall, Dublin

Alarums and Excursions opus 65 (1975)
Alto saxophone and piano. Dedicated to Sydney Egan
First performance: 8 January 1976, Sydney Egan (saxophone), Denis O'Sullivan (piano), Trinity College, Dublin

Ditto Daughter? opus 66 (1976)
SATB [with soli], flute/piccolo, oboe/cor anglais, horn, trumpet, percussion, harp and cello. Incidental music for play by Elsa Gress. Dedicated to Elsa Gress. A reworked and expanded version of music from 1973 (see under works without opus number)
First performance: October 1976, using recording of the Royal Theatre Group, conductor Verner Nicolet, Riddersalen Theatre, Copenhagen

Prelude for Brass Quintet opus 67 (1976)
2 trumpets, horn, trombone and tuba. Dedicated to the Georgian Brass Ensemble
First performance: June 1976, Georgian Brass Ensemble, St Patrick's cathedral, Dublin
This was later incorporated into Brass Quintet No. 2 (1986)
2 trumpets, horn trombone and tuba
First performance: 20 April 1991, Prelude Brass, Christ Church cathedral, Dublin

Concerto for percussion and orchestra opus 68 (1976)
Percussion and orchestra. Dedicated to Michael Czewinski
Destroyed by Wilson

Scapegoat (Donny Johnny) opus 69 (1977)
Soprano, tenor, flute/piccolo, cor anglais, percussion, harpsichord, guitar (acoustic and electric) string quartet. Incidental music for play by Elsa Gress

Songs of Welcome opus 70 (1978)
Soprano, Tenor, guitar, violin, cello and piano. Text: Francis Ledwidge. Dedicated to Her Majesty Queen Margarethe of Denmark
First performance: 25 April 1978, National Gallery of Ireland, Dublin

Nativity Ode opus 71 (1978)
Treble voices, SATB, trumpet, percussion, harp, organ, dancers. Text: from *The Coventry Pageant of the Shearmen and Tailors, The Wakefield Second Shepherd's Pageant, The Sun Dances* , ed. Alexander Carmichael, *Hymn on the Morning of Christ's Nativity* by John Milton. Dedicated to Cecil and Billy Wynne
First performance: 26 January 1985, Camerata Singers, David Milne, St Stephen's church, Mount Street Crescent, Dublin

The Rape of the Lock opus 72 (1978)
SATB and accordion. Text: Alexander Pope. Dedicated to Stephen Wilkinson
First performance: 1 December 1979, William Byrd Singers, Stephen Wilkinson, Royal Northern College of Music Manchester

Concerto for Four Flutes and String Orchestra opus 73 (1978)
4 flutes and strings. Dedicated to Doris Keogh
First broadcast performance: 24 July 1981, Deirdre Brady, Denise McInerney, Doris Keogh, Elizabeth Gaffney, RTÉCO, Hughes

Les Fiançailles opus 74 (1978)
Soprano and piano. Text: Guillaume Apollinaire
First performance: 27 April 1995, Jane Manning (soprano), David Mason (piano), British Music Information Centre, London

Arlecchino opus 75A (1979)
Flute. Dedicated to Verner Nicolet
First performance: January 1980, Verner Nicolet, Copenhagen

Two Little Choral Pieces opus 75B (1979)
SATB Text: Charles Dalmon and Eric Porter
First performance: 23 September 1980, RTÉ Singers, Eric Sweeney, National Gallery, Dublin

Concerto for Harpsichord and Chamber Orchestra opus 76 (1979)
Harpsichord and chamber orchestra. Dedicated to Gillian Smith
First performance: 24 June 1980, Gillian Smith, New Irish Chamber Orchestra, John Beckett, Trinity College Dublin

Epithalamion opus 77 (1979)
One free-bass accordion, one piano accordion. Dedicated to Mogens and Martha Ellegard
First Performance: 16 October 2005, Dermot Dunne and Patricia Kavanagh, National Concert Hall, Dublin

The Windhover opus 78 (1979)
Soprano and clarinet. Text: Gerard Manley Hopkins. Dedicated to Jane Manning
First performance: 29 March 1983, Jane Manning (soprano), Alan Hacker (clarinet), Wigmore Hall, London

The Witches' Ballad opus 79 (1979)
Mezzo-soprano and piano. Text: William Bell Scott. Dedicated to Gun Knouzell. Rededicated to Aylish Kerrigan

Air and Angels opus 80 (1979)
Soprano, flute and free-bass accordion. Text: John Donne. Dedicated to Dorothy Dorow
First performance: 1980 Dorothy Dorow (soprano), Rien de Reede (flute), Mogens Ellegaard (accordion), Ijsbreker, Amsterdam

Symphonic Variations opus 81 (1980)
Piano and orchestra. Dedicated to Philip Martin
First performance: September 1982, Philip Martin, RTÉSO, Colman Pearce

Arachne, ballet in one act opus 82 (1980)
Oboe/cor anglais, harp, percussion, cello. Scenario: Terez Nelson. Dedicated to Terez Nelson
First performance: 2 October 1980, Dublin City Ballet, members of the RTÉCO, Dublin Theatre Festival

Appendix 2

The Wedding on the Eiffel Tower opus 83 (1980)
Flute/piccolo/bass flute, trumpet, percussion, harp, piano. Incidental music for play by Jean Cocteau. Dedicated to Jytte Abildstrøm

Music for Castletown opus 84
Chamber Orchestra. Dedicated to Maria and Iain Balfour
First performance: 19 June 1980?, New Irish Chamber Orchestra, Bryden Thompson. Lost

Duo opus 85 (1982)
Treble recorder and piano

Nighttown opus 86 (1982)
Clarinet, bass clarinet, 2 saxophones, 2 bassoons, 2 trumpets, 2 trombones, percussion, harmonium and guitar
First performance: 24 January 1983, Dublin Sinfonia, William York, National Concert Hall, Dublin

Five Preludes opus 87 (1982)
Piano. Dedicated to John O'Conor
First performance: Anthony Byrne
No. 5 'Homeward' published by Bosworth in *Composers Series for Piano 3: Intermediate Collection*, ed. Richard Deering (1996)

Concerto Grosso 'Umbrage for Orchestra and Six Music Critics' opus 88 (1982)
Piano, percussion and orchestra
First performance: 31 December 1982, Fanny Feehan, Gus Smith, Ian Fox, James Maguire, RTÉSO, Proinnsías Ó Duinn

Plurabelle opus 89 (1982)
Soprano, flute, clarinet, harp, piano, guitar, violin, viola, cello. Text: James Joyce. Dedicated to Cadenza
First Performance: 24 June 1982, Anne Cant (soprano), Cadenza, Proinnsías Ó Duinn, National Concert Hall, Dublin

Variations on a French Tune opus 90 (1982)
Harp. Dedicated to Denise Kelly
First performance: 13 June 1984, Denise Kelly, Malahide Castle, Co Dublin

The Revenge of Truth opus 91 (1982)
Soprano, tenor, clarinet, cello, percussion. Incidental music to a puppet play by Isak Dineson
First performance: London, directed by Virginia Campbell

Letters to Theo opus 92 (1982)
Baritone, SATB, chamber orchestra. Libretto: James Wilson after Vincent Van Gogh's correspondence with his brother Theo
First performance: 26 November 1984, John Cashmore (Vincent Van Gogh, baritone), Camerata Singers, Ulysses Ensemble, Colman Pearce, St Stephen's church, Mount Street Crescent, Dublin

Brass Quintet No. 1 opus 93 (1983)
2 trumpets, horn, trombone and tuba. Dedicated to the Georgian Brass Ensemble
First performance: 17 December 1983, Dublin Georgian Brass Ensemble, St Stephen's church, Mount Street Crescent, Dublin

Two by Four by Two opus 94 (1983)
Bass clarinet/tenor saxophone and vibraphone/marimba
First performance: 12 April 1996, Concorde, John Field Room, National Concert Hall, Dublin

Solitaire opus 96 (1983)
Guitar
First performance: 1983, Royal Irish Academy of Music, Dublin

Three Playthings opus 97 (1983)
Clarinet. Dedicated to Alan Hacker
First performance: 25 February 1984, Alan Hacker, Stockton on Tees

Wind Quintet opus 98 (1983)
Flute, oboe, clarinet, bassoon and horn
First performance: 16 May 1985, Ulysses Wind Quintet, St Stephen's church, Mount Street Crescent, Dublin

Monkey opus 99 (1983)
2 accordions. Dedicated to Anny and Paula van Wanrooy.
First performance of movements 1 and 3: Swedish Radio, Anny and Paula van Wanrooy

The Cat that Walked by Himself, ballet opus 100 (1983)
Piano
First performance: 7 February 1984, Ian Montague (piano), New Dance Company, St Brigid's Community Hall, Blanchardstown

Grinning at the Devil opus 101 (1984)
Mezzo-soprano, baritone, SATB orchestra, later rescored for horn, percussion, piano, string quartet and synthesiser. Libretto: Elsa Gress. Dedicated to Elsa Gress
First performance (of reduced version): 23 February 1989, Edith Guillaume (Tania, mezzo-soprano), John Cashmore (Denys, baritone), Daimi, Ars Nova, instrumentalists, Verner Nicolet, Riddersalen Theatre, Copenhagen

Concerto for Cello and Orchestra opus 102 (1984)
Cello and orchestra
First performance: 19 July 1985, Aisling Drury-Byrne, RTÉSO, Colman Pearce, National Concert Hall, Dublin

Explorations opus 103 (1984)
Piano. Dedicated to Richard Deering
First performance: 1984, Richard Deering

1985 opus 104/*Music for a Mechanical Organ/The Temptations of Saint Anthony* (1984)
1985: SATB, children's choir, violin, double bass, 2 guitars, percussion and organ (mechanical).
The Temptations of Saint Anthony: flute, violin, double bass, guitar (electric and acoustic), percussion, piano
Music for a play by various including Elsa Gress and Hans Hartvich based on story by Hans Christian Andersen. These various pieces of music were all linked to a project which started as a collaboration between Elsa Gress, Clifford Wright and Wilson. Gress eventually dropped the project and Hartvich took over. In the event it seems only the *Music for Mechanical Organ* was used in the final production.
First performance of *Music for a Mechanical Organ*: 20 February 1985, Riddersalen Theatre, Copenhagen

Good Friday Journey opus 105 (1985)
Soprano and piano. Text: John Donne. Dedicated to Una Barry
First performance: 3 March 1986, Una Barry (soprano), John Gough (piano) Ashton, England

Runes opus 106 (1985)
Soprano and cello. Text: Anon and George Peele. Dedicated to Dorothy Dorow
First performance: October 1985, Dorothy Dorow (soprano), Aage Kvalbein (cello), Stockholm

The Little Mermaid opus 107 (1985)
Female voices, flute/piccolo, horn, percussion and harp. Dedicated to 'my friends at the Riddersalen Theatre'
First performance: 1986, Riddersalen Theatre, Copenhagen

Emily Singing opus 108 (1985)
Soprano and chamber orchestra. Dedicated to Virginia Kerr
First performance: 22 May 1986, Virginia Kerr (soprano), Ulysses Ensemble, Colman Pearce, St Stephen's church, Mount Street Crescent, Dublin

Breeze and Calm opus 109 (1985)
Violin and dancer. Choreographer Ian Montague
First performance 20 November 1988, Alan Smale (violin)

Duet for Ten opus 110 for double wind quintet (1986)
2 flutes, 2 oboes, 2 clarinets, 2 bassoons and 2 horns
First performance: 11 May 1987, Ulysses Wind Quintet and Falun Wind Quintet, St Stephen's church, Mount Street Crescent, Dublin

The King of the Golden River opus 111 (1987)
Soprano, 2 tenors, 2 basses, SA, chamber orchestra, later rescored (1992) for clarinet/bass clarinet, violin, cello, piano and DX7 synthesiser. Text: James Wilson after the story by John Ruskin. Dedicated to Barbara Gress

Angel One opus 112 (1987)
Strings. Dedicated to Clifford Wright

First performance: 8 March 1992, RTÉCO, Proinnsías Ó Duinn, Royal Hospital Kilmainham, Dublin

The Wonderful Stone opus 113 (1987)
Speaker, clarinet and piano. Text: P'u Sung-ling. Dedicated to Jytte Abildstrom

Ostinato opus 114 (1987)
Piano. Dedicated to Anthony Byrne

First Frost opus 115 (1988)
Bass and piano. Text: Kevin Nichols
First performance: 11 September 1988, Nigel Williams (bass), Roy Holmes (piano), Hugh Lane Municipal Gallery of Modern Art, Dublin

Shadow Play opus 115A (1988)
Viola

Stirabout opus 116 (1988)
Soprano and DX7 synthesiser. Dedicated to Aylish Kerrigan
First performance: 27 September 1988, Aylish Kerrigan (soprano), Gillian Smith (synthesizer), Sligo cathedral

Angel Two opus 95 (1988)
Orchestra. Dedicated to Elsa and H. C. Robbins Landon
First performance: 18 May 1990, RTÉNSOI, George Hurst, National Concert Hall, Dublin.
It would seem that reviewing his list of works Wilson realised he had omitted opus 95 and thus gave it to this work rather than another work from 1983

Rima opus 117 (1988, revised 1990)
Soprano, flute, clarinet, bassoon, guitar, harp, piano, violin, viola and cello. Revised version scored for soprano, flute, clarinet, horn, guitar, harp, piano, violin, viola and cello and dedicated to Jane Manning

Libberton Moonrise opus 118 (1988)
Oboe. Dedicated to Rocky Balfour
First performance: 21 March 1993, Aisling Casey, Nice, France

Boreas: Sonata for electronically amplified flute opus 119 (1989)
Amplified flute. Dedicated to Ron Cooney
First performance: Ron Cooney, Hugh Lane Municipal Gallery of Modern Art, Dublin

Pearl and Unicorn opus 120 (1989)
Violin and orchestra
First performance: 17 December 1990, Alan Smale, RTÉNSOI, Colman Pearce, National Concert Hall, Dublin

In Remembrance opus 121 (1989)
Flute, violin, cello, percussion and piano. Dedicated to Elisabeth Clarke. Music used for the ballet Dance Ritual
First performance: 14 October 1990, Elizabeth Clarke, Concorde, Ian Montague (choreography), John Field Room, National Concert Hall, Dublin

The Christmas Rose opus 122 (1989)
Speaker and viola. Text: Selma Lagerlof

Menorah opus 123 (1989)
Viola and orchestra
First performance: 18 November 1991, Rivka Golani, RTÉNSOI, Colman Pearce, National Concert Hall, Dublin. While the title page of the score states this is opus 122, it would seem opus 123 is the number Wilson intended giving the piece and this is the number he uses in his catalogue

Wildwood opus 124 (1990)
Soprano and viola. Text: Mgr Kevin Nichols
First performance: 6 April 1994, Aylish Kerrigan (soprano), Naomi Ogina (viola), Neuhausen
Arranged for soprano and violin in 1993 for Dorothy Dorow.
First performance: 23 April 1995, Tina Verbeke (soprano), Alan Smale (violin)

Undesirables opus 125 (1990)
Soprano and cello. Text: Leland Bardwell.
First performance: 27 September 1992, Dorothy Dorow (soprano), David James (cello), Hugh Lane Municipal Gallery of Modern Art, Dublin

String Quartet No. 2 opus 126 (1991)
2 violins, viola and cello

The Legend of the Third Dove opus 127 (1991)
Harp. Incidental music for a puppet play after a story by Stefan Zweig

The Leaden Echo and the Golden Echo opus 128 (1991)
Soprano and piano. Text: Gerard Manley Hopkins
First performance: 17 March 1999, Una Barry (soprano), John Gough (piano), Holy Trinity church, Hinckley

Three Poems by Susan Connolly opus 129 (1991)
Mezzo-soprano, Irish harp. Text: Sarah Connolly

Nine Very Small Songs opus 130 (1991)
Soprano, flute/piccolo, clarinet/bass clarinet, horn, violin and cello. Text: Ian Douglas. Dedicated to Virginia Kerr
First performance: 12 April 1996, Tina Verbeke (soprano), Concorde, John Field Room, National Concert Hall, Dublin

Animalphabet opus 131 (1992)
SATB and piano. Text: James Wilson. Dedicated to the National Chamber Choir
First performance: 23 February 1993, National Chamber Choir, Colin Mawby, Bank of Ireland Arts Centre

For Cliodhna opus 132 (1992)
Cello.
First Performance: Cliodhna Ní hAodáin

Keats on Keats opus 133 (1993)
SATB. Text: John Keats
First performance: 25 April 1993, Madrigal '75, Geoffrey Spratt, Cork City Hall

Quintet for Clarinet and Strings opus 134 (1993)
Clarinet, 2 violins, viola and cello. Dedicated to John Finucane and the RTÉ Vanbrugh Quartet
First performance: 12 May 1996, John Finucane (clarinet), RTÉ Vanbrugh Quartet, Irish Museum of Modern Art, Dublin

Vigil opus 135 (1993)
Mezzo-soprano, oboe, clarinet, horn, trumpet, violin, cello and double bass. Text: Ian Douglas

Maze opus 136 (1993)
Mezzo-soprano, Baritone, flute, cor anglais, piano, percussion, violin and cello. Text: Henry VIII, Anne Boleyn

Concertino opus 137 (1993)
Orchestra. Dedicated to Cecilia Stahl
First performance: 15 April 1994, RTÉNSOI, Colman Pearce, National Concert Hall, Dublin

Violin Sonata No. 4 opus 138 (1993)
Violin and piano. Dedicated to Alan Smale and Colman Pearce
First performance: 12 April 1996, Alan Smale (violin), Jane O'Leary (piano), John Field Room, National Concert Hall, Dublin

A Passionate Man opus 139 (1995)
three sopranos, two mezzo-sopranos, two tenors, four baritones, bass, clarinet/bass clarinet, horn, piano, synthesizer, two violins, viola and cello. Libretto: Bruce Arnold.
First performance: 21 June 1995, Philip O'Reilly (Jonathan Swift, baritone), Majella Cullagh (Vanessa, soprano), Colette McGahon (Stella, mezzo-soprano), Deirdre Cooling-Nolan (Duchess of Marlborough, mezzo-soprano), Paul Kelly (Duke of Marlborough, tenor), Martin Higgins (Robert Harley, baritone), John Scott (Patrick, tenor), Jane Manning (Rebecca Dingley, soprano) ad hoc ensemble, Colman Pearce, Samuel Beckett Centre, Trinity College, Dublin

Cloud Music opus 140 (1995)
two oboes, two clarinets, two horns and two bassoons. Dedicated to 'Dan'
First performance: 20 November 1995, Stuttgart Wind Octet, Bantry House, Co. Cork

House of Cards opus 141 (1995)
Bassoon and piano. Dedicated to 'Dorte'

Mr Dwyer's Fancy opus 142 (1995)
three guitars
First performance: 11 December 1995, Trio Cervantes, Bank of Ireland Arts Centre, Dublin

Concerto 'For Sarajevo' opus 143 (1996)
Violin, viola, cello and orchestra
First performance: 12 December 1997, Alan Smale (violin), Constantin Zanidache (viola), Aisling Drury-Byrne (cello), RTÉNSOI, Colman Pearce, National Concert Hall, Dublin

Calico Pie opus 144 (1998)
Soprano, horn, violin and piano. Text: Edward Lear
First performance: 5 March 1998, Jane Manning (soprano), Jane's Minstrels, Ulster Museum Belfast

Concerto for five wind instruments and orchestra 'Concerto Giocoso' opus 145 (1998)
Flute, oboe, clarinet, horn, bassoon and orchestra
First performance: 12 June 1998, Esposito Wind Quintet, RTÉNSOI, Alexander Anissimov, National Concert Hall, Dublin

Les Sylphides opus 146 (1998)
Orchestra. Orchestration of piano works by Chopin

Aceldama opus 147 (1998)
Cello. Incidental music for a play by Jimmy Murphy
First performance: 12 September 1998, Diane O'Keefe (cello), Andrew's Lane Theatre, Dublin

Tree and Moon opus 148 (1999)
Piano test piece for the AXA Dublin International Piano Competition
First performance: 13 May 2000, David Jalbert, National Concert Hall, Dublin.
Published by the Contemporary Music Centre

Sonatina opus 149 (1998)
Clarinet, accordion, violin, cello
First performance: 27 January 1999, Concorde, Galway

Sonata opus 150 (1998, revised 2001)
Harp. Dedicated to Andreja Malir
First performance: 19 April 2000, Andreja Malir, John Field Room, National Concert Hall, Dublin

Concerto for Clarinet and Orchestra opus 151 (1999)
Clarinet and orchestra. Dedicated to John Finucane
First performance: 28 January 2000, John Finucane, RTÉNSOI, Alexander Anissimov, National Concert Hal, Dublin

Piano Trio No. 2 opus 152 (1999)
Violin, cello and piano
First performance: 7 May 2000, Geraldine O'Grady (violin), David James (cello), Veronica McSwiney (piano), Hugh Lane Municipal Gallery of Modern Art, Dublin

Virata opus 153 (1999)
Soprano, two Trebles, two mezzo-sopranos (2nd optional), five Tenors (5th optional), two baritones (2nd optional), SATB and orchestra. Text: James Wilson after a short story by Stefan Zweig

The Fisherman and his Wife opus 154 (1999)
Speaker, clarinet, violin and piano

Dance Pieces (Ballet Suite) opus 155 (1999)
Violin and piano. Choreographed by Andrew Wilson as *The light, the night, the half light*
First performance, 18 March 2000, Irish National Youth Ballet Company, Michael D'Arcy (violin), Stuart O'Sullivan (piano), Samuel Beckett Theatre, Trinity College, Dublin

Impromptu for violin and piano opus 155A (1999)
Violin and piano. Choreographed by Anne Campbell Crawford as *Games*
First performance: 16 March 2000, Irish National Youth Ballet Company, Michael D'Arcy (violin), Stuart O'Sullivan (piano), Samuel Beckett Theatre, Trinity College, Dublin

Grimoire opus 156 (1999)
Two pianos, eight hands. Dedicated to Richard Deering
First performance: 28 August 2000, London Piano Quartet, Franz Liszt Academy, Budapest

Symphony No. 3 opus 157 (2000)
Orchestra. Dedicated to Colman Pearce
First performance: 4 March 2003, RTÉNSOI, Colman Pearce, National Concert Hall, Dublin

Dublin Spring opus 158 (2001)
Baritone and piano. Text: Micheal O'Siadhail
First performance: 7 April 2002, Conor Biggs (baritone), Pádhraic Ó Cuinneagáin (piano), Hugh Lane Municipal Gallery of Modern Art, Dublin

Trio opus 159 (2001)
3 voices, clarinet, cello, percussion, harp and piano. Text: James Wilson. Dedicated to Daimi Gentle, Jytte Abildstrom and Edith Guillaume

Weathercock opus 160 (2001)
Orchestra. Dedicated to Ian Balfour

Enjoying opus 161 (2001)
Soprano and flute. Text: John Gracen Brown. Dedicated to John Gracen Brown
First performance: 29 September 2002, Jane Manning (soprano), Madeleine Staunton (flute),
Hugh Lane Municipal Gallery of Modern Art, Dublin

String Quartet No. 3 opus 162 (2002)
2 violins, viola and cello

Sonata No. 5 opus 163 (2002)
Violin and piano. Dedicated to Catherine Leonard
First performance: 13 November 2002, Catherine Leonard (violin), Hugh Tinney (piano), Siamse Tire, Tralee, Kerry

Serenade opus 164 (2002)
Violin, cello and harp. Dedicated to Moya O'Grady
First performance: 22 November 2002, David O'Doherty (violin), Moya O'Grady (cello), Geraldine O'Doherty (harp), John Field Room, National Concert Hall, Dublin

Three Hans Andersen Tales opus 165 (2003)
The Teapot opus 165a for speaker, violin and piano
The Snail and the Rose Tree opus 165b for speaker, bassoon and harp
The Bell opus 165c for speaker, bassoon, harp, violin and piano
Text: Hans Christian Andersen

Utter Nonsense opus 166 (2004)
Soprano, contralto, tenor, bass, SATB and orchestra. Text: Edward Lear and Lewis Carroll

Orison opus 167 (2003–2005)
Piano
First performance of first movement: 16 October 2005, Hugh Tinney, National Concert Hall, Dublin
First complete performance: 29 September 2006, Hugh Tinney, St Mary's Church, New Ross, County Wexford

Chiaroscuro opus 168 (2003 or 2004)
Cello
First performance: 14 March 2004, Peter Hickey, Hugh Lane Municipal Gallery of Modern Art, Dublin

Consequences opus 169 (2004)
Flute, harp and viola
First performance: 16 January 2006, Ríona O'Duinnín (flute), Geraldine O'Grady (violin), Brendan Lawless (viola), National Concert Hall, Dublin

Contrariwise opus 170 (2004)
Violin and harp
First performance: 22 June 2007, Geraldine O'Grady (violin), Geraldine O'Doherty (harp), National Concert Hall, Dublin

Almanac opus 171 (2004)
SATB. Text: Samuel Taylor Coleridge, William Shakespeare, Geoffrey Chaucer and William Butler Yeats
First performance of first and final movements: 29 April 2005, National Chamber Choir, Celso Antunes, St Fin Barre's cathedral, Cork

Sonata in one movement opus 172 (2004)
Cello and piano

First performance: 11 April 2010, Martin Johnson (cello), Jane O'Leary (piano), Hugh Lane Municipal Gallery of Modern Art, Dublin

Violin Sonata no. 6 opus 173 (2004 or 2005)
Violin and piano
First performance: 16 October 2005, David O'Doherty (violin), Catherina Lemoni (piano), John Field Room, National Concert Hall, Dublin

The Lion Tamer's Night Off opus 174 (2005)
Speaker and orchestra. Text: Anne Makower
First performance: 4 March 2007, Kathryn McKiernan (narrator), RTÉCO, Gareth Hudson, National Concert Hall, Dublin

Two Pieces for Bass Clarinet and Piano opus 175 (2005)
Bass clarinet and piano
First performance: 9 October 2005, Concorde, National Gallery, Dublin

Stuffed Raspberries [opus 176] (2005, unfinished)
Soprano, contralto, tenor, bass and piano. Libretto: Anne Makower

Works Without Opus Number
Fantasy for Violin and Piano (1962)
Violin and piano. Probably written with Michael Chauveton in mind. Later destroyed by Wilson

Sinfonietta (1962?)
Scored for woodwind, percussion and strings. Probably destroyed by Wilson

Phoenix Park/Fand/The Whiteheaded Boy (1962?)
These three titles are listed in Wilson's catalogue notebooks, but are crossed out and no further details (such as scoring) are given

Tempo di valse (1962)
Harp

Après Trois Ans (1962)
Soprano and piano. Text: Paul Verlaine.
Dedicated to Virginia Zeani. Deale's catalogue mentions a performance in 1958 on Italian radio. Also arranged for baritone and orchestra in 1962. This version first performed: August 1975, Brian Kissane, RTÉLO, Bill Skinner, Capitol Cinema, Dublin

Ceremonies (1963)
String orchestra with 5-string basses in 14 movements. Probably destroyed by Wilson

String Quartet (1963)
Probably destroyed by Wilson

Sonatina for B-flat Clarinet and Piano (1964)
Clarinet and piano
1910 (W Burroughs) (1965)

It is not entirely clear what this work was. Wilson's own list of compositions suggests a work for piano and percussion. A note in his 1967 diary refers to 'Experience of sound montage (1910).' A tape exists labelled 1910 which contains about twelve minutes of material. The first half is principally constructed using a recording of Siegfried's funeral march from Wagner's *Götterdämmerung*, which is layered over itself several times. To this is added some drumming, which becomes the principal element of the second half of the track along with some other folk music. It cuts off abruptly, suggesting perhaps that the original was longer.

Jeu des Tierces (1966)
Organ. Dedicated to Brian Grimson

Elegy on a favourite cat drowned in a tub of gold fishes (1966)
SA and piano. Text: Thomas Gray

Spanish Arch (1966)
Two Irish harps. Dedicated to Sheila Cuthbert
First broadcast performance: 17 May 1975, Gráinne Yeats and Mercedes Bolger, Cáirde na Cruite. Published by Mercier (1975) in *The Irish Harp Book*

A Song of Light – Anthem (1967)
SATB (boys voices) Text: Marguerite Wilkinson, St Teresa

Ode to Autumn (1968)
Soprano, flute and piano. Also arranged for soprano and piano. Text: John Keats. Dedicated to Anne Makower
First broadcast performance: BBC Belfast, 4 November 1968, Anne Makower (soprano), Wendy Berry (flute), Havelock Nelson (piano)

The Solitary Reaper (1968)
Soprano and piano. Text: Sir Walter Scott. Dedicated to Mary Sheridan

When icicles hang by the wall (1970)
Soprano and piano. Text: William Shakespeare
First performance: 1971, Anne Makower (soprano), Denis O'Sullivan (piano)

Seventh Canticle (1972)
Mezzo-soprano and piano. Text: Thomas Traherne
First performance: 19 May 1978, Anne Woodworth (mezzo-soprano), Gillian Smith (piano), Monkstown parish church, Dublin.

Ditto Daughter? (1973)
Mezzo-soprano, tenor, flute and viola. Incidental music for play by Elsa Gress
First performance: March 1973, Cambridge. An expanded version of this became opus 66

Two Songs for Children with Orff Instruments (1975)
Texts: Eileen Nangle and Eric Porter. Lost

Carol in Thanks (1979)
SATB. Text: John Pudney

Three Pieces for Descant Recorder and Piano (1981)
Descant recorder and piano
Three pieces written for the Royal Irish Academy of Music for examination purposes

Endymion (1982)
Mezzo-soprano, guitar and piano. Text: Oscar Wilde. Dedicated to Sylvia Eaves

The Only Jealousy of Emer (1983)
Mezzo-soprano or baritone, horn and piano. Incidental music to a play by William Butler Yeats
First performance: 14 February 1983, Riddersalen Theatre, Copenhagen

Für Denise (1985)
Organ and string trio. Lost

Fanfare (2001)
Two trumpets, Two horns and trombone
First performance: 9 April 2001, Contemporary Music Centre, 19 Fishamble Street, Dublin

For Constantin (2001)
Viola
First performance: 3 February 2002, Constantin Zanidache (viola), Hugh Lane Municipal Gallery of Modern Art, Dublin

Select Bibliography

Arundell, Dennis, *The Story of Sadler's Wells, 1683–1977* (London: David and Charles, 1978)

Benser, Caroline Cepin, *Egon Wellesz: Chronicle of a Twentieth Century Musician* (New York: Peter Lang Publishing, 1985)

Blixen, Karen, *Out of Africa* (London: Penguin Books, 1999)

Boydell, Brian (ed.), *Four Centuries of Music in Ireland* (London: British Broadcasting Corporation, 1979)

Boyle, Brian, *Highbury County Revisited*, ed. David Perman (Hertfordshire: Rockingham Press, 2005)

Brontë, Emily Jane, *The Complete Poems*, ed. Janet Gezari (London: Penguin Classics, 1992)

Cox, David and John Bishop (eds.), *Peter Warlock: A Centenary Celebration* (London: Thames Publishing, 1994)

Cox, Gareth and Axel Klein, 'James Wilson', in Walter-Wolfgang Sparrer and Hans-Werner Heister (eds), *Komponisten der Gegenwart* (Munich: Ed. text und Kritik, 1992)

Cox, Gareth, Axel Klein and Michael Taylor, *The Life and Music of Brian Boydell* (Dublin: Irish Academic Press, 2003)

Cox, Gareth and Julian Horton (eds.), *Irish Musical Studies 11: Irish Musical Analysis* (Dublin: Four Courts Press, 2014)

De Barra, Séamas, *Aloys Fleischmann* (Dublin: Field Day, 2006)

Deale, Edgar (ed.), *Catalogue of Contemporary Irish Composers* (Dublin: Music Association of Ireland, 1973 [1968])

Dinesen, Isak [Karen Blixen], *Seven Gothic Tales* (London: Penguin Classics, 2002)

Drummond, John, *Speaking of Diaghilev* (London: Faber and Faber Ltd, 1997)

Dwyer, Benjamin, *Constellations: The Life and Music of John Buckley* (Dublin: Carysfort Press, 2011)

Ferriter, Diarmaid, *Occasions of Sin: Sex and Society in Modern Ireland* (London: Profile Books, 2009)

Fielding, Xan, *Hide and Seek* (Maidstone: George Mann, 1973)

Fitz-Simon, Christopher, *The Boys: A Biography of Micheál Mac Líammóir and Hilton Edwards* (Dublin: New Island Books, 2002)

Forsyth, Cecil, *Orchestration*, 2nd edn (London: Macmillan, 1935)

Gress, Elsa, *Philoctetes Wounded and other plays* (Denmark: Decenter, 1969)

—, *The Simurg* (London: Quartet Books Ltd, 1989)

Harrison, Bernard, *Catalogue of Contemporary Irish Music* (Dublin: Arch Printing, 1982)

Hotson, Leslie, *The First Night of Twelfth Night* (London: Mercury Books, 1961)

Houlbrook, Matt, *Queer London: Perils and Pleasures in the Sexual Metropolis, 1918–1957* (Chicago and London: University of Chicago Press, 2005)

Kington, Beryl, *Rowley Rediscovered: The Life and Music of Alec Rowley* (London: Thames Publishing, 1993)

Klein, Axel, *Die Musik Irlands im 20. Jahrhundert* (Hildesheim: Georg Olms Verlag, 1996)

—, 'Irish Composers and Foreign Education: A study of influences,' in *Irish Musical Studies 4: The Maynooth International Musicological Conference: Selected Proceedings Part One*, Patrick F. Devine and Harry White (eds.) (Dublin: Four Courts Press, 1996), 277.

Lagerlöf, Selma, *Gösta Berling's Saga*, trans., Lillie Tudeer (New York: Dover Publications, 2004)

Manning, Jane, *New Vocal Repertory: An Introduction* (London: Macmillan, 1982)

—, *New Vocal Repertory 2* (Oxford: Clarendon Press, 1998)

Moss, W. Stanley, *Ill met by Moonlight: The Classic Story of Wartime Daring* (London: Cassell Military Paperbacks, 2004).

Mountain, Peter, *Scraping a Living: A life of a Violinist* (Bloomington Indiana and Milton Keynes: Author House, 2007)

Neel, Boyd, *My Orchestras and Other Adventures: The Memoirs of Boyd Neel*, ed. J. David Finch (Toronto: University of Toronto Press, 1985)

O'Kelly, Pat, *The National Symphony Orchestra of Ireland: 1948–1998* (Dublin: Radio Telefís Éireann, 1998)

Pine, Richard, *Music and Broadcasting in Ireland* (Dublin: Four Courts Press, 2005)

Pine, Richard and Charles Acton (eds.), *To Talent Alone: The Royal Irish Academy of Music, 1848–1998* (Dublin: Gill & Macmillan, 1998)

Ruskin, John, *The King of the Golden River* (New York: Dover Publications, 1974)

Van Gogh, Vincent, *The Letters of Vincent van Gogh*, Mark ed. Roskill (London: William Collins, Sons & Co., 1974)

White, Harry and Barra Boydell (eds.), *The Encyclopaedia of Music in Ireland* (Dublin: UCD Press, 2013)

Winton, John, *Death of the* Scharnhorst (London: Cassell and Co., 2000)

Woodman, Richard, *Arctic Convoys 1941–1945* (London: John Murray, 2004)

Zweig, Stefan, *Jewish Legends*, trans. Eden and Cedar Paul (New York: Marcus Wiener Publishing, 1987)

DISCOGRAPHY

Thermagistris (1968)
Goasco (GXX 003–4), MC (1985) Nicholas O'Halloran (piano)

Runes (1985)
Simax (PSC1052), CD (1989), *Contemporary Music for Soprano and Cello*, Dorothy Dorow (soprano) and Aage Kvalbein (cello)

For Cliodhna (1992)
Contemporary Music Centre, Ireland (CD02), CD (1997), *Contemporary Music from Ireland 2*, David James (cello)

Arlecchino (1979)

Association of Irish Composers (AIC 0001), CD (1998), *Hugh Lane November Series 1998*, Anne O'Briain (flute)

Upon Silence (1972)

Priory Records Ltd [formerly Altarus] (AIR-CD-9010), CD (1999), *Songs by Nicola LeFanu, John Kinsella, James Wilson, John Buckley and Samuel Barber*, Penelope Price Jones (soprano) & Philip Martin (piano)

Pearl and Unicorn (1989), *Menorah* (1989) and *Concertino* (1993)

Marco Polo (8.225027), CD (2000) Constantin Zanidache (viola), Alan Smale (violin), National Symphony Orchestra of Ireland, Colman Pearce (cond.)

The Legend of the Third Dove (1991) and *The Fisherman and his Wife* (1999)

Focus Production (FP2001), CD (2001), *Jytte Abildstrøm Fortaeller for born og voksne: Konen i Muddergrøften & Legenden om den Tredje Due*, Jytte Abildstrøm (speaker), Vagn Sørensen (piano), Marianne Sørnesen (violin), Søren Elbo (clarinet), Tine Rehling (harp)

Upon Silence (1972), *The Windhover* (1979), *Arlecchino* (1979), *Three Playthings* (1983), *Calico Pie* (1998), *Sonatina* (1998) & *Enjoying* (2001)

JWCD01, CD (2003), *Songs and Chamber Music*, Jane Manning (soprano), Concorde (CD, 2003)

Three H.C. Andersen Fairytales (2003)

Focus Production (FPCD2010), CD (2004), *H.C. Andersen for children and adults told by Jytte Abildstrøm*, Jytte Abildstrøm (speaker), Vagn Sørensen (piano), Marianne Sørnesen (violin), Karen Lassen (bassoon), Tine Rehling (harp)

Arlecchino (1979)

Atoll Records (ACD111), CD (2010), *Breathe: Music by Irish and New Zealand Composers*, William Dowdall (flute)

Notes and References

1. Early Life in London

1 James Wilson, *From the Top* (unpublished memoir), p. 6.
2 James Wilson, *Looking back and looking forward*, RTÉ radio broadcast, 20 August 1982. Archive of the Contemporary Music Centre Dublin, RTÉ/277.
3 Wilson, *From the Top*, p. 13.
4 Ibid., p. 9.
5 Brian Boyle, *Highbury County Revisited*, ed. David Perman (Hertfordshire: Rockingham Press, 2005), back cover material.
6 It is possible that Wilson is incorrect in assigning this performance to his years at Miss Tappe's school. By the time he entered Highbury County, the school had formed the Highbury Theatre Group in collaboration with Highbury Hill Girls' School and their productions included works by Shakespeare. See Boyle, *Highbury County Revisited*, pp. 15, 43, 99. Near the end of his life, Wilson was considering creating an operatic version of *As You Like It*. See Michael Dungan, 'An Element of Recklessness,' *New Music News*, September 2002, pp. 9–11.
7 Wilson, *Looking back and looking forward*.
8 Wilson kept in contact with Mary Maskell and sent her recordings of some of his pieces, including his first symphony. She sent Wilson a copy of this piece and it is now housed with his papers in Trinity College, Dublin (TCD).
9 Wilson, *Looking back and looking forward*.
10 James Wilson in interview with Dermot Rattigan, RTÉ Radio 1 Broadcast, 13 October 1988. Archive of the Contemporary Music Centre Dublin, RTÉ/91.
11 Wilson, *From the Top*, p. 14.
12 Boyle, *Highbury County Revisited*, p. 99.
13 Wilson, *Looking back and looking forward*.
14 Wilson, *From the Top*, p. 15.
15 Ibid., pp. 16–17.
16 Wilson, *Looking back and looking forward*.
17 Wilson, *From the Top*, p. 19.
18 Ibid., p. 18.
19 John Drummond, *Speaking of Diaghilev* (London: Faber and Faber, 1997), pp. 314–15.
20 For more details about the Sadler's Wells Company, see Dennis Arundell, *The Story of Sadler's Wells, 1683–1977* (London: David and Charles, 1978).
21 Wilson, *From the Top*, p. 20. Against the background of depression and with an intake from mixed backgrounds it is not surprising that the school placed such an emphasis on 'safe' employment. This is reflected in the 1934 school magazine, where it was noted with 'satisfaction that 18 out of 21 boys who had left with matriculation the previous June had found employment.' Boyle, *Highbury County Revisited*, p. 42.

22 Wilson, *Looking back and looking forward*.

23 Wilson, *From the Top*, p. 14.

24 de Basil's company was another offshoot of the dismantled Ballet Russes. It began as the Ballets Russes de Monte Carlo and later became the Original Ballets Russes. While Leonid Massine created many works for the company it did not commission new works from contemporary composers. A certain amount of Diaghilev ballets were kept in its repertoire. See Drummond, *Speaking of Diaghilev*, pp. 311–12.

25 Wilson, *Looking back and looking forward*.

26 Its origins lie in a suite of orchestrations by Aleksandr Glazunov of piano pieces by Frédéric Chopin entitled Chopiniana. With the addition of one further waltz this became the first version of the score. However, the choreographer Mikhaíl Fokine then decided to create a second version of the ballet with a different selection of music. The majority of the orchestration was undertaken by a *répétiteur* of the Mariinsky Theatre, Maurice Keller. When Diaghilev took it into his repertoire he commissioned a new set of orchestrations from Anatoly Liadov, Sergei Taneyev, Nikolai Tcherepnin and Igor Stravinsky. This new score was never published, resulting in the various versions current today. Richard Taruskin, *Stravinsky and the Russian Traditions: A biography of the works through Mavra, Volume I* (Oxford University Press, 1996), pp. 546–547.

27 TCD MS11240, undated draft of a response to a government White Paper on the arts for Aosdána.

28 Wilson, *Looking back and looking forward*.

29 I am indebted to Nicholas Wilson for further details regarding Clarice Wilson née Jeffery. E-mail to the author, 22 August 2009.

30 Wilson letter to Clarice Wilson, 29 December 1944.

31 Soviet Russia's army had been badly damaged by the Winter War with Finland in 1939 and its command structure destroyed by Stalin's purges; it was taken by surprise by the launch of Operation Barbarossa on 22 June 1941. Having lost a huge number of aircraft and with the Germans pressing in from the east and cutting off supplies from the south, Stalin demanded that the British supply the Soviet Union with munitions and other necessary supplies. See Richard Woodman, *Arctic Convoys, 1941–1945* (London: John Murray, 2004), p. 9.

32 Wilson, *From the Top*, p. 26.

33 Woodman, *Arctic Convoys*, pp. 355–75. For more detail see John Winton, *Death of the Scharnhorst* (London: Cassell and Co., 2000).

34 Woodman, *Arctic Convoys*, pp. 383–85.

35 Wilson, *From the Top*, p. 27.

36 TCD MS 11240 Wilson, *From the Top* early draft; this passage is omitted from the final version. Vaughan Williams and Sibelius were two of the most popular contemporary composers in 1930s London. *Orchestration* by Cecil Forsyth was written in 1913 and a second edition had been published in 1935. While providing a standard introduction to the instruments of the orchestra, much of the text, particularly when dealing with wind, brass and percussion instruments, was out of date by the 1940s as the original text had never been revised. The second edition merely added an extra chapter that is mainly concerned with clarifying and adding historical information rather than adding any information regarding improvements in instruments, new possibilities or new repertoire. See Cecil Forsyth, *Orchestration*, 2nd edn (London: Macmillan, 1935).

37 Wilson letter to Clarice Wilson, 15 October 1944.

38 Brian Thomas (Director of Education and Adult Learning for The Marine Society and Sea Cadets), e-mail to the author 22 August 2006.

39 In interview with Dermot Rattigan, Wilson states that his teacher was Peter Mountain, a violinist who later became leader of the Liverpool Philharmonic Orchestra. However, Mountain did not work for the College of the Sea and in 1943 was enlisted in the Royal Marines. After the war he worked with the Boyd Neel Orchestra and it is possible that Wilson encountered him then and confused the name with some other person in the interview. Peter Mountain, *Scraping a Living: A life of a Violinist* (Bloomington Indiana and Milton Keynes: Author House, 2007), and e-mail from Mountain to the author, 21 November 2008.

40 Wilson letters to Clarice Wilson, 15 October, 3 November, 7 December 1944.

41 Wilson letter to Clarice Wilson, 29 December 1944. Wilson's interest in using the harpsichord had been sparked by seeing Christopher Wood play with the Dolmetsch family before he was called up for active service.

42 James Wilson in interview with Jonathan Grimes, 11 July 2005, www.cmc.ie/articles/article1034.html.

43 Wilson, *From the Top*, p. 30.

44 Brian Grimson recalled Wilson reacting in an uncharacteristically violent manner to a television comedy set in wartime, with Wilson declaring that war was never a laughing matter. Brian Grimson to the author, 6 August 2009.

45 Wilson in interview with Dermot Rattigan.

46 Wilson, *Looking back and looking forward*.

47 It is impossible to date with any certainty when Wilson enrolled at Trinity College of Music London or how long his lessons lasted, as Trinity no longer holds records for this period.

48 Beryl Kington, *Rowley Rediscovered: The Life and Music of Alec Rowley* (London: Thames Publishing, 1993), pp. 9, 68–69. It is interesting to note how closely this parallels Wilson's own tastes.

49 Wilson, *From the Top*, p. 31.

50 These are presumably the Ronsard settings Wilson composed while studying with Alec Rowley, gathered together as a gift for Isla Morante, the sister of his then partner John Campbell, in return for her hospitality on Ischia when Wilson visited with John Campbell. For details regarding Wilson's Mediterranean trip see chapter two, pages 17–19.

51 Wilson in interview with Dermot Rattigan.

52 James Wilson, 'Personal View, The James Wilson Column: A View from the Hebrides', *Soundpost*, no. 6, February/March 1982, p. 9.

53 Wilson letter to Clarice Wilson, 29 December 1944.

54 Dungan, 'An Element of Recklessness', p. 10.

55 Colman Pearce to the author, 19 December 2005.

56 Wilson, *From the Top*, p. 29.

57 A letter to Clarice Wilson, 15 October 1944 refers to a performance as 'the great event of recent times while another on 7 December 1944 states 'I may be mistaken but it strikes me as one of those works which, though completely different, cannot fail to impress with their undeniable greatness, and the queer, splendid melodies will get you.'

58 Wilson to the author, 4 August 2005.

59 Wilson letter to Clarice Wilson, 29 December 1944.

60 Wilson, Pre-concert talk on the occasion of the premiere of *Concerto For Sarajevo*, op. 143, 12 December 1997. Archive of the Contemporary Music Centre Dublin, 98/13.

61 Wilson in interview with Jonathan Grimes.

62 Wilson letter to Clarice Wilson, undated 1940s.

63 Wilson in interview with Ciaran Carty, *Sunday Independent*, 3 February 1985.

64 James Wilson in interview with Ray Lynott, RTÉ radio, 17 July 1995. Archive of the Contemporary Music Centre Dublin, 95/27, 95/23. Ian Balfour recalls his almost violent reaction on first hearing Arvo Pärt's *Cantus in memory of Benjamin Britten* in Aldeburgh, when Wilson exclaimed loudly 'No, no!', which Balfour states 'would have been audible several rows away'. Ian Balfour to the author 24 January 2006.

65 Wilson to the author, 4 August 2005.

66 Neel had commissioned the Bridge Variations when the Boyd Neel String Orchestra was asked to perform at the Salzburg Festival in 1937, the main condition being that the concert would contain a new specially commissioned work by an English composer. With less than three months to the performance date Neel asked the young Britten, who managed to draft the work in about ten days. The performance made Britten's name in Europe and wrote a number of other works with the orchestra in mind. *Les Illuminations* was premiered in 1940 with a scratch orchestra as many of the members of the original orchestra were in active service. See Boyd Neel, *My Orchestras and Other Adventures: The Memoirs of Boyd Neel*, ed. J. David Finch (Toronto: University of Toronto Press, 1985), pp. 91–96, 106.

67 Information taken from letters to Clarice Wilson, 14 June 1945, and Ian Balfour (private collection), undated 1995.

68 Wilson to the author, 4 August 2005, and TCD MS11240 diary 1948. Despite his strong aversion to Wagner in later life, he attended the Wagner Prom in 1948.

69 Wilson to the author, 4 August 2005.

70 'Re Rape of Lucretia', Wilson to the author, 4 August 2005. The list is in a letter from 1978 and also includes Mozart's *Don Giovanni* and Stravinsky's *Pulcinella* along with Proust's *Swann's Way*, George and Weedon Grossmith's *Diary of a Nobody* and Pope's *The Rape of the Lock*. Wilson to Clarice Wilson, undated.

71 TCD MS11240 'John Campbell Obituary' in King's College, Cambridge, Annual Report of the Council under Statute D, III, 10 on the General and Educational Condition of the College November 1976, pp. 30–31.

72 TCD MS11240 John Campbell, *Fragments of Stone* (unpublished war memoir).

73 A full account of this operation is to be found in W. Stanley Moss, *Ill met by Moonlight: The Classic Story of Wartime Daring* (London: Cassell Military Paperbacks, 2004). This was made into a film in 1958 by Michael Powell and Emeric Pressburger, staring Dirk Bogarde.

74 TCD MS11240 John Campbell, *Fragments of Stone*.

75 Xan Fielding, *Hide and Seek* (Maidstone: George Mann, 1973), p. 26.

76 Wilson, *Looking back and looking forward*.

77 Wilson, *From the Top*, p. 31. Extra detail taken from TCD MS11240 early draft of *From the Top*.

78 Wilson, *From the Top*, p. 35.

79 Wilson in interview with Dermot Rattigan. Nicholas Wilson recalled Wilson making similar remarks about London, in interview with the author 22 March 2006.

80 Matt Houlbrook, *Queer London: Perils and Pleasures in the Sexual Metropolis, 1918–1957* (Chicago and London: University of Chicago Press, 2005), pp. 33–36. This period culminated in the notorious prosecution of journalist Peter Wildeblood, Major Michael Pitt Rivers and Lord Montagu of Beaulieu in 1954, which eventually led to the publication of the Wolfendon Report in 1957.

81 Patrick Zuk, unpublished interview with James Wilson, 31 August 2004.

82 For more details on homosexuality in Ireland at this Period, see Diarmaid Ferriter, *Occasions of Sin: Sex and Society in Modern Ireland* (London: Profile Books, 2009).

83 It has proved impossible to pinpoint the exact date of Wilson's arrival in Ireland, but it is clear that the date given in more recent articles and interviews of 1948 is incorrect. The Republic was formally inaugurated on Easter Monday 1949.

2. ARRIVAL IN DUBLIN

1 TCD MS11240 Letter from Chatto and Windus, 16 October 1950. In 1956, Campbell attempted to interest Weidenfeld and Nicolson but by this stage, with a market saturated with colourful war memoirs, Campbell's book was again turned down for reasons of its repetition and lack of narrative direction. It was also criticised for a lack of local colour. No further attempt seems to have been made to publish it, but, with its exactitude and detail, it remains an important source of information on Aegean operations.

2 Zuk, unpublished interview with Wilson.

3 James Wilson, 'Dublin to Athens in *Vistona* Part 1', *The Rudder*, June 1951, pp. 5–9, 50–56.

4 The exact chronology and sequence of events is, like so many other things, unclear in *From the Top*. Further information and dates come from TCD MS11240, guest book of the *Vistona* and TCD MS11240 diary 1952. The first part of the journey was documented by Wilson in a three-part article that appeared in *The Rudder* in June, July and August 1951.

5 In his articles in *The Rudder*, Wilson notes two occasions when he heard other music: once when he heard *Les Sylphides* from a radio on a passing steamer, and, a visit to a radio shop in Capri where the proprietor played Rossini's *Thieving Magpie* Overture at Wilson's request. James Wilson, 'Dublin to Athens in *Vistona* Part II', *The Rudder*, July 1951, pp. 28–31, 29–30.

6 Ibid., p. 29.

7 Wilson in interview with Dermot Rattigan.

8 TCD MS11240 *Éire Ireland: Bulletin of the Department of External Affairs*, 23 January 1968.

9 Wilson letter to Gerard Gillen, 1 August 1968.

10 Wilson in interview with Dermot Rattigan.

11 Zuk, unpublished interview with Wilson.

12 Dr Noël Browne's plans to introduce a universal health-welfare system for mothers and children failed in the main due to opposition from the Catholic hierarchy.

13 For more information see Michael Adams, *Censorship: The Irish Experience* (Dublin: Scepter Books, 1968).

14 Mary Boydell to the author, 23 July 2007.

15 James Wilson 'Personal View, The James Wilson Column: The composer in Ireland today,' *Soundpost*, no. 1 (April/May 1981), p. 30. Like many things associated with Wilson's early years in Ireland, the dating of this is unclear. In the article for *Soundpost*, Wilson states that Norah McGuinness also introduced Wilson to Boydell. Mary Boydell suggests that they met via a mutual friend, Aleck Crichton. The earliest mention of Wilson in Boydell's engagement diaries is on 7 December 1952. I am grateful to Mary Boydell for providing this information. The engagement also appears in Wilson's diary.

16 Porter had studied at the Slade School of Art with Henry Tonks and exhibited his works, which included landscapes, portraits and works utilising broken coloured glass in Dublin, Wexford and London. He was also the author of *Saturn's child: a romantic novel based on the life of Francisco Goya y Lucientes, 1746–1828* (London: Rockliff, 1947). Phyllida McAlpine e-mail to the author, 17 April 2009.

17 The reviews come from the scrapbooks of reviews of the concerts given by the Dublin Orchestral kept by Brian Boydell, TCD MS11128.

18 Wilson, 'The Composer in Ireland Today', p. 30.

19 Wilson, *From the Top*, p. 36.

20 It is interesting to note that as late as 1978 he was still considering this story as the basis of a possible opera, and suggested it to Elsa Gress when discussing possible collaborations. Royal Library Denmark, Acc 1978/142 Supp 1, Wilson letter to Elsa Gress, 2 October 1978.

21 Wilson had no training in large-scale composition. However, this may not have been as big a problem as it may at first seem, the example of *Esther* suggesting a ballet constructed from a series of short dances rather than a through-composed piece.

22 Phyllida McAlpine e-mail to the author, 17 April 2009.

23 Phyllida McAlpine e-mail to the author, 19 March 2009. Julian Braunsweg (1897–1978) was the founder of the London Festival Ballet (later, English National Ballet) and was the director from 1950 until 1965. He had previously worked with the Original Ballet Russe among other companies. Anton Dolin (1904–1983), born Patrick Healy-Kaye, was an English dancer who had been a star of Diaghilev's company in the 1920s as well as being one of Diaghilev's lovers. At this period he was principal dancer and artistic director of the London Festival Ballet. For more information see Drummond, *Speaking of Diaghilev*. When in 1980 Wilson's short ballet *Arachne*, choreographed by Terez Nelson, was premiered in the Dublin Theatre Festival, Wilson noted with particular pleasure the praise the music received from Dolin, who was producing Adolph Adam's *Giselle* in the same programme, perhaps recalling privately how he had been rejected by Dolin many years before. Wilson letter to Clarice Wilson, undated October 1980.

24 Donald McAlpine to the author, 2 October 2009.

25 Neel, *My Orchestras and Other Adventures*, pp. 150–59.

26 Bernard Harrison (ed.), *Catalogue of Contemporary Irish Music* (Dublin: Arch Printing, 1982).

27 Donald McAlpine to the author, 2 October 2009.

28 *Oxford Dictionary of Music*, revised edition, ed. Michael Kennedy (Oxford University Press, 1997) and Caroline Cepin Benser, *Egon Wellesz: Chronicle of a Twentieth Century Musician* (New York: Peter Lang Publishing, 1985), pp. 58–59.

29 National Library of Ireland Acc6000, Box 19.

30 Wilson letter to Robert and Clarice Wilson, 1960. For more detail on Tibor Paul see Richard Pine, *Music and Broadcasting in Ireland* (Dublin: Gill & Macmillan, 2005), pp. 420ff. A concert hall was not to materialise until the conversion of the Great Hall of University College, Dublin in Earlsfort Terrace into the National Concert Hall in 1981.

31 Wilson letter to Clarice Wilson, undated 1961.

32 Zuk, unpublished interview with Wilson.

33 Wilson, *From the Top*, p. 56. When the symphony was eventually performed in 1967, not only did the horn players have no difficulty with the parts, the principal horn player Patrick McElwee commissioned a concerto from Wilson.

34 Jonathan Grimes, 'What's it like to be James Wilson', www.cmc.ie/articles/ article 1035.html.

35 For example, Brian Boydell's compositional training before he set himself up as a composer in Ireland was limited to a year of study (1938–1939) with Patrick Hadley and Herbert Howells (he also took a MusB in TCD in 1942), while Gerard Victory's first attempts at orchestral composition were dismissed by the then head of RTÉ for their technical incompetence. See TCD MS10839/1/1 and Klein, 'Irish Composers and Foreign Education, p. 277.

36 Mary Boydell to the author, 23 July 2007.

37 Brian Grimson to the author, 6 August 2009.

38 TCD MS11240 *Éire Ireland*. The other seven works were by Bodley, Boydell, Fleischmann and Victory. A further two works by Séan Ó Riada and Proinnsías Ó Duinn were added to the list.

39 Attempts to discover exactly what the work vaguely referred to as a 'musical' in one letter was have yielded no positive results.

40 Brian Grimson to the author, 6 August 2009.

41 Wilson, *From the Top*, 48.

42 Eve O'Kelly, 'Wilson at Seventy', *New Music News,* September 1992, pp. 10–12 .

43 Wilson in interview with Jonathan Grimes.

44 TCD MS11240 Wilson letter to Dorothy Mayer, 4 April 1963.

45 Brian Grimson to the author, 6 August 2009.

46 TCD MS11240 Wilson letter to Dorothy Mayer, 4 April 1963.

47 Wilson letter to Clarice Wilson, undated early summer 1963.

48 Wilson letter to Robert and Clarice Wilson, undated late 1963.

49 The Dagg Hall has recently been renamed the Katherine Brennan Hall.

50 TCD MS11240 Herbert Moulton letter to Wilson, 9 May 1963.

51 Phyllida McAlpine e-mail to the author, 19 March 2009.

52 TCD MS11240 Brian Grimson letter to James Wilson, 22 October 1964.

53 Brian Grimson e-mail to the author, 6 August 2009. He recalled her 'launching fearlessly, like the rearing horse in that statue of Peter the Great, into a score she had never seen before.'

54 Mary Boydell to the author, 23 July 2007. It is perhaps indicative of the characters of the two men that in interviews people generally referred to Wilson as 'Jim' and Campbell as 'the Commander'.

55 Captained by The Bellman they are a Boots, a Bonnet-maker, a Barrister, a Broker, a Billiard-marker, a Banker, a Beaver, a Butcher who can only kill beavers and a Baker who can only bake bridecake.

56 James Wilson, 'Wax Bananas and Snarks', *Counterpoint*, March 1974.

57 Wilson letter to Clarice Wilson, March 1965.

58 In a letter from 1967 Wilson suggested a range of cuts. Some of these were simply omissions of repeats or second verses of sections. However, in the Bonnet Maker's scene he suggested cuts totalling 111 bars out of 283 bars. When the work was revived in 1974 however, this was reduced to a cut of thirty-eight bars. The only other section omitted was the Bellman's 'Friends, Romans, countrymen' address. Wilson to Geoffrey Russell-Smith, 7 July 1967. I am grateful to Brian Grimson for showing me a copy of this letter.

59 TCD MS11240 Dorothy Mayer letter to Wilson, 21 December 1963.

60 TCD MS11240 Letter from Edwards to Wilson. Telefís Éireann had been launched on 31 December 1961.

61 After this he also had to go to Spain where, in the event, he had to abandon a role in a film version of *Chimes at Midnight* due to illness. Christopher Fitz-Simon, *The Boys: A Biography of Micheál Mac Líammóir and Hilton Edwards* (Dublin: New Island Books, 2002), pp. 273–77. Wilson reports the results of his meeting with Edwards in a letter to Randal Henry dated 10 June 1964. In this letter Wilson notes that Edwards was 'most encouraging . . . and it might possibly get on to television.' Randal Henry's letters concerning the premiere of *The Hunting of the Snark* are held by the archive of the Royal Irish Academy of Music, Dublin.

62 After the premiere of his first symphony Wilson played a tape of the piece to Edwards, who immediately proposed a cycle of three Greek plays with music for small orchestra provided by Wilson, but nothing came of this project. Wilson letter to Robert Wilson, March 1967.

63 Charles Acton, 'Hunting of the Snark Delightful Entertainment,' *The Irish Times*, 6 January 1965.

64 Wilson recalls in his memoirs that the percussionist Janos Keszei of the RTÉ Symphony Orchestra thought at first glance that the percussion part was unplayable. Although he is not listed in the programme, he played in some of the performances and autographed Brian Grimson's programme (Brian Grimson e-mail to the author, 7 August 2009). Wilson recalls playing in some of them and the listed percussionist also from the Symphony Orchestra was Stanislaus Stack.

65 Wilson to Geoffrey Russell-Smith, 7 July 1967. I am grateful to Brian Grimson for showing me this letter.

66 TCD MS11240 Letter from Britten to Andrew, Winser 24 April 1965, © Britten-Pears Foundation. Text reproduced by kind permission of the Britten Pears Library. Winser, who worked in Stone House Preparatory School in Broadstairs, had originally been contacted by Wilson in January 1965 in the hope that he would get his school to perform *The Hunting of the Snark*.

67 Wilson letter to Britten, 5 July 1965. Text reproduced by kind permission of the Britten-Pears Foundation.

68 Wilson letter to Clarice Wilson, April/May 1973.

69 Wilson, Programme note for *Grinning at the Devil*.

70 Jytte Abildstrøm had produced a staging of the tale in the 1997–98 Riddersalen season with incidental music by Lars Iver Shiller.

71 TCD MS11240 Notebook with sketches for *A Christmas Canticle*.

72 Wilson, *From the Top*, pp. 65–66.

73 This is presumably a recording of the premiere in 1975. For a description see Wilson, *From the Top*, p. 66.

3. FIRST COMPOSITIONAL SUCCESSES

1 Gregor Koenig, Obituary: John Gregory, the *Independent*, 31 October 1996.
2 TCD MS11240 *Evening Echo*, Bournemouth, 16 November 1965.
3 Donald McAlpine to the author, 2 October 2009.
4 Wilson letter to Robert and Clarice Wilson, undated March 1965. The flute and cello pieces do not seem to have materialised.
5 Wilson letter to Clarice Wilson, undated December 1966.
6 O'Kelly, 'Wilson at Seventy', p. 11.
7 Wilson in interview with Dermot Rattigan.
8 Wilson letter to Robert and Clarice Wilson, undated 1966. The religious work is *Three Canticles* opus 14. Eric Porter's poems were used for a piece for the RTÉ Singers, *Idle Winds* opus 16. The work with Chinese verse was never composed.
9 Wilson, *From the Top*, p. 51.
10 The description of male beauty in 'Antique' is dedicated to K.H.W.S., the young Wulff Scherchen whom Britten had been besotted by, while 'Being Beauteous' is dedicated to P.N.L.P., his future partner Peter Pears.
11 Undated letter to Clarice Wilson, November 1966. Naturally, this second rebuff did nothing to improve relations between Paul and Wilson, and Wilson rather gleefully reported Paul's dismissal from RTÉ to his family in the same letter. Undated letter to Clarice Wilson, November 1966.
12 Charles Acton, 'James Wilson's new choral work', *The Irish Times*, 25 January 1967.
13 Wilson in interview with Jonathan Grimes.
14 Wilson, Programme note for *A Woman Young and Old*.
15 Wilson, *From the Top*, p. 58.
16 Ibid., pp. 58–59.
17 Ibid., p. 58.
18 Wilson notes in his memoirs that he paralleled the reference to Mantegna in the text of this song with music derived from the music of the furies in Gluck's *Orfeo ed Euridice*, perhaps an arcane reference to Mantegna's depiction of Orpheus taming Cerberus and a fury in the *Camera degli Sposi* in the Castel San Giorgio, Mantua. Wilson, ibid., p. 59.
19 Wilson, 'Writing a Song Cycle', *Hibernia*, 20 November 1970.
20 Charles Acton, 'Good voice in Song Recital,' *The Irish Times*, 25 November 1968.
21 Wilson, *From the Top*, pp. 53–4. Wilson's setting of the lines highlighted here places a long pause in the vocal line after the word 'fall', and although he then places a phrasing mark after the word 'towers,' as there are no rests before the rest of the line, the resultant sound is 'Angels fall. They are towers from heaven.'
22 Royal Library Denmark, Acc 1978/142 Suppl. Wilson recalled this in a letter to Elsa Gress while discussing the power of her work.
23 Wilson, *From the Top*, p. 54.
24 Robert Johnson, 'Irish Composer at Work', *Sunday Press*, 25 August 1968.
25 Wilson, *From the Top*, p. 54.
26 Ibid., p. 39.
27 Ibid., p. 64.
28 Wilson, 'Writing for the accordion', *Counterpoint*, October 1970, pp. 7–8.

29 Wilson letter to Ian Balfour, undated.

30 Wilson, *From the Top*, p. 64.

31 'Music in Toronto', *Counterpoint*, June 1969, p. 2.

32 Wilson letter to Clarice Wilson, 14 February 1969.

33 In 1970, Wilson reworked these studies as a set of bagatelles for chamber orchestra op. 45.

34 Wilson to the author, 4 August 2005.

35 The influence of Prokofiev's music can still be heard clearly as late as 1967 in the Horn Concerto Wilson wrote shortly after the belated premiere of the symphony.

36 Wilson letter to Robert Wilson, March 1967.

37 Wilson, *From the Top*, p. 57.

38 Wilson letter to Robert and Clarice Wilson, undated September 1967.

39 O'Kelly, 'Wilson at Seventy', pp. 10–11.

40 Intonation in the first performance in 1967 was a problem as the broadcast recording testifies.

41 Wilson letter to Clarice Wilson, 21 August 1971.

42 TCD MS 11240 Wilson letter to C.F.T. Birnie, 16 September 1967.

43 TCD MS11240 notebook with concept sketches for *The Pied Piper of Hamelin*.

44 TCD MS11240 Wilson letter to Julian Budden, undated.

45 Wilson referred to the performance as an inadequate representation of his intentions on a number of occasions. See for example his comments in *From the Top*, p. 59.

46 Wilson letter to Clarice Wilson, undated July/August 1967.

47 Indeed most of the staples of the twentieth-century opera repertoire from Berg to Ligeti have never been performed in Ireland.

48 Royal Library Denmark, Acc 1978/142 Suppl.

49 Robert Johnstone, Premiere of New Opera by Dublin Composer', *Sunday Press*, 31 January 1965.

50 Tony Ó Dálaigh to the author, 5 July 2007.

51 TCD MS11240 Red Notebook of concept sketches.

52 TCD MS11240 Tony Ó Dálaigh undated letter to Wilson, early 1968.

53 Wilson letter to Clarice Wilson, undated March 1968.

54 TCD MS11240 Wilson letter to Tony Ó Dálaigh, 4 December 1968.

55 Wilson letter to Clarice Wilson, undated January/February1969.

56 Wilson letter to Clarice Wilson, November 1969.

57 TCD MS11240 Draft of letter from Wilson to 'Joe,' dated 28 October [?1969].

58 James Wilson, 'A View from the Hebrides', p. 9.

59 Leslie Hotson, *The First Night of Twelfth Night* (London: Mercury Books, 1961), p. 166.

60 Ibid., pp. 143–144, 167–172.

61 TCD MS11240 James Wilson, 'Thoughts on *Twelfth Night*'.

62 TCD MS11240 Libretto for *Twelfth Night*.

63 TCD MS11240 draft of letter from Wilson to 'Joe', dated 28 October [1969?].

64 The references to Italian opera in many reviews give an interesting insight into what was expected by Irish critics in a contemporary opera in the late 1960s and early 1970s.

65 Tony Ó Dálaigh to the author, 5 July 2007.

66 J.J. Finegan, 'Abbey's Weekend of Opera', *Evening Herald*, 22 June 1970.

67 Charles Acton, 'Wexford 1980', *The Irish Times*, 31 October 1980.

68 TCD MS11240 Wilson letter to Chris de Souza, 8 September 1980. Wilson was responding to a letter detailing why the work had been turned down by the BBC for studio recording. While the work was praised for its atmospheric music, it was felt that it lacked both dramatic pacing and contrast.

4.Consolidation of Career

1 Nicholas Wilson to the author, 22 March 2006.

2 O'Kelly, 'Wilson at Seventy', p. 11.

3 Wilson in interview with Jonathan Grimes.

4 Wilson, *From the Top*, p. 70.

5 John Buckley interview with the author, 16 January 2006.

6 Anne Makower to the author, 18 November 2005.

7 Wilson letter to Gerard Gillen, 1 August 1969.

8 Wilson in interview with Ciaran Carty.

9 Wilson, 'Writing a song cycle', p. 13.

10 Royal Library Denmark, Acc1978/142. Wilson letter to Elsa Gress, 12 May 1976.

11 William Mann, 'Inimitable Irish Festival' *The Times*, 4 November 1969.

12 'The Hunting of the Snark' *The Irish Times*, 22 March 1974. This was in response to Charles Acton, 'James Wilson's *Snark* revived', *The Irish Times*, 16 March 1974, in which Acton wrote that 'Wilson had set too many important consonants to percussive sounds . . . In the case of Brian Kissane's authoritative Bellman much of the tessitura was uncomfortably low. I suspect that Brendan Cavanagh . . . was finding that the composer's notes lie very uneasily for the voice . . . Apart therefore from the beautiful Act II sets, the one wholly enjoyable portion was Fit the 7th, where Christine Morris wordlessly mimed "The Banker's Fate" grippingly to clever percussion writing. I liked Anne Makower's production, but came away sure that this slight frolic of an opera needs some hard cutting back, far more taut musical direction and a really slick cast.'

13 Royal Library Denmark, Acc1978/142, Wilson letter to Elsa Gress, 12 May 1976. Acton had noted that the quartet 'sounded well made' and added 'the finale ought to build on these foundations but somehow I did not feel that it was more than good construction.' Charles Acton, 'Testore Quartet's Monkstown Recital', *The Irish Times*, 12 May 1976.

14 Wilson, *From the Top*, p. 107.

15 Ibid., p. 106.

16 See Charles Acton, 'The Music of Modern America', *The Irish Times*, 6 September 1956.

17 Wilson, programme note for *Capricci*.

18 Wilson letter to Clarice Wilson, August 1967.

19 Wilson, *From the Top*, p. 74.

20 Wilson, *Looking back and looking forward*.

21 Ian Fox to the author, 1 June 2006.

22 Reviewer Fanny Feehan detected in this and 'A Glass of Beer' 'many a comfortable dig at the female sex', Feehan, 'The Artistes Deserved a Big Ovation,' *Evening Press*, 5 March 1971.

23 For more on *Inisfail* and its significance see Chris Morash, 'The Little Black Rose

revisited: Church, empire and national destiny in the writings of Aubrey de Vere',
Canadian Journal of Irish Studies, vol. 20, no. 2 (1994), pp. 44–52.

24 Wilson, *From the Top*, p. 65.

25 Ian Fox to the author, 1 June 2006.

26 TCD MS11240 Ian Fox letter to Wilson, undated.

27 Wilson letter to Clarice Wilson, September 1971 and *From the Top*, p. 65. In a pre-
concert talk before the premiere of his third symphony he stated 'there is nothing to
do with war in my music'. Archive of the Contemporary Music Centre Dublin,
CD03/15.

28 Wilson letter to Clarice Wilson, 8 July 1972.

29 Wilson, programme note for *The Táin*.

30 Wilson letter to Clarice Wilson, 8 July 1972.

31 Wilson to Clarice Wilson, undated September 1974. The premiere of Wilson's
Second Symphony followed in 1976.

32 Wilson to Clarice Wilson, undated early 1974.

33 Wilson, Programme note for *Le Bateau Ivre*.

34 Wilson, Programme noote for the premiere of *Le Bateau Ivre*, 15 October 1972.

35 Wilson, *From the Top*, p. 26.

36 The references here are to the lines 'Et l'éveil jaune et bleu des phosphores chanteurs!'
and 'J'ai vu des archipels sidéraux! et des îles/Dont les cieux délirants sont ouverts au
vogueur.'

37 Wilson interview in with Dermot Rattigan.

38 Wilson, Programme note for *Le Bateau Ivre*.

39 Derek Ball to the author, 30 March 2006.

40 I am grateful to Viki Moltke for information regarding Wilson's Danish friends.

41 Royal Library Denmark, MS 2004/81. Elsa Gress to Wilson 8 February 1973 and
14 March 1973. As a result of this loose arrangement with O'Horgan it is his name
rather than Wilson's that appears in the published text as composer of the incidental
music.

42 The patent states that it was designed to work 'efficiently in large, low-speed types, in
small high-speed types and in any intermediate sizes with minimal loss of power
through turbulence or fluid friction . . . wear due to friction will be very slight so that
the pump can operate over long periods without requiring overhaul.' Patent specifi-
cation 1074171, published 28 June 1967.

43 Wilson letter to Clarice Wilson, January 1971. Wilson had previously acted as exam-
iner for the Academy.

44 Wilson letter to Clarice Wilson, 24 January 1973.

45 Derek Ball interview with the author, 30 March 2006.

46 John Buckley interview with the author, 16 January 2006. For more on Buckley's
studies with Wilson see Benjamin Dwyer, *Constellations: The Life and Music of John
Buckley* (Dublin: Carysfort Press, 2011), pp. 15–18.

47 Wilson letter to Clarice Wilson, undated November 1974.

48 Wilson, Programme note for *For Cliodhna*.

49 Wilson, Programme note for Violin Sonata no. 3.

50 Wilson, *From the Top*, p. 70.

51 Wilson letter to Clarice Wilson, undated July 1975.

52 Wilson, Programme Note for Symphony no. 2.

53 In a note in the score Wilson subdivides the second section (giving a total of six sections), noting that the second part 'is centred entirely on the brass', but this subdivision does not reflect a substantive change of material.

54 O'Kelly, 'Wilson at Seventy', p. 10.

55 TCD MS 11240 Wilson letter to Scotus Music Publications Ltd., 1 June 1980.

5. CONNECTIONS WITH DENMARK AND RETURN TO OPERA

1 Wilson letter to Clarice Wilson, 10 June 1977.

2 Wilson, *From the Top*, pp. 72, 76.

3 Jytte Abildstrøm to the author 23 March 2007.

4 Elsa Gress, *The Simurg* (London 1989), p. 191. There is also a later mention of his 'lovely music' for a puppet show based on Wilson's collaboration with Virginia Campbell on a production of Karen Blixen's marionette play *The Revenge of Truth*.

5 Jytte Abildstrøm to the author, 23 March 2007.

6 TCD MS11240 Letter from Stephen Wilkinson to Wilson, January 1972.

7 Wilson, *From the Top*, p. 29.

8 Ibid., p. 52.

9 TCD MS11240 Letter from Stephen Wilkinson to Wilson, 30 January 1978.

10 Wilson, *From the Top*, p. 15.

11 TCD MS11240 Red Notebook with sketches for *The Rape of the Lock*.

12 Ibid.

13 Wilson, *From the Top*, p. 99.

14 Ibid.

15 Ibid.

16 Wilson to Clarice Wilson, undated 1978.

17 Wilson to Clarice Wilson, 8 January 1978.

18 Of course Wilson had used the harp as accompanist for *A Woman Young and Old*, but this is used in the traditional manner as an accompanying instrument rather than as an equal with the voice.

19 Anne Makower to the author, 18 November 2005.

20 Hilary Finch, 'Jane Manning: Wigmore Hall', *The Times*, 30 March, 1983.

21 Gillian Smith to the author 26 March 2010. RTÉ television broadcast a performance of Smith playing one of the Dances in Bulgarian Rhythm on 13 May 1980, after the concerto had been written.

22 Wilson, Programme note for Harpsichord Concerto.

23 Charles Acton, 'NICO Concert in TCD', *The Irish Times*, 26 June 1980. Amusingly when the concerto was repeated at the 1982 Dublin Festival of Twentieth Century Music Acton was to complain that the work contained too much Stravinsky.

24 Wilson to Ian Balfour, undated.

25 This group had originally been founded as the Association of Young Irish Composers by a group of composers including Derek Ball, Gerald Barry, Brian Beckett, Raymond Deane and John Gibson to organise concerts of music by composers of their generation.

26 Eve O'Kelly to the author, 18 July 2007.

27 TCD MS11240 Response to White Paper on Aosdána.

28 Charles Acton, 'Stockhausen brings festival to its climax,' *The Irish Times*, 14 January 1982.

29 Bernard Levin, 'The Nicest Bandwagon you ever saw', *The Times*, 18 March 1981.

30 Ibid.

31 James Wilson, 'Personal View, The James Wilson Column: Aosdána', *Soundpost*, no. 2, June/July 1981, p. 24.

32 The other composers were Seóirse Bodley, Frank Corcoran, Aloys Fleischmann, John Kinsella, Frederick May, Jane O'Leary and Gerard Victory. See Áine Sheil, 'Aosdána', in Harris White and BarraBoydell (eds), *The Encyclopaedia of Music in Ireland* (Dublin: UCD Press, 2013), pp. 27–8.

33 TCD MS11240 Wilson letter to Chris de Souza, 8 September 1980.

34 Ian Fox to the author, 1 July 2006.

35 Zuk, unpublished interview with Wilson.

36 Wilson in interview with Jonathan Grimes.

37 Most Irish composers of this generation who dabbled with twelve, note 'rows' invoked Berg in programme notes to explain their unsystematic approach. For more on this see Gareth Cox, 'The bar of legitimacy? Serialism in Ireland', in Gareth Cox and Julian Horton (eds), *Irish Musical Studies 11: Irish Musical Analysis* (Dublin: Four Courts Press, 2011), pp. 187–201.

38 Particularly if one is to include Berg's early student compositions, the vast majority of his output is vocal.

39 Zuk, unpublished interview with Wilson. He later described the Darmstadt 'school' as 'a totally unmusical thing'. Wilson in interview with Ray Lynott.

40 Wilson in interview with Ciaran Carty.

41 Ian Balfour to the author, 7 December 2005. Wilson, *From the Top*, p. 107.

42 Royal Library Denmark, Acc 1978/142 Supp. 1, Wilson letter to Elsa Gress, 3 March [?].

43 Wilson, Programme note for *Letters to Theo*.

44 Ronit Lentin, 'Making an opera from Van Gogh', *The Irish Times*, 23 November 1984.

45 Though he did point out in a number of interviews how Theo died within months of Vincent of 'a broken heart'.

46 Lentin, 'Making an opera from Van Gogh.'

47 Wilson in interview with Ray Lynott.

48 Wilson letter to Clarice Wilson, undated 1985.

49 *Letters to Theo*, Scene iv.

50 Vincent Van Gogh, *The Letters of Vincent Van Gogh*, ed. Mark Roskill (London: William Collins Sons & Co., 1974), p. 259.

51 Michael Dervan, 'Overkill Opera', *Sunday Tribune* and Charles Acton, 'James Wilson's *Letters from Theo*' [sic], *The Irish Times*, 27 November 1984.

52 The other winners were Felim Egan, Bob Geldof, Seamus Heaney, Neil Jordan, Tom MacIntyre, Pat O'Connor, Graham Reid and Costello Murray and Beaumont architects. Ciaran Carty, 'Our 1984 Arts Awards', *Sunday Independent*, 30 December 1984.

53 Ciaran Carty, 'Getting over a public fear of modern music', *Sunday Independent*, 3 February 1985.

54 Ann Makower to the author, 18 November 2005. TCD MS11240 response to White Paper on Aosdána.

55 Ann Makower to the author, 18 November 2005.

56 James Wilson, Programme note for *Emily Singing*.

57 TCD MS11240 Text sketches for *Emily Singing*.

58 For the arguments about this poem see Emily Jane Brontë, *The Complete Poems*, ed. Janet Gezari, (London: Penguin, 1992), pp. 284–285. While it may be tempting to link these last poems to Wilson's sexuality or to other personal matters it seems clear within the context of this work, and also his *Letters to Theo*, that he was considering the role of the artist and his oft-expressed view that great artists are only recognised by an apathetic public after they are dead.

59 The concert also featured Weill songs and Gerald Barry's *Sur les Points*.

60 Wilson, *From the Top*, p. 93.

61 Charles Acton, 'Cadenza in Irish Programme at Concert Hall', *The Irish Times*, 25 June 1982.

62 John Buckley interview with the author, 16 January 2006. Martin O'Leary interview with the author, 20 July 2006.

63 In 2001 he attended part of the course and gave a lecture. For more on the foundation of the composition summer school see Dwyer, *Constellations*, pp. 84–6.

64 Dwyer, ibid., p. 84 and Wilson, Preliminary notes for *From the Top*.

65 John Buckley interview with the author, 16 January 2006. A good example of what Buckley is talking about is the short piece *Breeze and Calm* (1985) for solo violin and dancer. The work is a compendium of different effects achievable on the violin, encompassing in its seven minute duration every type of pizzicato including normal pizzicato, nail pizzicato, left-hand pizzicato, Bartók pizzicato, a guitar-style pizzicato, and pizzicato glissandi, all forms of harmonics and glissando techniques and various combinations of double, triple and quadruple stopping.

66 Zuk, unpublished interview with Wilson.

67 TCD MS11240 Dorothy Dorow to Wilson, 17 February 1985.

68 Wilson, programme note for *Runes*.

69 Wilson letter to Clarice Wilson, undated November/December 1963.

70 The actress and artist Virginia Campbell had also been a friend of Blixen. *The Revenge of Truth* is mentioned in *The Roads round Pisa*, one of the stories utilised by Gress in her libretto.

71 Royal Library Denmark, Acc 1978/142 Supp 1. Wilson letter to Elsa Gress, undated.

72 Jytte Abildstrøm to the author, 23 March 2007 and TCD MS11240 letter from Wilson to Jytte Abildstrøm with accompanying legal documentation regarding the dispute from 1988.

73 Isak Dinesen, 'The Deluge of Norderney', in idem, *Seven Gothic Tales* (London: Penguin Classics, 2002), p. 187.

74 Gress, *The Simurg*.

75 Gress, *Grinning at the Devil*, Act 1.

76 Gress takes the opportunity to ridicule McCullers, whose work she did not like and felt had been in some cases plagiarised from Blixen's stories and Wilson underpins her lines with a lurching waltz.

77 The story appears in Isak Dinesen, *Carnival: Entertainments and Posthumous Tales* (Chicago: University of Chicago Press, 1977). This section was cut in performance.

78 In his memoirs Wilson recalled 'At an interview with a reporter I mentioned that these two sections had presented problems for me. Elsa turned to me and said "Why didn't you say so? I would have changed them." The humility of a great artist.' Wilson, *From the Top*, p. 89. Ann Makower similarly recalls his reluctance to ask

Gress for any changes. Anne Makower to the author, 18 November 2005.

79 Poul Erik Pind, 'Grinning at the Devil,' *Opera*, vol. 40, no. 6, (June 1989), pp. 716–717.

80 Ian Fox, 'Wilson's Blixen opera scores with the Danes,' *Sunday Tribune*, 12 March 1989.

81 Gus Smith, 'Acclaim for Wilson opera,' *Sunday Independent*, 19 March 1989.

82 Wilson, *From the Top*, p. 76.

6. LATE WORKS

1 In *A Passionate Man* Wilson used synthesiser to fill in percussion parts and to imitate other instrumental sounds. *Stuffed Raspberries* is composed in vocal score but the composer outlined the intended instrumentation and why he chose this combination in conversation with the author, 4 August 2005.

2 Wilson, *From the Top*, p. 87.

3 Wilson in interview with Jonathan Grimes. Wilson remained in contact with Dutilleux and at various times sent him recordings of *Letters to Theo*, *Angel One* and *Menorah*. See Wilson–Dutilleux correspondence TCD MS 11240.

4 Wilson, *From the Top*, p. 107.

5 Dungan, 'An Element of Recklessness', p. 10.

6 Wilson, *From the Top*, pp. 77–78. The pieces referred to are Mozart's *Eine kleine Nachtmusik* K525, Dvořák's Serenade for Strings op. 22, Elgar's Introduction and Allegro for Strings op. 47 and Vaughan Williams' *Fantasia on a Theme by Thomas Tallis*.

7 Wilson letter to Maria Balfour, undated 1991 or 1992. Wilson used *Angel and Harlequin* to illustrate the cover of his CD of chamber and vocal works JWCD01, 2003.

8 Wilson letter to Ian and Maria Balfour, undated.

9 Ronit Lentin, 'Adventures on the viola,' *The Irish Times*, 5 May 1988.

10 Information conflated from an introduction given by Wilson to a 1991 radio broadcast of the work (Archive of the Contemporary Music Centre, RTÉ 389) and *From the Top*, p. 78.

11 'Who's who in the celebration of new Irish music', *The Irish Times*, 16 February 1994.

12 Wilson, Programme note for *Menorah*.

13 Axel Klein, *Die Musik Irlands im 20. Jahrhundert* (Hildesheim: Georg Olms Verlag, 1996), pp. 322–323.

14 Notes by James Wilson for Marco Polo CD8.225027, 2000.

15 The original reads 'Im zweiten Satz dagegen droht die Stimme der Menschlichkeit angesichts einer absurden und unerbittlichen Todesmaschinerie zu verstummen.' Marco Polo CD8.225027, 2000.

16 Gareth Cox, and Axel Klein, 'James Wilson,' in Walter-Wolfgang Sparrer and Hans-Werner Heister, eds., *Komponisten der Gegenwart* (Munich, 1992). Similarly parallels are drawn by Cox between the trumpet fanfares at the close of the work and those from Stravinsky's *Petrouchka* (Stravinsky again being a composer known to have held anti-Semitic views), but it is not likely that the remote resemblance to *Petrouchka* was intentional.

17 These veiled echoes of a universally known melody may have been influenced by the example of Shostakovich's Viola Sonata op. 147, the final movement of which is

haunted by the memory of Beethoven's Piano Sonata op. 27 no. 2 (the 'Moonlight' Sonata). In this context it is worth noting that Wilson, in his programme note, compared the second movement to a Shostakovich scherzo.

18 Gareth Cox, 'Review of *Die Musik Irlands im 20. Jahrhundert* by Axel Klein', in *Music and Letters*, vol. 78, no. 4 (November, 1997), pp. 624–625.

19 Information regarding the original version from TCD MS11240 Letter from Dorothy Dorow to the British Council, 5 October 1992.

20 Wilson letter to Clarice Wilson, undated October 1992.

21 O'Kelly, 'Wilson at Seventy', p. 12.

22 Wilson letter to Ian Balfour, undated 1995.

23 Michael Dervan, 'Celebration', *The Irish Times*, 26 September 1992

24 Wilson letter to Ian Balfour, undated.

25 Jyyte Abildstrøm to the author, 23 March 2007.

26 TCD MS11240 Bruce Arnold and James Wilson, 'Submission to the Opera Development Group, May 27 1996'. I am grateful to Mr Arnold for giving me a copy of the original play to compare with the opera libretto.

27 Wilson, *From the Top*, p. 104.

28 Ibid.

29 Wilson, 'Personal View, The James Wilson Column', *Soundpost*, no. 3, August/September 1981, p. 7.

30 O'Kelly, 'Wilson at Seventy', p. 11. The importance of simplicity is again highlighted in a talk he gave on the music of Michael Tippett, where discussing *The Midsummer Marriage*: he notes, 'It contains a lot of splendid music, but I am reminded of what Verlaine said – at least I think it was Verlaine: "Poetry is not made of ideas it is made of words." And opera is not made of ideas it is made of notes. If the ideas are too complicated, you run the risk of being unintelligible.' TCD MS 11240. I am grateful to Viki Moltke for first drawing my attention to this talk.

31 Wilson's feelings about the plot of *Così fan tutte* fluctuated over the years. In the *Soundpost* article he described it as being, apart from Archie Potter's *The Wedding*, the 'one other opera that I like, whose characters are completely unattractive'.

32 TCD MS11240 Red Notebook with concept sketches.

33 Swift suggested to Gay the idea of creating a 'Newgate Pastoral, among the thieves and whores there'.

34 A similar approach can be found for Vincent's final letter before he commits suicide in *Letters to Theo* or at the moment when Virata addresses the Young Woman having realised that one cannot escape action and responsibility in the eponymous opera. In a letter to Jytte Abildstrøm he described unaccompanied singing as 'a telling device in opera'. I am indebted to Anne Makower for sending me a copy of this letter.

35 One copy of the libretto among Wilson's papers has cuts marked in three different hands.

36 Jane Manning e-mail to the author, 22 August 2009.

37 Anne Makower to the author, 18 November 2005, and Wilson, *From the Top*, p. 91

38 TCD MS 11240 Clarice Wilson letter to James Wilson, 23 May 1994.

39 Information taken from the programme booklet for the premiere of the concerto on 12 December 1997. Smailovič had been playing the Albinoni/Giazotto Adagio.

40 Wilson letter to Maria Balfour, undated June or July 1997.

41 Wilson letter to Ian Balfour, undated.

42 Wilson, *From the Top*, p. 80.

43 Wilson, Programme note for Concertino for Orchestra.

44 Anne Makower to the author, 12 August 2009.

45 Dungan, 'An Element of Recklessness,' p. 10. It is interesting to contrast his association of national identity in these islands with the use of folk music and his dismissal of use of such music with his use of folk music from Mediterranean lands in his earlier years.

46 Wilson letter to Clarice Wilson, undated September 1971.

47 Raymond Deane e-mail to the author, 21 July 2014. The letter signed by Deane, Wilson, Frank Corcoran, Roger Doyle, Fergus Johnson and Ian Wilson stated: We the undersigned composer members of Aosdána, wish to encourage the Irish government to use its position on the UN Security Council to work towards ending the bombing of Afghanistan. While we utterly deplore the September 11th assaults on New York and Washington, we feel that the current campaign, with its mounting toll of civilian fatalities, is inherently unjust and as likely to encourage international terrorism as to defeat it, *The Irish Times*, 14 November 2001.

48 Wilson, Programme note for Symphony no. 3.

49 Wilson, *From the Top*, p. 107.

50 Wilson in conversation with Colman Pearce on the occasion of the premiere of Symphony no. 3, 4 March 2003. Archive of the Contemporary Music Centre, CD03/15.

51 Bruce Arnold e-mail to the author, 20 August 2009.

52 Eve O'Kelly to the author, 18 July 2007.

53 Dungan, 'An Element of Recklessness', p. 9.

54 Jytte Abildstrøm to the author, 23 March 2007.

55 Dungan, 'An Element of Recklessness', p. 9.

56 Anne Makower to the author, 18 November 2005.

57 Wilson to Jytte Abildstrøm, undated 2004/2005.

58 Ibid.

59 Wilson to the author, 4 August 2005.

7. CONCLUSION

1 Royal Library Denmark, Acc1978/142.

2 Anne Makower to the author, 18 November 2005.

3 O'Kelly, 'Wilson at Seventy', p. 12.

4 Wilson letter to Clarice Wilson, 10 January 1970.

5 Cox, 'The bar of legitimacy? Serialism in Ireland', pp. 187–201. Of these only Seóirse Bodley can be said to have engaged thoroughly with serial and integral serial techniques.

6 Mark Fitzgerald, 'Modernism', in White and Boydell (eds), *Encyclopaedia of Music in Ireland*, p. 671.

7 TCD MS11240 On his libretto Wilson noted that the choral writing at the opening was to be modelled on *Così fan tutte*.

8 Ian Balfour, programme note for *Voyage into Darkness*, an operatic treatment of Donald Crowhurst's voyage, a work composed at Wilson's suggestion.

9 Wilson letter to Clarice, Rob and Nicholas Wilson, 16 January [1968?].

10 Wilson letter to Aloys Fleischmann, 17 March 1969, Fleischmann family archive. I

am grateful to the Fleischmann family for providing me with this correspondence.

11 Joe Kehoe, 'RTÉ National Symphony Orchestra', in White and Boydell (eds), *Encyclopaedia of Music in Ireland*, p. 907.

12 Wilson, 'A View from the Hebrides', p. 9. Similarly in interview with Michael Dervan he declared that his response to being passed over in his early years was 'to become angry' and this 'sustained him until he found a public platform'. Michael Dervan, 'Celebration', *The Irish Times*, 26 September 1992.

13 See Gareth Cox, 'Brian Boydell', in White and Boydell, *The Encyclopaedia of Music in Ireland*, p. 115.

14 Anne Makower to the author, 18 November 2005.

15 Zuk, unpublished interview with Wilson.

16 O'Kelly, 'Wilson at Seventy', p. 12.

17 Wilson letter to Clarice Wilson, December 1944.

18 Wilson in interview with Ciaran Carty.

19 Wilson, 'Arts Grants Cuts', *The Irish Times*, 22 February 1986.

20 In the case of Victory his *Olympic Festival* and *Cyrano de Bergerac* overtures and in Potter's *Finnegans Wake* and *Rhapsody under a High Sky*.

21 See http://www.corkcitylibraries.ie/fleischmann100/aloysfleischmann-theworks/digitisationproject/ for further details.

Index

À la recherche du temps perdu (Proust) 9
Abbey Lecture Hall, Dublin 20
Abbey Theatre, Dublin 68, 70
Abildstrøm, Jytte 105, 106, 155, 156, 166, 167–8, 169, 172
Aceldama (Murphy) 163
Aceldama: incidental music (Wilson) 163
Acton, Carol 20
Acton, Charles 20, 29, 49, 70, 74, 116–17, 123, 130, 174
Addinsell, Richard: *Warsaw Concerto* 181
Admiralty, the 5–6, 10, 15, 16
Aeolian Harp (Cowell) 77
Afghanistan 167
Agnew, Elaine 131
Air and Angels (Donne) 111
Air and Angels (Wilson) 111
'Akond of Swat, The' (Lear) 168
Albert Herring (Britten) 13
Alcorn, Michael 131
Almanac (Wilson) 171, 172, 182
Amsterdam 111
Andersen, Hans Christian
    The Bell 169
    Girl Who Trod on a Loaf 106
    The Little Mermaid 167
    The Snail and the Rosetree 169
    The Teapot 169
Angel and Harlequin (Wright) 141, 169
Angel One (Wilson) 141–6
Angel Two (Wilson) 176
Anna Liffey (Wilson) 114
Another Direction (Wilson) 88, 112–13
Aosdána 118–20, 167
Aprahamian, Felix 81, 112, 174
Arabella (Strauss) 64
Áras an Uachtaráin 92
Ariadne auf Naxos (Strauss) 64
Arlecchino (Wilson) 168, 182–3
Arles 9, 122
Arlésienne, L': incidental music (Bizet) 2

Armstrong, Lindsay 114
Arnold, Bruce 156–7, 167
    A Most Confounded Tory 156–7
Arnold, Malcolm 175
Arts Council 68, 74, 81, 117, 118, 119, 125, 165, 166, 168, 180
'As kingfishers catch fire, dragonflies catch flame' (Hopkins) 112
As You Like It (Shakespeare) 171
Association of Irish Composers (AIC) 117, 118, 179
Aufstieg und Fall der Stadt Mahagonny (Weill) 61
Avni, Tzvi 114

Bach, Johann Christian 20
Bach, Johann Sebastian 50, 51
    Die Kunst der Fuge 13
    Mass in B Minor 13
Bachauer, Gina 22–3, 25
Bagatelles for Orchestra (Wilson) 118
Baiser de la fée, Le (Stravinsky) 4
Balfour, Ian 54, 176
Balfour, Maria 162
Ball, Derek 88, 91
Ballets Russes 4
Bardwell, Leland 153
Barrie, J.M.: *Peter Pan* 40
Bartered Bride, The (Smetana) 12
Bartók, Béla 10, 12, 77, 121
    Mikrokosmos 114
    Sonata for Two Pianos and Percussion 12
    Violin Concerto no. 2 12
Bateau Ivre, Le (Wilson) 87–90, 118, 146, 167, 178
BBC (British Broadcasting Corporation) 22, 35, 62, 70–71, 106–7
BBC Midland Orchestra 22
BBC Northern Ireland 22
BBC Northern Singers 107
BBC Philharmonic 146

237

Beckett, Brian 91

Beethoven, Ludwig van 2, 3, 12
    Fidelio 63, 64
    Symphony no. 1 20

Beggar's Opera, The (Gay) 13, 14, 159

Belfast Chamber Opera Group 23, 25

Belfast Festival 49

Bell, The (Andersen) 169

Berg, Alban 13, 25, 120–21, 128

Berliner Requiem (Weill) 128

Berlioz, Hector 15
    Harold en Italie 146

Bernstein, Leonard: *Fancy Free* 13

Birtwistle, Harrison: *Deowa* 114

Bizet, Georges
    L'Arlésienne: incidental music 2
    Carmen 4

'Black Rose, The' (de Vere) 83, 84

Bliss, Arthur: *Checkmate* 4

Blixen, Karen 133–8
    Out of Africa 134
    The Revenge of Truth 133
    Seven Gothic Tales 133, 134, 136

Bodley, Seóirse 21, 118, 120, 174

Bohème, La (Puccini) 4

Boosey & Hawkes 35, 36

Bosnian Community Development Project
    163

Bournemouth 40

Boydell, Brian 20, 21, 26, 179–80, 181–2
    The Maiden and the Seven Devils 180

Boydell, Mary 19, 25, 29, 179

Brahms, Johannes 12–13, 149
    Guten Abend, Gute Nacht 151–2
    Piano Concerto no. 2 22
    Symphony no. 3 8, 12
    Symphony no. 4 8

Braunschweg, Julian 22

Breeze and Calm (Wilson) 154

Bridge, Frank 10, 12

Britten, Benjamin 13–14, 36–7, 76, 173,
    175
    Albert Herring 13
    The Beggar's Opera 13, 14
    Les Illuminations 13, 14, 43
    Let's Make an Opera 23, 26
    The Little Sweep 26, 30–31, 36
    A Midsummer Night's Dream 70
    Noye's Fludde 25–6
    Peter Grimes 13, 14, 58

    The Rape of Lucretia 13, 14
    Variations on a Theme of Frank Bridge 13
    Young Person's Guide to the Orchestra 13

Brontë, Charlotte 126–7

Brontë, Emily 126–8

Browne, Noël 19

Browning, Robert: *The Pied Piper of Hamelin*
    60

Bruch, Max: *Violin Concerto no. 1* 20

Buckley, John 72–3, 91, 92, 131

Budden, Julian 71

Burlesque for Piano and Orchestra (Strauss)
    13

Burns Night (Wilson) 42–4, 107, 177

Burns, Robert 42–3

Burton, Humphrey 35

Byron, George Gordon, Lord 106

Cadíz 17

Cage, John 131

Calder, John 35

Calico Pie (Wilson) 168–9

Callas, Maria 176

Campbell, John 5, 14–16, 17–19, 25, 28,
    29, 35, 43, 91, 95–6, 105, 167

Campbell, Virginia 133

Canada 22, 56, 57

Canticle for Christmas (Wilson) 39, 104

Čapek, Karel 3

Capricci (Wilson) 76, 77–81

Carmen (Bizet) 4

Carrion Comfort (Wilson) 49–53, 62, 107

Carroll, Lewis
    The Hunting of the Snark 26, 30
    Jabberwocky 30

Cashmore, John 125, 134

Catholic church 19

censorship 19

Ceremonies (Wilson) 25, 141

Chamisso, Adelbert von 45–6

Chappell 81

Chaucer, Geoffrey: 'Now welcome summer'
    171

Chauveton, Michel 25

Checkmate (Bliss) 4

Chekhov, Anton 3

Chesterton, G.K.: *The Man who was Thurs-*
    day 176

Childers, Erskine 36, 92

Chopin, Frédéric: *Les Sylphides* 5

Index

Christmas Rose, The (Lagerlöf) 168
Christmas Rose, The (Wilson) 168
Churchill, Winston 6, 7
City Shower, A (Swift) 83, 84
Civic Museum, Dublin 23–4
Clarke, Rhona 131
Cleary, Siobhán 131
Cocteau, Jean: *The Wedding on the Eiffel Tower* 106
Coláiste Mhuire, Ennis 131–2, 174, 179
Coleridge, Samuel Taylor: 'Frost at Midnight' 171
Colette 31
College of the Sea 8–9
Collegiate Theatre, London 87
Colloquy (Wilson) 92–3
Concertino (Wilson) 163–5
Concerto for Harpsichord and Chamber Orchestra (Wilson) 114–17, 118
Concorde 168, 182
Contemporary Music Centre 117, 163, 168, 177, 181, 182
Copenhagen 38–9, 104–5, 133–4, 138, 156, 171–2
Copenhagen String Quartet 56
Corbett, Geoffrey 22
Corcubión 17
Cork Ballet Company 60
Cork International Choral Festival 106–7
Così fan tutte (Mozart) 158, 172
Côte d'Azur 18
Counterpoint 54, 57
Coward, Noel 19
Cowell, Henry 77
Cox, Gareth 151, 153, 174
Crete 14
Crowhurst, Donald 176
Cultural Relations Committee of Ireland 25
Cunningham, Merce 131
Curwen Edition 81
Cynara (Dowson) 22

Damrosch, Walter 23
Dance around the Golden Calf (Schoenberg) 174
Dances for a Festival (Wilson) 118
Darley, George: 'Sea Ritual' 83–4
Davies, Peter Maxwell 120
    Eight Songs for a Mad King 120
    Miss Donnithorne's Maggot 120

de Basil, Wassily 5
de Bromhead, Jerome 91
de Souza, Chris 71
de Valois, Ninette 4, 60
de Vere, Aubrey: 'The Black Rose' 83, 84
Deane, Raymond 167
Debussy, Claude 3, 10, 12, 77, 175
    Jeux 164
Deering, Richard 118
Delibes, Léo: *Sylvia* 18
Denmark 8, 38–9, 56, 90–91, 104–6, 121, 133–4, 138, 156, 171–2
Deowa (Birtwistle) 114
Derry 9
Diaghilev, Sergei 4
Dickens, Charles 3
Dickie, Brian 64
Dinesen, Isak *see* Blixen, Karen
Dingley, Rebecca 157, 161
Ditto Daughter? (Gress) 90–91, 104–5
Ditto Daughter?: incidental music (Wilson) 90–91, 104–5
Diversions on a Theme by Handel (Wilson) 73, 81
Divertimento for Strings (Wilson) 22, 24, 40, 141
Dolin, Anton 22, 40
Don Carlos (Schiller) 159
Don Carlos (Verdi) 159
Don Giovanni (Mozart) 4, 137
Don Juan (Strauss) 13
Donizetti, Gaetano: *Lucia di Lammermoor* 158
Donizetti Variations (Wilson) 182
Donne, John: *Air and Angels* 111
Donoghue, Denis 21
Donohue, Peter 107
Dorow, Dorothy 111, 132–3, 153–4
Dowden, Edward: 'Swallows' 83, 84, 86
Dowson, Ernest: *Cynara* 22
Doyle, Deirdre 117
Doyle, Roger 91–2
Drinkwater, John 3
Drury Byrne, Aisling 162
Dublin 15, 16, 17, 19–30, 40, 45, 62, 64, 68, 70, 77, 81, 91–2, 104, 111–12, 118, 173, 177
Dublin Festival of Twentieth Century Music 81, 111–12, 118, 120, 140, 154, 174, 175

Dublin Grand Opera Society 62
Dublin Orchestral Players 19, 20, 24, 26,
    27, 29, 57, 180
Duffy, Gerry 63
Dún Laoghaire 17
Dunne, Veronica 82, 84, 85–6
Dutilleux, Henri 140, 175
    Metaboles 140
Dvořák, Antonín 12

'Echo' (Moore) 83
Edwards, Hilton 35, 60
Eight Songs for a Mad King (Davies) 120
Elgar, Edward 11, 140, 146
Eliot, T.S.: *The Waste Land* 2, 8–9, 11
Ellegaard, Mogens 53, 56, 57, 111
Ellesborough, Buckinghamshire 1, 6
Emily Singing (Wilson) 126–8
Enfant et les sortilèges, L' (Ravel) 31
Enjoying (Wilson) 168
Epithalamion (Wilson) 57
Erdesz, Otto 146
Esther (Wilson) 20–21, 57
Explorations (Wilson) 154

Faber Music 81
Façade (Walton) 13, 168
Falla, Manuel de 114
Fancy Free (Bernstein) 13
Fand (Wilson) 86
Fantasia on a Theme by Thomas Tallis
    (Vaughan Williams) 8, 11
Fauré, Gabriel 10
Faust (Gounod) 63
Feis Ceoil 117
Fermor, Paddy Leigh 14
Fidelio (Beethoven) 63, 64
Fielding, Xan 14–15
Fiery Angel (Prokofiev) 158
Finchley Children's Group 37
Finnegans Wake (Joyce) 129–30
Firebird, The (Stravinsky) 18
Fisherman and his Wife, The (Brothers
    Grimm) 168
Fisherman and his Wife, The (Wilson) 168
Fleischmann, Aloys 176–7, 181–2
folk music 18–19, 22, 85, 166
For Cliodhna (Wilson) 163
For Sarajevo (Wilson) 161–3, 166
Forrester, Maureen 153

Forsyth, Cecil: *Orchestration* 8
Fourth Canticle (Wilson) 44, 53
Fox, Ian 62, 83, 84–5, 138
Fragments of Stone (Campbell) 17
France 9, 18
Frauenliebe und Leben (Schumann) 45–6
'Frost at Midnight' (Coleridge) 171

Gaiety Theatre, Dublin 40
Gallagher, Mary 93
Galsworthy, John 3
Gardner, Stephen 131
Gate Theatre, Dublin 35, 64, 138
Gauguin, Paul 122
Gay, John: *The Beggar's Opera* 13, 14, 159
Gentile, Daimi 105, 166
Gibraltar 17–18
Gielgud, John 16
Gilbert, W.S. 15
Gillen, Gerard 73
Ginsberg, Alan 106
Girl Who Trod on a Loaf (Andersen) 106
'Glass of Beer, A' (Stephens) 83, 84
Gluck, Christoph Willibald: *Orfeo ed*
    Euridice 106
Glyndebourne 70
Goehr, Walter 13
Golani, Rivka 146–7, 153
Gordon, Gavin: *The Rake's Progress* 4, 67
Gösta Berling's Saga (Lagerlöf) 21
Gounod, Charles
    Faust 63
    Mireille 158
Gramophone 81
Great Ormond Street Hospital 40
Greece 14, 18, 32
Greer, Germaine 106
Greevy, Bernadette 44, 53, 63, 104
Gregory, John 40
Gresham Hotel, Dublin 28
Gress, David 90–91
Gress, Elsa 82, 90–91, 104–6, 121, 133–9
    Ditto Daughter? 90–91, 104–5
    Grinning at the Devil 133–9, 140, 178
    Scapegoat 105–6
    The Simurg 105
Grimm, brothers: *The Fisherman and his*
    Wife 168
Grimoire (Wilson) 182
Grimson, Brian 19, 25, 26, 27, 29, 36

Grinning at the Devil (Gress/Wilson) 133–9, 140, 178
Guevara, Ernesto 'Che' 106
Guillaume, Edith 134, 166
Gulbenkian Foundation 74
Gulliver's Travels (Swift) 157
Guten Abend, Gute Nacht (Brahms) 151–2

Hacker, Alan 53, 114
Hadley, Patrick 180
Handel, George Frideric 23–4
    Semele 137
Handley, Vernon 87
Harawi (Messiaen) 114
Harboe, Thorkild 8, 91
Harkin, Jim 62, 96
Harlequin Ballet 40
Harley, Robert 159
Harold en Italie (Berlioz) 146
Harrison, Bernard 117
Hatton, Denys Finch 135–7
Hemingway, Ernest 106
Hess, Myra 6
Highbury County School 1–3, 5
Hill, Derek 64
Hilvershum 111
Hinchcliffe, Irving 9
Hindemith, Paul 13
Holocaust 140, 146–7, 151
Honegger, Arthur 12, 13
    Le roi David 12
Hopkins, Gerard Manley 49–50, 53, 107
    'As kingfishers catch fire, dragonflies catch flame' 112
    'I wake and feel the fell of dark, not day' 50
    'The Leaden Echo and the Golden Echo' 53
    'Moonrise' 112
    'My own heart let me more have pity on' 50
    'No worst, there is none' 50
    'Not, I'll not, carrion comfort, Despair, not feast on thee' 50
    'Patience, hard thing! the hard thing but to pray' 50
    'The shepherd's brow, fronting forked lightning' 50
    'Thou art indeed just, Lord, if I contend with thee' 50

'The Windhover' 112
The Wreck of the Deutschland 53
Horn Concerto (Wilson) 118
Horoscope (Lambert) 4
Hotson, Leslie 65
Hugh the Drover (Vaughan Williams) 4
Hunt, Leigh: *Jenny Kissed Me* 10
Hunting of the Snark, The (Carroll) 26, 30
Hunting of the Snark, The (Wilson) 26–37, 62, 72, 75–6, 81, 91, 92, 158, 173
Huxley, Aldous 3

'I am of Ireland' (anon.) 132–3
'I wake and feel the fell of dark, not day' (Hopkins) 50
Ibsen, Henrik 3
'If all the world were paper' (anon.) 132
Ijsbreker, Amsterdam 111
Illuminations, Les (Britten) 13, 14, 43
Impulsive, HMS 7–9
Ingoldsby, Marian 131
Inori (Stockhausen) 118
Irish Composers Centre 117
Irish Independent 20–21
Irish Music Rights Organisation 117
Irish National Opera 62–4, 68, 70, 74
Irish Press 20, 62
Irish Songs (Wilson) 82–4, 86
Irish Times 20, 43–4, 75–6, 146
Ischia 18, 22
Israel 146–7
'It was a lover and his lass' (Shakespeare) 171
Italy 18

J&W Chester Ltd 35–6
Jabberwocky (Carroll) 30
Jacob, Gordon 8
Jagger, Mick 106
James, David 154
'Jamie come try me' (Burns) 43
Janáček, Leoš 125, 140
Järnefelt, Armas 20
Jeux (Debussy) 164
Jellett, Bay 29
Jellett, Mainie 29
Jenny Kissed Me (Hunt) 10
Johnson, Esther 156, 157
Johnstone, Robert 20
Josef Weinberger Ltd 81
Joyce, James 128–30

Julius Caesar (Shakespeare) 74, 176
Julius Caesar (Wilson) 74, 176

Kagel, Mauricio 118
Kerr, Virginia 126
Kerrigan, Aylish 153
King of the Golden River (Ruskin) 37–8
King of the Golden River (Wilson) 37–9
Kinsella, John 174
Klee, Paul 141
Klein, Axel 147
Kontarsky, Alfons 118
Kontarsky, Aloys 118
Kraglund, John 57
Kunst der Fuge, Die (Bach) 13
Kvalbein, Aage 132–3

Lady Macbeth of Mtsensk (Shostakovich) 158
Lake Isle of Innisfree (Yeats) 2
Lagerlöf, Selma
    The Christmas Rose 168
    Gösta Berling's Saga 21
Laing, David 25
Lambert, Constant: *Horoscope* 4
Lawrence, D.H. 3, 132
Le Fanu, Nicola 114
'Leaden Echo and the Golden Echo, The'
    (Hopkins) 53
Leaden Echo and the Golden Echo, The
    (Wilson) 53
Lear, Edward 168
Leeson, Victor 25, 28
Legend of the Third Dove (Wilson) 155, 168
'Legend of the Third Dove' (Zweig) 155, 168
Leonard, Catherine 93
Let's Make an Opera (Britten) 23, 26
Letters to Theo (Wilson) 50, 120, 121–6,
    127, 140
Lever, Charles: 'The Widow Malone' 83
Levin, Bernard 118–19
Ligeti, György 77
Lisbon 17
Little Mermaid, The (Andersen) 167
Little Mermaid, The (Wilson) 167
Little Sweep, The (Britten) 26, 30–31, 36
London 1–2, 6, 9–16, 35, 82, 87, 173
London Festival Ballet 22
London Philharmonic Orchestra 87, 178
Lucia di Lammermoor (Donizetti) 158
Lutosławski, Witold 140, 142, 175

Lynch, Charles 77, 81, 104

McAlpine, Donald 21–2, 40
McAlpine, Phyllida (née Porter) 21–2, 27, 29
McBrien, Peter 63
McCullers, Carson 136
McDonagh, Donagh 25
McElwee, Patrick 64
McGuinness, Norah 20
MacLiammóir, Micheál 35
Magic Flute, The see *Zauberflöte, Die* (Mozart)
Mahratta, HMS 7
Maiden and the Seven Devils, The (Boydell)
    180
Mailer, Norman 106
Majorca 18
Makower, Anne 35, 36, 63, 64, 73, 104,
    112, 125, 134, 156, 171–2, 180
Man who was Thursday, The (Chesterton)
    176
Mann, William 74
Manning, Jane 45, 53, 87, 111–12, 113,
    114, 161, 168, 178
Mantra (Stockhausen) 118
Marcerollo, Joe 57
Marienborg Castle, Denmark 90–91
Markova, Alicia 40
Marten Toonder Award 165–6
Martin, Frank 13
Martin, Philip 76
Masham, Abigail 159
Maskall, Mary 2
Mass in B Minor (Bach) 13
May, Frederick 21
'May in Monkstown' concerts 104, 177
Mayer, Dorothy, Lady (née Moulton) 23,
    26–7, 28, 35
Mayer, Sir Robert 23
Mediterranean 17, 167, 173
Menorah (Wilson) 146–53, 162, 163, 166
Merton, Philip 14, 17
Messiaen, Olivier: *Harawi* 114
Metaboles (Dutilleux) 140
Meyerbeer, Giacomo 3
Midsummer Night's Dream, A (Britten) 70
Midsummer Night's Dream, A (Shakespeare) 70
Mid-West Arts 131
Mikrokosmos (Bartók) 114
Milhaud, Darius 10
Miller, Arthur 136

Milner, Guy 27
minimalism 13, 175
Mireille (Gounod) 158
Miss Donnithorne's Maggot (Davies) 120
Mitchell, Donald 81
modernism 121, 174–5
Moltke, Peter 91
Monkstown 15, 104, 177
Monroe, Marilyn 136
Monteverdi, Claudio: *Vespers of 1610* 13
'Moonrise' (Hopkins) 112
Moore, Henry 2
Moore, Thomas 106
    'Echo' 83
    'Music at Night' 83, 84
Morante, Isla 10, 21
Moriarty, Joan Denise 60
Most Confounded Tory, A (Arnold) 156–7
Mother and Child Scheme 19
Moulton, Gun (née Kronzell) 44, 63
Moulton, Herbert 28–9, 39, 44, 49, 62, 63,
    67–8, 70, 74
Mount Jerome Crematorium, Dublin 172
Mount Temple School, Dublin 36
Mozart, Wolfgang Amadeus 3, 6, 12, 63
    Così fan tutte 158, 172
    Don Giovanni 4, 137
    Le Nozze di Figaro 63, 64
    Oboe Quartet 6, 172
    Piano Concerto in C Minor 18
    Die Zauberflöte 18, 157, 158
Mulvey, Gráinne 131
Murmansk 7
Murphy, Jim: *Aceldama* 163
Music Association of Ireland (MAI) 19–20,
    21, 23, 25, 28, 77, 81, 180
'Music at Night' (Moore) 83, 84
Music for a Mechanical Organ (Wilson) 106
Music for a Temple (Wilson) 57, 81
Music hath Mischief, The (Victory) 62
Musikverlag Josef Preisler 57
'My own heart let me more have pity on'
    (Hopkins) 50

National Gallery, London 6
National Symphony Orchestra 154, 163, 165
Nativity Ode (Wilson) 104
Naxos/Marco Polo 163, 165
Neel, Boyd 13, 15, 22, 24, 25, 56, 57
Nelson, Havelock 23, 25, 26, 27, 50–51

Netherlands 111, 122
New Irish Record Company 77
New Simplicity 175
Nichols, Kevin 153
Nicolet, Verner 134, 140, 182
Nighttown (Wilson) 128–9
'No worst, there is none' (Hopkins) 50
Noces, Les (Stravinsky) 13, 60
Nordheim, Arne 118, 132
Northern Ireland 166
Norway 5
'Not, I'll not, carrion comfort, Despair, not
    feast on thee' (Hopkins) 50
Novello 81
'Now welcome summer' (Chaucer) 171
Noye's Fludde (Britten) 25–6
Nozze di Figaro, Le (Mozart) 63, 64
Nutcracker, The (Tchaikovsky) 4

'O whistle, an' I'll come to ye, my lad' (Burns)
    43
Oboe Quartet (Mozart) 6, 172
O'Conor, John 104
Ó Dálaigh, Tony 63
*Ode on a Favourite Cat, Drowned in a Tub of
    Goldfishes* (Wilson) 42
O'Doherty, David 93
Ogina, Naomi 153
O'Grady, Geraldine 93, 104
O'Horgan, Tom 91, 133
O'Kelly, Eve 41
O'Kelly, Pat 138
Old Wives' Tale (Peele) 132
O'Neill, Joseph 20–21
Only Jealousy of Emer (Yeats) 106
Only Jealousy of Emer: incidental music
    (Wilson) 106
Opera Theatre Company 62, 138
Orchestration (Forsyth) 8
Orfeo ed Euridice (Gluck) 106
Orford Quartet 57
Ó Riada, Seán 21, 175
Out of Africa (Blixen) 134
Oxford University Press 35

Parr, James 112
Passionate Man, A (Wilson) 9, 14, 140, 155,
    156–61
'Patience, hard thing! the hard thing but to
    pray' (Hopkins) 50

Paul, Tibor 24, 43, 63, 178
Pearce, Colman 12, 57, 58, 59, 86, 125,
    156, 163, 167, 177
Pearl and Unicorn (Wilson) 146, 163
Peele, George: *Old Wives' Tale* 132
'Peg Nicholson' (Burns) 42–3
Performing Rights Society (PRS) 82, 117
Pergolesi, Giovanni Battista: *Stabat Mater* 8
Peter Grimes (Britten) 13, 14, 58
Peter Pan (Barrie) 40
Piano Concerto (Wilson) 22–3
Piano Concerto in C Minor (Mozart) 18
Piano Concerto no. 2 (Brahms) 22
Pied Piper of Hamelin (Browning) 60
Pied Piper of Hamelin (Wilson) 60–62, 107
Pierrot Lunaire (Schoenberg) 13, 52
Pind, Poul Erik 138
Pitcairn, HMS 9
Plurabelle (Wilson) 128, 129–31
Poema Sarda (Wilson) 23, 24
Pope, Alexander 106, 108–9
popular songs 159–60
Porter, Eric Horsbrugh 20, 21, 29, 42
Portugal 17
Potter, Archie 21, 91, 174, 180, 181–2
Poulenc, Francis 10
Prokofiev, Sergei 11, 12, 57–8
    The Fiery Angel 158
    Symphony no. 2 58
    Symphony no. 3 58
Promenade Concerts 13
Proust, Marcel: *À la recherche du temps perdu*
    9
Puccini, Giacomo 63
    La Bohème 4
    Turandot 158

'Quangle Wangle's Hat, The' (Lear) 168
Quick, Simon 29
Quintet for Accordion and Strings (Wilson)
    53–7, 59, 81, 182

Radio Éireann symphony orchestra *see* RTÉ
    Symphony Orchestra
Rake's Progress (Gordon) 4, 67
Rape of Lucretia (Britten) 13, 14
Rape of the Lock (Pope) 108–9
Rape of the Lock (Wilson) 108–11
Ravel, Maurice 3, 5, 12, 14, 31, 48, 77,
    128, 175

Records and Recording 81
Reede, Rien de 111
Residente Orchestra, The Hague 111
Revenge of Truth (Blixen) 133
Revenge of Truth: incidental music (Wilson)
    133
Reykjavik 7
Rheingold, Das (Wagner) 151
Riddersalen Theatre, Copenhagen 38–9,
    104–5, 121, 134, 138, 171–2
Rima (Wilson) 76
Rimbaud, Arthur 87
Rimsky-Korsakov, Nikolai: *The Snow Maiden*
    4
Ring, Patrick 63
Roi David, Le (Honegger) 12
Roi de l'Ille, Le (Wilson) 21
Ronsard, Pierre de 10
Rosen, Albert 87, 125, 178
Rosen, Hans Waldemar 41–2, 43, 62, 64
Rosenkavalier, Der (Strauss) 13, 64
Rossini, Gioachino 63
Rowley, Alec 9–11, 173
Royal College of Surgeons 172
Royal Dublin Society 76
Royal Irish Academy of Music 28, 91, 117,
    120, 179
Royal Navy 6–9, 88
Royal Theatre, Copenhagen 133–4, 178
RTÉ (Radió Telefís Éireann) 24, 25, 35, 53,
    68, 81, 82, 125–6, 162–3, 177,
    181
RTÉ Singers 41, 43, 60, 62, 64, 109
RTÉ Symphony Orchestra 19, 24, 57, 62,
    63, 64, 87, 178, 180, 181–2
Runes (Wilson) 132–3, 154
Rungstedlund Foundation 134
Ruskin, John: *The King of the Golden River*
    37–8
Ryan, Paddy 63

Sadler's Wells, London 4, 5, 13, 21–2, 60,
    70
St Patrick's Hospital, Dublin 156
St Stephen's Church, Dublin 125
Salzedo, Carlos 163
Sandford Park School 27, 29
Sarajevo 161
Sardinia 18
Scapa Flow 7

Scapegoat (Gress/Wilson) 105–6
Scharnhorst (German battleship) 7
Schiller, Friedrich: *Don Carlos* 159
Schoenberg, Arnold 23, 120, 174
    Dance around the Golden Calf 174
    Pierrot Lunaire 13, 52
Schubert, Franz 3, 8, 12
Schumann, Elizabeth 8
Schumann, Robert 12
    Frauenliebe und Leben 45–6
Scottish Opera 70
Scotus Music Publications 118
'Sea Ritual' (Darley) 83–4
Second World War 5–9, 14, 155, 180
Semele (Handel) 137
serialism 120–21, 174–5
Seven Gothic Tales (Blixen) 133, 134, 136
Seventh Canticle (Wilson) 104
Shakespeare, William
    As You Like It 171
    'It was a lover and his lass' 171
    Julius Caesar 74, 176
    A Midsummer Night's Dream 70
    Sonnet no. 55 95–6
    Twelfth Night 64–5, 67, 70, 174
Shaw, George Bernard 3
'Shepherd's brow, fronting forked lightning,
    The' (Hopkins) 50
Sheridan, Mary 104
Sherriff, R.C. 3
Shostakovich, Dmitri: *Lady Macbeth of
    Mtsensk* 158
Sibelius, Jean 8, 12
Simurg, The (Gress) 105
Sinfonia Domestica (Strauss) 13
Sirius (Stockhausen) 114
Sitwell, Edith: *Street Songs* 8
Six Chansons de Ronsard pour des voix divers
    (Wilson) 10
Sleeping Princess, The (Tchaikovsky) 4, 18
Smailovič, Vedran 161, 163
Smale, Alan 93, 131, 146, 153, 162, 163
Smetana, Bedřich: *The Bartered Bride* 12
Smith, Gillian 114
Smith, Olive 25, 28, 114
Smyth, Ethel: *The Wreckers* 4
Snail and the Rosetree, The (Andersen) 169
Snake (Lawrence) 132
Snow Maiden, The (Rimsky-Korsakov) 4
Society for the Promotion of New Music 87

Sonata for Cor Anglais and Piano (Wilson)
    114
Sonata for Two Pianos and Percussion (Bartók)
    12
Sonatina (Wilson) 168, 182
Sonatina for Alto Flute (Wilson) 182
Sonnet no. 55 (Shakespeare) 95–6
Soundpost 118–20, 157–8
Spain 17, 18
Spanish Arch (Wilson) 182
Stabat Mater (Pergolesi) 8
Stahl, Hendrik 133
Stephens, James: 'A Glass of Beer' 83, 84
Stiven, Nadia 29
Stockhausen, Karlheinz
    Inori 118
    Mantra 118
    Sirius 118
Stockhausen, Markus 118
Stockholm 133
Strauss, Richard 157
    Arabella 64
    Ariadne auf Naxos 64
    Burlesque for Piano and Orchestra 13
    Don Juan 13
    Der Rosenkavalier 13, 64
    Sinfonia Domestica 13
Stravinsky, Igor 3, 12, 23, 116–17, 121,
    175
    Le baiser de la fée 4
    The Firebird 18
    Les Noces 13, 60
    Symphonies of Wind Instruments 147
Street Songs (Sitwell) 8
Streich, Rita 76
String Quartet no. 1 (Wilson) 76, 104
String Quartet no. 3 (Wilson) 169
Stuffed Raspberries (Wilson) 140, 171–2
Suite for Brass Band (Wilson) 22
Sullivan, Arthur 15
Sunflowers (Van Gogh) 126
Swallow, Keith 107
'Swallows' (Dowden) 83, 84, 86
Swan Lake (Tchaikovsky) 106
Swift, Jonathan 156, 158–60
    A City Shower 83, 84
    Gulliver's Travels 157
Sylphides, Les (Chopin) 5
Sylvia (Delibes) 18
Symphonic Variations (Wilson) 76, 129

Symphonies of Wind Instruments (Stravinsky) 147

Symphony no. 1 (Beethoven) 20

Symphony no. 1 (Wilson) 12, 24–5, 57–9, 82, 174, 177

Symphony no. 2 (Prokofiev) 58

Symphony no. 2 (Wilson) 72, 95–103, 183

Symphony no. 3 (Brahms) 8, 12

Symphony no. 3 (Prokofiev) 58

Symphony no. 3 (Wilson) 146, 167

Symphony no. 4 (Brahms) 8

Symphony no. 6 (Tchaikovsky) 87

Symphony no. 6 (Vaughan Williams) 13

Táin, The (Wilson) 81, 84–6

Tait, Reg 3, 6

Tam O'Shanter (Wilson) 42, 107, 177

Tappe, Clara 2

Tauber, Richard 181

Tchaikovsky, Pyotr Ilyich 53
   The Nutcracker 4
   The Sleeping Princess 4, 18
   Swan Lake 106
   Symphony no. 6 87

Tcherepnin, Alexander 56–7

Teapot, The (Andersen) 169

Thames Publishing 82

Thermagistris (Wilson) 76–7, 81

Three Birds (Wilson) 44

Three Hans Andersen Tales (Wilson) 169

Three Playthings (Wilson) 168, 182

Three Yeats Songs (Wilson) 53

'Thou art indeed just, Lord, if I contend with thee' (Hopkins) 50

Times, The 75, 114, 118–19

Timoney, Therese 93

Tippett, Michael 162

Tom O'Bedlam (Wilson) 42

Toronto 22, 56, 57

Trefoil (Wilson) 44, 49

Trinity College, Dublin 21, 25, 44, 180

Trinity College of Music, London 9–11

Trio (Wilson) 166–7

Trovatore, Il (Verdi) 4, 158

Trumpet Concerto (Wilson) 118

Turandot (Puccini) 158

Turkey 18

Twelfth Night (Shakespeare) 64–5, 67, 70

Twelfth Night (Wilson) 12, 59, 62–71, 74, 82, 158

Two Pieces for Bass Clarinet (Wilson) 182

Umbrage for Orchestra and Six Music Critics (Wilson) 180

Undesirables (Wilson) 153–4, 182

United States 56–7, 136, 167

Upon Silence (Wilson) 168

Van Gogh, Vincent 9, 120, 121–6

Vanhomrigh, Hester 156, 157, 159–60

Variations on a Theme of Frank Bridge (Britten) 13

Vaughan Williams, Ralph 11
   Fantasia on a Theme by Thomas Tallis 8, 11
   Hugh the Drover 4
   Symphony no. 6 13

Verbecke, Tina 153

Verdi, Giuseppe
   Don Carlos 159
   Il Trovatore 4, 158

Vespers of 1610 (Monteverdi) 13

Victory, Gerard 24, 121, 174, 180, 181–2
   The Music hath Mischief 62

Violin Concerto (Wilson) 25

Violin Concerto no. 1 (Bruch) 20

Violin Concerto no. 2 (Bartók) 12

Violin Sonata no. 2 (Wilson) 92, 104

Violin Sonata no. 3 (Wilson) 93–5, 154

Violin Sonata no. 5 (Wilson) 169

Violin Sonata no. 6 (Wilson) 169–71, 182

Virata (Wilson) 9, 155–6, 166

'Virata or the Eyes of the Dying Brother' (Zweig) 155

Wagner, Richard: *Das Rheingold* 151

Walker, James 75

Walton, William 57
   Façade 13, 168

Warlock, Peter 10

Warsaw Concerto (Addinsell) 181

Waste Land, The (Eliot) 2, 8–9, 11

Waterloo Music Company 57

Wedding on the Eiffel Tower (Cocteau) 106

Wedding on the Eiffel Tower: incidental music (Wilson) 106

Weill, Kurt
   Aufstieg und Fall der Stadt Mahagonny 61
   Berliner Requiem i128

Wendover 6

Wesley College, Dublin 26, 27, 28
Wexford Festival 22, 62, 64, 70
'Widow Malone, The' (Lever) 83
Wigmore Hall, London 77, 114
'Wild swans at Coole, The' (Yeats) 171
Wildwood 153–4, 182
Wilkinson, Stephen 106–8, 177
William Byrd Singers 107–8
Wilson, Alex 1, 3
Wilson, Clarice (née Jeffery) 6, 24, 27, 86,
    111–12, 133
Wilson, Edgar 1
Wilson, James
  atheism 3, 50
  birth 1
  considers career in music 8
  death and funeral 172
  early compositions 8–9, 10, 11–12, 20–
    23
  early life 1–5
  education 1–3, 5
  fails civil service interview 14
  family background 1
  Irish citizenship 166
  and John Campbell 14–16, 17–19, 28,
    91, 95–6, 105, 167
  moves to Dublin 17, 19–21, 173, 177
  musical education 2, 3–5, 8–12
  musical influences 11–14, 57–8
  nominated to Aosdána 120
  publishing of works 35, 57, 81–2, 118
  radio work 104, 120
  receives Marten Toonder Award 165–6
  recordings of works 62, 81, 82, 111,
    133, 153, 154, 163, 165, 167–
    9, 182–3
  reviews of works 20–21, 35–6, 62, 68,
    70, 75–6, 81, 86, 116–17, 123,
    130, 138, 161
  service with Royal Navy 6–9, 88
  sexuality 8, 15–16, 19, 25
  social life 19
  Soundpost column 118–20, 157–8
  teaches at Ennis summer school 131–2,
    174, 179
  teaches at Royal Irish Academy 91–2,
    120, 179
  travel 5, 9, 17–19, 146–7
  work at the Admiralty 5–6, 10, 15, 16
  work with music organisations 117–18

works
  Aceldama: incidental music 163
  Air and Angels 111
  Almanac 171, 172, 182
  Angel One 141–6
  Angel Two 176
  Anna Liffey 114
  Another Direction 88, 112–13
  Arlecchino 168, 182–3
  Bagatelles for Orchestra 118
  Le Bateau Ivre 87–90, 118, 146,
    167, 178
  Breeze and Calm 154
  Burns Night 42–4, 107, 177
  Calico Pie 168–9
  Canticle for Christmas 39, 104
  Capricci 76, 77–81
  Carrion Comfort 49–53, 62, 107
  Ceremonies 25, 141
  The Christmas Rose 168
  Colloquy 92–3
  Concertino 163–5
  *Concerto for Harpsichord and
    Chamber Orchestra* 114–17, 118
  Dances for a Festival 118
  Ditto Daughter?: incidental music
    90–91, 104–5
  Diversions on a Theme by Handel 73,
    81
  Divertimento for Strings 22, 24, 40,
    141
  Donizetti Variations 182
  Emily Singing 126–8
  Enjoying 168
  Epithalamion 57
  Esther 20–21, 57
  Explorations 154
  Fand 86
  The Fisherman and his Wife 168
  For Cliodhna 163
  For Sarajevo 161–3, 166
  Fourth Canticle 44, 53
  Grimoire 182
  Grinning at the Devil 133–9, 140,
    178
  Horn Concerto 118
  The Hunting of the Snark 26–37, 62,
    72, 75–6, 81, 91, 92, 158, 173
  Irish Songs 82–4, 86
  Julius Caesar 74, 176

The King of the Golden River 37–9
The Leaden Echo and the Golden Echo 53
Legend of the Third Dove 155, 168
Letters to Theo 50, 120, 121–6, 127, 140
The Little Mermaid 167
Menorah 146–53, 162, 163, 166
Music for a Mechanical Organ 106
Music for a Temple 57, 81
Nativity Ode 104
Nighttown 128–9
Ode on a Favourite Cat, Drowned in a Tub of Goldfishes 42
The Only Jealousy of Emer: incidental music 106
A Passionate Man 9, 14, 140, 155, 156–61
Pearl and Unicorn 146, 163
Piano Concerto 22–3
The Pied Piper of Hamelin 60–62, 107
Plurabelle 128, 129–31
Poema Sarda 23, 24
Quintet for Accordion and Strings 53–7, 59, 81, 182
The Rape of the Lock 108–11
The Revenge of Truth: incidental music 133
Rima 76
Le Roi de l'Ille 21
Runes 132–3, 154
Scapegoat 105–6
Seventh Canticle 104
Six Chansons de Ronsard pour des voix divers 10
Sonata for Cor Anglais and Piano 114
Sonatina 168, 182
Sonatina for Alto Flute 182
Spanish Arch 182
String Quartet no. 1 76, 104
String Quartet no. 3 169
Stuffed Raspberries 140, 171–2
Suite for Brass Band 22
Symphonic Variations 76, 129
Symphony no. 1 12, 24–5, 57–9, 82, 174, 177
Symphony no. 2 72, 95–103, 183
Symphony no. 3 146, 167

The Táin 81, 84–6
Tam O'Shanter 42, 107, 177
Thermagistris 76–7, 81
Three Birds 44
Three Hans Andersen Tales 169
Three Playthings 168, 182
Three Yeats Songs 53
Tom O'Bedlam 42
Trefoil 44, 49
Trio 166–7
Trumpet Concerto 118
Twelfth Night 12, 59, 62–71, 74, 82, 158, 174
Two Pieces for Bass Clarinet 182
Umbrage for Orchestra and Six Music Critics 180
Undesirables 153–4, 182
Upon Silence 168
Violin Concerto 25
Violin Sonata no. 2 92, 104
Violin Sonata no. 3 93–5, 154
Violin Sonata no. 5 169
Violin Sonata no. 6 169–71, 182
Virata 9, 155–6, 166
Wedding on the Eiffel Tower: incidental music 106
Wildwood 153–4, 182
The Windhover 112, 113–14, 168
Witches Ballad 182
A Woman Young and Old 45–9, 81, 111–12
Xanadu 76
Wilson, Margaret Alice (née Eldridge) 1, 3–4, 6
Wilson, Rob 1, 3, 6
'Windhover, The' (Hopkins) 112
Windhover, The (Wilson) 112, 113–14, 168
Winser, Andrew 36
Witches Ballad (Wilson) 182
Woman Young and Old, A (Wilson) 45–9, 81, 111–12
Woman Young and Old, A (Yeats) 45–9
Wood, Christopher 9
Wood, Henry 13
Wreck of the Deutschland, The (Hopkins) 53
Wreckers, The (Smyth) 4
Wright, Clifford 90–91, 105, 106, 141, 169
Angel and Harlequin 141, 169
Wurmser, Leo 22
Wynne, Richard William Maurice 104

Xanadu (Wilson) 76

Yeats, Gráinne 45, 53
Yeats, W.B. 44, 53
   The Lake Isle of Innisfree 2
   The Only Jealousy of Emer 106
   A Woman Young and Old 45–9
   'The wild swans at Coole' 171
'Yonghy Bonghy Bo, The' (Lear) 168
Young Person's Guide to the Orchestra (Britten)
   13

Zanidache, Constantin 162, 163
Zauberflöte, Die (Mozart) 18, 157, 158
Zweig, Stefan
   'The Legend of the Third Dove' 155,
     168
   'Virata or the Eyes of the Dying Brother'
     155